Lone Voyager

Annie Forbes

HOWARD BLACKBURN
Back from Newfoundland

Lone Voyager

JOSEPH E. GARLAND

Revised Edition
With Maps and Illustrations

Nelson B. Robinson, Bookseller
Rockport, Massachusetts 01966

Maps by Samuel H. Bryant
Cover illustration by Don Stone
Revised cover design by LineWork

PRINTING HISTORY

Little, Brown & Co., Boston, 1963
Hutchinson & Co., London, 1964
As *Le Solitaire du Large* by Éditions Denoël, Paris, 1966
Éditions Gallimard, Paris, 1975
Nelson B. Robinson, Rockport, Massachusetts, 1978
Second Printing, 1984
Third Printing, 1995

LIBRARY OF CONGRESS CATALOG CARD NUMBER 63-13452
ISBN 0-930352-05-X

Published by

NELSON B. ROBINSON, BOOKSELLER
51 Main Street, Rockport, Massachusetts 01966

Printed in the U.S.A. by Courier Companies Inc., Westford, Massachusetts

Preface
to the
Third Printing

I was ten when Howard Blackburn died. My family vacationed in the Gloucester summer cottage of my grandmother, whose late husband had treated the hero when he returned from Newfoundland. My father, also a doctor, had every reason to bring me around to have my wee hand grasped by that huge maimed fist, but he never did, perhaps thinking me too young for a fisherman's hangout.

Thirty-one years after Blackburn's death, *Lone Voyager* was first published. The hardcover book went through two French editions under the intriguing title *Le Solitaire du Large*. Eight years out of print in English, it was resurrected in 1978 as this expanded paperback by Nelson Buck Robinson, founder of Rockport's environmentally supportive Toad Hall Bookstore, and Eleanor Hoy, the manager, who have kept it before the public ever since.

A source of anguish for me has been the loss of the lone voyager's last sloop, *Cruising Club,* which I'd acquired and restored in 1976. During a gale on October 26, 1980, she chafed through her mooring pennant off my house on Gloucester Harbor and broke up on the rocks before my eyes.

Of almost compensating satisfaction is the enshrinement on July 30, 1992, of his most famous sloop, *Great Republic*, in the new maritime exhibition hall of the Cape Ann Historical Association next door to my grandparents' home in Gloucester.

I leave the reader with this bonus run across in the *Cape Ann Weekly Advertiser* of June 23, 1893: "On Saturday a young child named Robeshaw fell from the wharf into the dock in the rear of Howard Blackburn's. Mr. Blackburn saw the accident and ran to the rescue, jumping on a raft to reach for the lad, but it sank under him and he found himself in the water. Nothing daunted he saved the little one and was soon on shore. It was a brave act and considering the crippling condition of Mr. Blackburn's hands, meritorious in the extreme."

Joseph E. Garland

Black Bess
Gloucester, Massachusetts
January 1995

Foreword

A WILD ATLANTIC NORTHEASTER is driving a scud of rain and spray across this spit of land called Eastern Point. Out there to the southward, a thousand yards beyond the lighthouse, the whistling buoy groans on the back of the ocean swell. The great waves have been making up at sea for two days. They heave by the land's end in relentless procession and explode into plumes of surf against the ledge across the harbor. Sometimes one sideswipes the breakwater at the entrance, lifts its white crest fifteen feet, twenty feet, clear over the top and buries the granite under a concussion of solid spume that boils along the length of it for half a mile.

The house creaks and wrenches from the storm, but it is snug inside, like the bridge of a big ship. Through the salt-sprayed windows I see the whole of Gloucester Harbor stretching out, north to south from the rocks close in front, empty and gray, until it vanishes behind the gale.

Into this same harbor, past the arm of land where my house stands, sailed Champlain on a wandering voyage of discovery three hundred and fifty years ago. And past it — out to the sea and the banks — have sailed ten thousand fishermen of Gloucester to their deaths.

Past it sailed Howard Blackburn.

This was his kind of weather, the way it is outside today.

A few ancient mariners who dory-trawled from schooners and drank beer in his saloon remember him, and to them he was "the finest kind" — the Man of Iron. He remains the special possession of all the fishermen of Gloucester — the symbol of their hard courage and their stoic love, and hatred, of the sea.

Something in this place of my forebears has pulled me back. A hundred and fourteen years ago my great-grandfather came here to practice medicine, and the people elected him their mayor and christened a schooner after him. My grandfather, for whom another schooner and I were named, was also a doctor — and my father, a doctor too, born and raised here. Young Blackburn, back from Newfoundland, was Grandfather's patient, but he reached the end of his lone voyage while I was a child, and I had not met him.

The gale howls on. Two fishing draggers lurch in from the monstrous seas and labor by the house, just visible through the sheets of rain and spray, homeward bound.

What a beating the Atlantic has given them, these men and their boats! And their fathers and grandfathers before them, in schooners and pinkies and dories, in sloops and shallops and sharpshooters.

Howard Blackburn belongs to them all, to the fishermen of all time.

JOSEPH E. GARLAND

Eastern Point
Gloucester, Massachusetts

Contents

Gloucester: January 1883

SUDDENLY the great sails are there.

Gray as the winter Atlantic, they slide into view from behind the drifted snow on Eastern Point's far shore. They are still a long way off.

The black hulls lunge by the lighthouse and swing off the swells to the quiet water of the lee. The rollers surge onward into detonations of destruction against the crags of Norman's Woe.

Down the length of their harbor lean the schooners of Gloucester, hard on the wind. Heavy with fish, and silent, they schoon through the tide.

They are coming fast, sheeting in around the ice-strewn rocks of Ten Pound Island.

Now they have made the anchorage and are turning to face the wind, losing way, tall sails luffing aloft.

The anchors splash and sink with a rattle of cable. The flapping spreads of canvas collapse in heaps to the decks.

The fishing fleet is home.

In from the winter sea the wind still sweeps. It shrieks through the shrouds of the sleeping ships and whines across the wharves. It groans up the streets and moans at the doors, and the lamps in the windows shiver.

It sighs up the stairs and breathes cold on the beds of the men that went down to the sea.

Sch. *Hattie S. Clark* from Georges, on Friday, reports the loss of one of her crew, John Powers, who was washed off the mainboom and drowned. He was a native of Nova Scotia.

Sch. *Herbert M. Rogers* arrived home from a Newfoundland herring trip Saturday morning, and reports that on the previous Tuesday, James Keefe, one of the crew, was lost overboard while engaged in reefing the mainsail, and was drowned. He was thirty years of age, and leaves a widow and three children in this city.

No news has been received in relation to the sch. *Willie H. Joyce*, reported overdue on a Newfoundland herring trip, and the conviction is becoming a settled one that she struck upon the reefs at Sable Island and was lost with all on board.

Mr. Michael Brien, one of the crew of sch. *Hattie L. Newman* of this port, died at St. Jacques, Newfoundland, January 16, from the effects of exposure. He had been on a visit to the sch. *Henri M. Woods,* and while returning to his own vessel in a dory became chilled, was driven ashore and perished on the beach.

Sch. *Gatherer* arrived home from a halibuting trip on Sunday and reports speaking on Grank Bank sch. *Mary F. Chisholm* of this port with loss of two of her crew, Angus McIsaac and Martin Flaherty, while visiting their trawls.

An improbable story and one calculated to arouse false hopes and occasion unnecessary anguish, was circulated in this community on Tuesday evening, when it was reported that Charles Ray and John Whitman, two of the men lost from sch. *James A. Garfield* January 10, had arrived at St. Pierre, having rowed ashore.

Sch. *Grace L. Fears* came in Wednesday afternoon with flag at half-mast to the memory of Thomas Welch, one of her crew, who was frozen to death in a dory January 26.

Seventeen vessels and two hundred and nine lives have been lost in the Gloucester fisheries during the year. Forty of the men are known to have left widows, and the number of fatherless children of which there is a record is sixty-eight. Seventy-one men capsized or gone astray in dories have reached the shore or been rescued from a watery grave, many of them after exposure and sufferings that defy description.

1
Burgeo Bank

SHE SLICED THROUGH the North Atlantic, nodding her head with the swell. The wind thundered off the taut curve of her sails, and she heeled away. Spray boomed from her plunging bow in cascades of exploding water. The sea poured over the rail and frothed along her lee deck and fell off past her quarters. The white wake boiled up under her counter as she surged on, and it simmered and faded astern, and the ocean was whole again.

The Gloucester schooner *Grace L. Fears*, queen of the fresh halibut fleet, was beating past the south shore of Nova Scotia. She was snug-rigged against the winter weather, her stately topmasts having been lowered and left home, along with her topsails and fisherman's staysail. But even her shortened canvas — jib, jumbo, foresail and main — was enough to put her deck under, and she rushed toward the fishing banks with a power that flung spume high into her rigging, where it froze and sparkled like crystal in the sun.

This two-masted beauty with the lines of a clipper ship was eighty-one feet from stem to stern, yet the proud lift of her bowsprit and the rakish slant of her fifty-six-foot mainboom made her look twice as long. With her sails flying and the ocean leaping from her forefoot, she was a sight to make the heart beat faster.

The master of this mistress, Captain Nathaniel Greenleaf, was the king of the halibut killers. The previous spring he and the *Fears* had brought home a fare of upwards of fifty tons in one record five weeks at sea, and it fetched the biggest money ever stocked on a single halibut trip in the history of the fisheries. The giant flounder, which sometimes attained a weight of three hundred and fifty pounds, was in premium demand; competition among the schooners to be the first into market for the highest prices was fierce, and fierce risks were taken in its name. First fare meant top money for all hands, and a highliner like Greenleaf could hand-pick his crew from the ablest men on the coast.

But Skipper Nat was not aboard this trip. A few days earlier he had sailed the *Fears* into Liverpool, down below Halifax, to put an ailing member of the crew ashore; then he decided to swallow the anchor himself for a trip, at least, and turned the command over to Alec Griffin, his first mate and cook. Looking for new hands to make up his complement, Griffin met up with a young fisherman he had known from Gloucester who was spending the holidays in his home town of Port Medway down the line. His name was Howard Blackburn, and he signed him on.

With a few thousand herring for bait and a load of ice in her hold to keep the catch fresh, the schooner cleared Liverpool on the twenty-first of January. Captain Griffin set a northeast course along the coast past Halifax and Cape Canso, around the cliffs of Cape Breton Island and into Cabot Strait, where the Gulf of St. Lawrence loses itself in the Atlantic off Newfoundland's south shore. The hunting ground he sought was Burgeo Bank, a mound on the ocean floor, dwarfed by the broad underwater mesa of the Grand Banks directly to the eastward and bigger than Newfoundland itself.

At the swirling junctions of the Gulf Stream and the Labrador Current the wandering silt had settled to build the shallow banks; the mixing of the waters, warm and cold, created on the ocean's bottom a feeding farm for fish by the billion, and on its surface a turbulent wilderness, now white from the lash of the gale, now black with the stealth of the fog.

Burgeo Bank lay sixty miles south of the fjords of Newfoundland, and on Burgeo lurked the prey.

The *Fears* sailed over the southern slope of Burgeo during

the night of the twenty-fourth, three days out of Nova Scotia. Alec Griffin hove the lead rhythmically, fingering his way along the earth a hundred fathoms below. The lead line chopped off the chart depth. But only the tallow told where the fish would be. As the bob plunked to the bottom, a sticky plug of the fat picked up samples of mud and sand so typical that when it was hand-over-handed back aboard, an old salt — eyeing, feeling, smelling, tasting the soil of the sea — could lay his mark on infinity and not miss by a hundred yards.

By daybreak the skipper had found his spot below. He threw the wheel hard over and brought the schooner into the wind. The anchor splashed off the bow, and the men, heavy in their oilskins, pulled down the wings of snapping canvas.

Amidships, the fishing dories were nested in stacks to port and starboard. A hoist from the mainmast was snapped to the rope handle, the becket, in the stern of the one on top, another from the foremast to the becket of the painter; with a heave the men swung the dory up and out of the nest and lowered it to the deck.

It was a tough-looking boat. Eighteen feet long, with flared sides and flat bottom, it was hard to tell bow from stern in profile, and it moved about as fast one way as the other, at that. The thwarts were removable so that the boats could be nested to save space on deck. The oars were twice as long as its beam on the gunwale — ten feet of stiff spruce. The bank dory was built to take a beating.

Trawl tubs and gear were hove aboard, and with one more haul on the hoists and a shove from the deck, the dory swung over the rail and dropped into the sea. It bobbed like a cork until its crew of two jumped in, cast off the lines and bent to the oars. Their weight gave it stability, and a load of fish would give it even more; yet it was steadiest when it was tipping, and the farther it leaned — even to the gunwale — the more stable it would be . . . a strange boat.

Five more dories were loaded and lowered away. The six crews had drawn lots for position, and they rowed out from the *Fears* across the wind, which was coming light from the southeast. The sea ran easy. The dawn of the north was about to leap from the night. The cold was bitter.

Tom Welch, a husky Newfoundland lad with tousled hair and a broad, cheerful face, had been assigned the newcomer Blackburn as his dorymate. As they swung away from the schooner, rowing in powerful unison, he watched with satisfaction the sweep of the oars in the big man's hands.

When each dory had reached its position on the line, the crew shipped their oars and prepared to set the trawl. All were fishing against the light breeze in parallel lanes. This way, when it came time to haul, they would pick up the far end of the trawl first, and the wind would help them back to the ship.

One man went forward and dropped the trawl anchor overboard, paying the trawl out of the first tub until the anchor hit bottom. Next went the keg buoy, topped with a flag and attached to the anchor by a separate line. The trawl was a tarred cotton rope the thickness of a pencil, coiled in the tubs in fifty-fathom sections called skates, six skates to a tub, four tubs to a dory. At fifteen-foot intervals ganging lines were tied to the trawl, four feet long, a baited hook at the end of each. The hooks were flicked out of the tub with a supple stick as the trawl spun off the coil. As each skate went over the side, the ends were knotted, one to the next, from tub to tub, until nearly a mile and a half of trawl and four hundred and eighty hooks lay on the ocean floor. When the last of the trawl was reached, a second anchor and buoy were dropped over.

After setting, the men rowed their dories back to the schooner for a mug-up. The rest was up to the fish; twenty-nine hundred innocent-looking dinners were awaiting them in the murk of Burgeo Bank.

But in only two hours Skipper Alec ordered his crew back over the side. There was a feel to the heavy air and a look to the sky that meant wind. Fish or no, the trawls would have to be

Gordon W. Thomas

The *Grace L. Fears* under construction in the David A. Story yard (later John Bishop's) on Vincent Cove, Gloucester. The cove has long since been filled in. The *Fears* was launched July 2, 1874, and sold to Captain Greenleaf and the Atlantic Halibut Company in 1879.

Goode's Fisheries, *1887*

At anchor on the banks in the early 1880's, the crew of a typical Gloucester halibut schooner cuts bait and baits trawls before setting out in the dories.

hauled before their time. The catch would be thin, but he wanted none of his dories caught in a nasty sea away from their vessel.

Just as the boats shoved off, the first snowflakes fluttered down. The wind had died to a breath. The sky was leaden and faded into the smooth gray sea at the horizon. For the second time this morning the men left the schooner astern, heading now for the outermost buoys.

Welch and Blackburn drove their dory with surging strokes through the glassy sea. The snow was coming a little thicker. Some of the others had already reached their markers and were commencing to haul as the two men passed. A few more strokes, and they glided up to the keg and pulled it aboard. Up came the buoy rope, then the anchor and the end of the trawl. Welch hove the heavy line up on the gurdy, a metal roller set on a pin in the port gunwale of the bow. Blackburn stood in the waist, his killer club at the ready.

The gurdy twirled and the water spun from the line as Welch hauled in the straining trawl. It jerked and jumped in his grip. A thrashing halibut broke the surface. Blackburn seized the ganging line, yanked the big, flat, flapping fish to the gunwale and clubbed it on the head. He dragged it over the side, worked the hook from its mouth with his killer and dropped the quivering body in the bottom. Then he coiled the freed line in the tub, while his dory-mate turned back to the trawl.

When half a mile of trawl was back aboard, and a few fish slithered in the bilge, the two paused to remark that the southeast breeze was freshening. But this was all right, since it favored them all the more as they worked their way toward the *Fears*. They could see the nearest dories through the snow, ahead of them with the hauling. They returned to their task.

Just as they fetched the second buoy, the wind fell back to a flat calm, ominously. The other men were already pulling for the schooner. Blackburn and Welch got the last of the trawl aboard, grabbed the oars and headed for their ship.

Then the squall hit. But it came from the wrong direction, from the northwest, as they had feared. Now they were to leeward of the vessel, fighting the wind. In an instant the schooner was out of sight in the flying snow . . . they weren't sure where; the sudden shift had fouled their bearings.

As the snow thickened, the wind increased. It kicked the sea into a chop, flicking spindrift from the whitecaps. The wind-driven snow and spray blasted against their oilskins. A few dory lengths away the ocean disappeared behind a dizzy, whirling curtain of white. It was as if they were rowing with all their might against a rock.

After an hour's hard pulling they agreed that they must have passed beyond their objective and could only be to windward of her; they might have rowed on by within a few yards without seeing the ghostly vessel or hearing her horn above the shrieking gale. They decided the smart thing was to anchor and wait for the snow to let up; then they would be able to see the schooner and could make an easy job of rowing back to her with a following wind.

Soon after darkness the snow came to an end. There, not down-wind as they had expected but as far to the windward as ever, they saw the torch raised in the shrouds of the *Fears* to guide them home. They had been rowing on an ocean treadmill.

They broke out the anchor and strained for the flare. But the wind was too fierce and the sea too rough; they made no more headway against the combination than before. Again they threw over the anchor. At first it refused to take a bite, and the dory drifted to leeward. Suddenly it caught on the bottom and fetched them up short. Head to the wind, the dory backed off tight against the line, bouncing up in each trough and plowing into every wave; water poured in over the bow.

Welch dove for the bailing scoop and flailed at the rising water. But it was useless; the sea crashed into the boat faster than he could throw it back. They kicked in the head of a buoy keg and, using it as a bucket, were just able to dump the ocean out as it swept aboard.

The gale honed the edge of the cold. Spray froze where it struck and glazed the dory in a gnarled plate of ice. The boat grew churlish under the burden and settled lumpishly into the sea. They hove the trawls and tubs over the side and all the fish save a cod; they could eat him raw if it came to that.

Now and again during the wild night an obliging sea lifted them high on its back, and for a hovering instant they glimpsed the dim spark of the torch before they were plunged back into the valley of the trough.

At dawn there was nothing to see but the frenzy of the waves, nothing to hear but the scream of the gale.

They were alone.

Newfoundland lay somewhere to the north — sixty miles, maybe more. They were big men, tough from hardship. Blackburn was twenty-three years old; he stood six feet two, weighed over two hundred pounds, and was all bone and muscle. Welch was younger and not so heavy, but strong and full of the will to live. They would have all they could do to keep afloat. There was neither food nor fresh water, only the codfish, by now frozen stiff. The cold was intense.

Again they broke out the anchor and tried to row, this time for the coast. It was no use. The seas were running so high that at any instant a cresting giant might suck them to itself, flip them over and bury all in a thundering avalanche of water.

And so they gave it up. While Welch kept the dory head to the wind and sea with the oars, Blackburn kicked in the head of the other key buoy and tried to tie the end of the bow painter to its flagstaff. His thick mittens made him clumsy; he pulled them off and dropped them in the bilge to keep them from freezing. When he had made the painter fast to the buoy's staff, he pulled the gurdy from the gunwale and tied it to the keg to weight it down. Then he threw this sea anchor overboard. The open end of the keg cupped against the water and kept enough tension on the line to hold their bow to the wind and the oncoming seas.

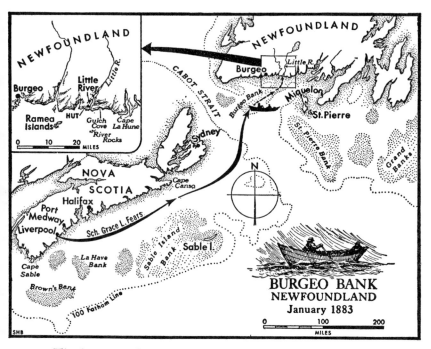

BURGEO BANK
NEWFOUNDLAND
January 1883

The boat was filling with water. The instant the drag stretched the painter to its length and swung them head to the waves, Welch shipped his oars, seized the bailing keg and turned to furiously.

With his first bailerful, the mittens went over the side and floated away. Neither man noticed what had happened until Welch paused for breath and Blackburn began searching through the slosh of the bilge. The mittens were gone. There was no helping it. He took his turn with the bailer.

For an hour or more they bailed. Blackburn hardly missed the sodden mittens until Welch remarked that his dorymate's hands looked peculiar. The color had drained from them, and they were the ashen gray of a cadaver. Although his hands, especially the fingers, were frigid to the touch, they didn't hurt, and the only sensation Blackburn felt, now that Welch had called his attention to them, was numbness.

His hands were freezing to death. Blackburn knew that without the protection of mittens they would petrify as the cold drove in. The water in the tissues, and the blood, would crystallize to ice, and the fingers would be bone-encasing casts of frozen flesh. Without fingers, without hands, he would be a dead weight in the dory, a grotesque cargo. What if a vessel should chance by and save them? It would find Tom at the oars, and him crouched on a thwart, his hands as stiff as sticks, a helpless old woman.

He leaned over and picked up his oars. Slowly, slowly, he bent the resisting fingers and thumbs around the handles. In twenty minutes they were frozen claws. He slipped them off, replaced the oars in the bottom and took his turn bailing.

All that second day the two men spelled each other bailing and pounding ice with the killer. It froze as fast as they knocked it off. Blackburn could hardly grasp the club. He held it so crudely that sometimes the claw of his hand itself smashed down on the jagged crusts.

Welch was a game man. He would often say — don't give up, we will soon be picked up. But a vessel could have passed within fifty yards of us and not see us as the vapor was so thick, and the boat shipped so much water and made ice so fast that it kept one of us busy about all the time, and he knew as well as I did that no vessel would be moving about in such weather.

Blackburn had missed the ice so often with the killer that the little finger of his right hand was pulpy. He kicked away his right boot, worked the sock off and put his bare foot back in. With his teeth, he drew the stocking over the swollen hand, but it stuck at the turn of the heel. Each time he dipped the bailer, the toe of the sock dragged through the water. A ball of ice formed in the toe and grew so heavy it pulled the stocking down with every sweep of his arm. Each time he worked it back on with his teeth. In exasperation he whacked the lumpy toe across the gunwale to break the ice. The sock flipped off and disappeared. He had robbed his foot to save his hand, uselessly.

It was my turn just before dark, and after bailing out the boat I was just about to lie down in the bow with Welch so to get a little shelter from the wind, which cut us like a knife, when a sea broke on the boat, half filling her. It was now Welch's turn to bail, but he made no attempt to get up, and when I said — Tom, jump quick, he said — I can't see. As the water had to be bailed out before another sea broke on her, there was no time for an argument, so I jumped up and bailed out the water. I then said — Tom this won't do. You must do your part. Your hands are not frozen and beating to pieces like mine — showing him my hand with the little finger just hanging by the skin between the fingers. I have always been sorry that I showed him the hand, for he gave up altogether then and said — Howard, what is the use, we can't live until morning, and might as well go first as last.

Blackburn shook his head. He told the weakening man to shove over, and lay back in the bow beside him.

The seas engulfed the dory in the blackness of the second night, and the gale drove the spray like bullets across the bow. Blackburn bailed ceaselessly, flopping down with Welch only long enough to catch his breath before stumbling back to the battle.

His mate was slipping away. Once he roused himself and put his feet over the side into the sea. Blackburn lifted them back and settled him in his place; then he decided to turn over the bow to him altogether and moved to the stern. Tom asked for a drink of water, over and over. He asked for a piece of ice. Blackburn picked a salty chunk from the bilge and handed it to him; he bit some off and threw the rest away.

As cold crept in and life seeped out, he moaned and muttered, a dark and shapeless form in the pounding bow. Once he mumbled something that sounded like a prayer; twice he called out to Blackburn by name.

But the big man had all he could do to keep the dory from sinking. The crash of breaking seas and the thunder of wind and spray beat down the groans from the bow. About two hours after dark he called to Tom. There was no stir nor sound that could be heard.

He stumbled forward and tilted back the lolling head. He peered down into the white, wet face, into the staring eyes. His dorymate was dead.

There was a lull in the heaving sea. He picked up the body, staggered aft and dropped it in the stern. He clawed off one of the mittens and tried to put it on. But his hand was too swollen and distorted. The freezing spray wrapped the body in a winding sheet of ice. Its weight raised the bow and steadied the boat. It was ballast.

For the rest of the night he bailed and pounded ice. When he could, he slumped into the bow, his claws between his legs and his face down out of the wind and spray. Suddenly a wave would flood the boat, and he would drag himself back to the bailing.

Before dawn of the third day the wind died, and the seas subsided. By sunrise the ocean was nearly calm. The dory rose and fell on the long swells. The cold relaxed its bite to a grinding gnaw.

His mouth and throat were dry, and his tongue was thick, but he had no hunger. He pulled in the drag. One pair of oars had been lost overboard during the storm; one pair remained. He set them in the wooden tholepins in the gunwales and forced the claws over the handles. The dory was a gross sculpture of ice, ponderous as a barge to row.

He shipped the oars and pounded the planks with one until the armor plates of ice worked loose and splashed into the sea. Where the becket of the painter looped through the bow, rope and wood were welded by a solid hunk of ice. When he struck it with the oar, and it fell away, he found that two of the rope's three strands had parted. The bond of ice had saved the drag that night, and the drag had saved him.

With clumsy claws he repaired the painter. Then he worked them back on the oars and resumed rowing . . . for Newfoundland.

From A Fearless Fisherman

On Burgeo Bank the storm thickens. Welch hauls in the trawl as Blackburn clubs a halibut.

From A Fearless Fisherman

Bailing for life, Blackburn fights to keep his ice-sheathed dory afloat. Welch lies dead in the stern.

By noon the steady twist of the oars had worn away the insides of his fingers. First the skin, then the frozen flesh crumbled off in a dry powder. The wood was rasping on his bare bones.

The friction of the oar handles had wore away so much flesh from the inside of my hands that I could hardly hold the oars, and often my hands would slip off the ends of the oars. When I, forgetting that I could not open my hands, would make a grab for the oar handle and when the backs of my fingers would strike the oar, it would sound just like so many sticks.

So to hold the oars I had to put the outside of each hand upon the thick part of the oar, and by so doing the oarhandles would stick out between my forefinger and thumb two or three inches. When bending forward to take a stroke I would keep one hand a little higher than the other, but sometimes I would forget and take a stroke as if my hands were all right. Then the end of the oar would strike the side of my hand and knock off a piece of flesh as big around as a fifty cent piece, and fully three times as thick. The blood would just show and then seem to freeze.

He rowed thus all day. His thirst increased, but still not his hunger. Just before dusk, far out on the horizon, he saw what appeared to be a great rock covered with snow. He pulled on until dark. Afraid of losing the oars overboard in the night if he kept on rowing, he dropped the drag over and huddled in the bottom to await daylight.

The wind arose and blew hard during the third night. But the dory shipped little water. To keep awake and warm he hooked his arms around a thwart and rocked back and forth, back and forth. The night was long, and Tom Welch poor company.

At dawn of the fourth day — it was Sunday — he hauled in the drag and bent again to the oars. The night wind had expired. The sea was calm, and the cold was not so sharp. What he had taken to be a massive rock the previous evening turned out to be an island, cloaked with snow.

He rested on the oars and inspected it. There were no signs of life, neither harbor nor house. He concluded it was barren, and since it lay away from the direction in which he presumed the mainland to be, he oared on by at a distance.

All morning he rowed, and in the early afternoon he passed a cluster of rocks jutting unexpectedly out of the sea. All afternoon he rowed. Every stroke must be bringing him closer to the land. The rhythm was mechanical, a perpetual motion easier to maintain than to stop. Now and then he glanced over his shoulder without breaking the clockwork of his body and the oars.

Late in the afternoon a white stretch of coast rose thinly out of the horizon.

He rowed on.

At the edge of dusk the dory moved into a strong tide rip. The ocean was black and turbulent from the seaward surge of a brackish current, out and over the incoming tide. He figured he was outside the mouth of a rapidly emptying river. The boat was buffeted by the maelstrom of opposing waters, and he struggled on. Now he could see the outline of the narrow entrance. Sheer rock portals overhung with snow climbed a quarter of a mile out of the banging surf.

At dusk the wind arose, and the sea erupted into whitecaps. Every stroke an agony, he fought the current and crawled through the narrows. The bluffs towered over him. He feared to miss even a stroke lest the river disgorge him back to the sea.

Searching the snow-laden banks in the last glimmer of twilight as he rowed, his eyes stopped at a broken wharf. There was a shed on it. In back, on the shore, was a hut, steeped in snow, silent and deserted.

His thirst rushed in on him.

I could tell by the color of the water running out that fresh water could be found if I could only row up the river against the tide, and at that time I would give ten years of my life for a drink of water. I rowed some distance up the river, when all at once my mind gave way.

I seemed to think that some former shipmates was laughing at the little headway I was making.

Abruptly, he turned back and rowed for the wharf and the lifeless hut.

The moon had risen, and by its frigid light he worked up to the landing. Next to it the waves were breaking against a flat rock. He guided the dory alongside and shipped the oars. He stood up. His hips and knees crackled, and he nearly fell as he stepped out. He hooked an arm through the becket, pulled the boat partway onto the rock and hove the drag over the wharf. Then he clambered up himself.

The deadness in his feet told him they were frozen.

He stumbled into the shed and found a barrel half full of salt codfish. He was sure that if he ate some now the salt would drive him crazy, so he broke through the ice on top and buried a couple in the snow, hoping it would draw out the salt and freshen them by morning. The thought of the fish in the dory never crossed his mind.

He waded through the snow to the hut and pushed in the rotten door. The roof was patched with sky, and the snow on the dirt floor came up to his knees. There was a table in one room, a bedstead in the other, both drifted with snow.

As he turned back to the doorway, his eyes wandered toward the river narrows and out beyond to the ocean. There, in the frame of the cliffs, a silhouette against the moonlit sea, was a schooner passing to the east. It had not been in view when he entered the river, and he thought it must be making for a harbor not far away. He resolved to spend the night in the shack and at daybreak to get back in the dory, row out of the river and search for life to the eastward.

He clawed the boards from the bed, brushed away the snow and turned them over for something dry to lie on. In a corner he found some fishlines rolled up on reels. A torn net hung from a beam. He put the lines and reels at the head of the bed for a pillow, lay down and drew the net over his body.

The cold pierced him. He shivered so, he thought his teeth would break, and every muscle in his body joined the uncontrollable contagion of his shaking.

Yet the cold, the stillness, the utter fatigue . . . they were a curtain closing around his consciousness. His very eyelids begged for rest.

He knew that if he slept he would never wake up.

Pushing the net away, he dragged himself from the boards and commenced to walk the drifted floor. He ate snow from the table; the more he ate, the more he craved. All that fourth night he walked the floor and ate snow, and his thirst was merciless.

The earliest light of the fifth day brought him outside. He floundered back to the wharf. The night wind had moderated, but before it fell off it had pushed the sea up into the river and against the shore.

The dory was awash with water. The body was a weird shape in the bottom. The thwarts and the oars revolved in an eddy under the wharf.

The waves had pounded the boat against the rock. The plug had been knocked from the drainhole, and the water had poured up through. One plank below the port waterline was splintered; another, under the gunwale, was smashed.

2
Frostbite

I COULD THEN SEE what a terrible mistake I had made, in not making both ends of the boat fast to the wharf and by giving her so much slack. I looked all around me but could see no escape and said to myself, it is too bad that it must end like this after such a struggle. The thoughts of it made me desperate.

He got down on the rock. Each breaking wave pushed the oars and thwarts beneath the wharf; then the undertow carried them back toward him. When the chance came, he reached out as far as he dared without slipping and clawed in one of the oars. With the next chance, he used it to pole in the other, and the thwarts, and laid them up on the stage.

Suddenly the silence was shattered by a report that bounced and rebounded across the hills. It sounded like the shot of a gun. He climbed up on the wharf and shouted as loud as he could, but the only answer was an echo.

He had heard something of the habits of the fishermen thereabouts. Those who had caught enough cod during the warm months to pay for provisions moved with their families to cabins in the deep woods of the hills for a winter of hunting. If hunters were around, he had to find some way to attract their attention.

He remembered seeing a flint, file and some tinder in a rough closet in the hut; perhaps he could set it on fire. He waded back through the snow and scraped them off the shelf. But the rigid claws refused to close around the flint and file, and the tinder was so wet that it didn't matter.

His hopes had for a moment drowned his thirst, but now they were gone and it rushed back. Someone must live in this place in the summer, so somewhere under the snow there had to be a well. Half delirious, he charged out of the hut and into the drifts. Like a quicksand of powder, the snow enveloped him to his hips. But he bulled through into every low place between the shack and the steep rise of the hills in back. Here and there he sank to his shoulders in the drifts and his heart leaped and he knew he had found the well; when he dragged himself out of the hole it was only a bowl in the ground, leveled over with ice and snow. At last his senses returned, and he fought heavily back to the hut.

Now he saw it clearly: he must concentrate on his plan of the night before; somehow he had to get the dory afloat and row to the eastward.

He went back down to the landing. There was the battered boat, gunwales awash, bumping and grinding against the rock. There was Tom's body, crumpled in the bottom, rolling slightly with the motion of the waves.

Leaning out from the rock, he reached in the dory to his shoulder and found the iron gaff. He jabbed it into the toe of a boot and pulled the body up in the stern. He laid down the gaff and hauled it by the legs partway over the transom, crooked his arms under the shoulders and dragged it onto the rock. He rested a moment. Again he hooked under the armpits, lifted it to its feet, and with all his strength lurched toward the landing. As he tried to raise it over the edge of the wharf, a dagger of pain slashed through his guts. It doubled him over, and the corpse slid from his arms into the water with a splash and slowly sank two fathoms to the bottom.

Gasping with agony, he clutched at his groin. The sudden strain had ruptured his abdomen. He worked the bulging hernia of intestine back inside with his claws, and straightened up.

The dory's stern painter was long enough to run around one of the posts that supported the wharf and back to the rock where he was standing. He clenched the end of it between his teeth. Every sea that came in lifted the swamped boat almost to the level of the rock. Sliding an arm through the loop of the stern becket, he hauled the dory a little farther up the rock with each rise of the water and took in the slack of the painter with his teeth to hold the boat until the next wave came along.

He got it up far enough so that some of the water gurgled out the drainhole; he pounded the plug back and bailed out the rest. He replaced the thwarts and the oars and filled with snow the keg he had used as a drag. He took a last look at his dorymate, stirring on the bottom with the eddies. Shoving the dory off the rock, he stepped in, jammed the claws on the oars and pulled for the narrows.

The sea spurted through the long crack near the bottom in a row of thin geysers, and he had to sit off center on the thwart, throwing his weight to starboard so as to keep the smashed plank on the opposite side out of the water. The boat leaked so badly that he was compelled to ship the oars every little while and bail.

Outside the river, he turned to the eastward and rowed along the coast for five or six miles until he rounded a cape and entered a cove. Pulling up the near side to the head of the inlet, he saw a house but no sign of life. He continued along the shore and rowed down the far side of the cove, which was formed by a second headland.

Just as he reached this promontory, he saw two schooners beating slowly to the westward against the light breeze. They were standing in for the cape he had passed already on his way from the river. He pulled straight back across the mouth of the cove to intercept them. He got close enough to see a man on the deck of the nearest vessel. But before he could head them off, the breeze backed around to the east and freshened. Their sails filled, and with a following wind they were soon out of sight around the cape.

He rested on the oars. It was late in the day. The leak was getting worse. The shift in the wind favored a return to the river. Best try to get back before dark, spend another night in the shack, then in the morning row east or west, depending on the whim of the wind.

But it was breezing up fast, and the sea was turning choppy. He kept as close inshore as he dared. Every few minutes he shipped the oars and bailed. Clouds of snow cascaded down on him as the wind swirled across the drifts that hung over the brow of the bluffs, high above the sea.

The fifth night had fallen, and the same cold moon was on the rise when he battled back into the torrential narrows of the river. This time he followed the opposite bank, the east one. It was the same struggle all over again.

A machine, he heaved on the oars. But from this shore, by the white lunar light, he saw what had previously been hidden from his view, a cove tucked behind a point on the western side, perhaps three quarters of a mile beyond the mark he had reached the night before. He could dimly make out a few cabins huddled on its shore. The moon, bleak as the distant scene it illuminated, revealed no life.

Chunks of ice grated past the dory with the current. They might be tumbling into the river from a brook, possibly one that sluiced down the hills into the cove. If he could fight up the river as far as the cabins, there was a chance of fresh water.

Dodging the ice pans, he continued along the east shore. But far short of the mark where he had given up last night, he found again he could no more than hold his own against the coursing stream.

He crossed the river to the other side; the current there was weaker, and he made some progress. But soon he rowed where it again flowed free and strong against him, and he crossed back.

For three hours he zigzagged up the river, seeking eddies of quieter water behind the jutting points. He paused frequently to bail, and to lose ground each time as the dory was carried back.

Late in the night he approached the cove. It was frozen solid. But beyond, there was life.

Some persons crossing the cove on the ice from one house to another saw the dory with only one man in it and came out to the edge of the ice and waited for me to land. As soon as the boat struck the ice they caught hold of her and two of the men was going to jump into the boat which was half full of water at the time. I stopped them and asked one man to get in and go with me to get my companion. I told them that I had left him at the house down the river. I wanted to make them think that I did not feel so bad as I looked, but they said — you come out and go to the house, and we will go down for him. I got onto the ice. They bailed out the water and three men got into the dory and started for the mouth of the river. I then told them where they would find him, and they said — oh, he is dead?

The men told Blackburn he had come to Little River, a fishing settlement about twenty-five miles to the east of the town of Burgeo, for which the fishing bank was named. The apparently barren island he had passed two days earlier was Ramea, and there was a village on it, hidden from his view. The rocks he had skirted were called River Rocks, seven miles from the coast. The inlet he had entered this morning was Gulch Cove, and they told him that if he had continued rowing to the eastward around that cape — Cape La Hune, it was — instead of trying to head off the schooners, he would have come to a town where the people were prosperous and even had a doctor.

As they stood there talking, a group of thin and tattered folk and a pack of yelping, scrawny dogs approached across the ice. And then a dozen children. He stared at the young ones. Their feet were bare. They ran a few steps at a time and stopped; each child put a hand on another's shoulder for balance and rubbed first one red foot and then the other against the opposite leg; then they danced on toward him again.

The people led him over the ice to shore. Wisps of smoke curled from the chimneys of half a dozen log cabins

Hands frozen to his oars, Howard rows up Little River under a bleak moon and the snowy cliffs of Newfoundland the fifth night. (Illustrations from *A Fearless Fisherman.*)

Howard Blackburn
July 1883

Thomas Welch

clumped in a moonlit clearing. Behind them the forest climbed into the sky, deep in snow.

He was taken to the largest of the cabins, the home of Frank Lishman and his family. The Lishmans took him in hand swiftly and bluntly. There was no time to waste. They had seen many cases of exposure and frostbite. But this one . . . they shook their heads.

While her husband seated him on a bench across the room from the heat of the fireplace and cut away his clothing and boots with a knife, Mrs. Lishman gave him a few sips of cold water. He begged for more, but she refused. Instead, she brewed a tea by steeping young spruce boughs in hot water and gave him a large bowl of this, which he drank greedily.

A tub made from half a flour barrel was placed in front of the fire, and as they filled it with cold water, he looked about him.

The walls of the cabin were of logs; the floor was dirt, and in the middle of it stood the huge stone fireplace. The chimney, plastered with mud, tapered up and through the roof. A stack of three-foot logs snapped and smoked on the hearth. He saw neither candles nor lamps; the fireplace was the only source of illumination. A table, a couple of benches and a few stools were fashioned of timber slabs, with legs pegged through the corners. Mrs. Lishman's chair was a flour barrel set on its butt. It had been sawed halfway through the waist and the cut staves knocked out so that those remaining served as the back. The lower half was stuffed with green brush and covered with tarpaulin to form the seat.

The rear of the cabin behind the fireplace was divided into two sleeping rooms by partitions of rough planks. The beds were pallets of straw. The Lishmans and two of their daughters slept in one room; two sons slept in the other. Four more children were married and lived with the grandchildren in neighboring cabins.

When the tub had been filled, Mrs. Lishman stirred in some salt, brought him up to the fireplace and told him to sit on a bench facing the tub. She wrapped him in a dry coverlet and ordered him to dip his hands and feet in the cold brine.

In a few minutes I was wishing myself in Welch's place. I will say no more about the agony I was compelled to undergo while the frost was being slowly drawn out. I asked them how long I would have to keep my hands and feet in the brine. They said — your poor hands and feet are so badly frost burned that you must keep them in the water for about one hour. I still think that was the longest hour I ever spent.

All the time that I sat there they fed me on bread and hot spruce tea, and although I had not tasted food of any kind for one hundred and fourteen hours, the bread and tea did not taste good, and when I would ask for water they would only say — we don't want to kill you, poor man. At last what they called an hour was up.

Mrs. Lishman had been preparing a paste of flour and cod-liver oil which she spread on clean strips of cloth. She wrapped the raw hunks of hands and feet with this poultice. Her husband brought a straw pallet bed up to the fireplace and threw an old sail over it. They helped him to lie down, draped another sail over him and retired for the rest of the night.

From where he lay he could see the stars twinkling at him through the black square of a small window. The fire settled, and the flickering light from the embers rose and fell against the murk of the log walls. He tossed and turned and dozed fitfully, but the pain clamored at his brain and shut out sleep.

The next morning the Lishmans bathed him with warm water and homemade soap.

Then they lifted me out of the bed and sat me on the bench, and when they took the wrappings off the right hand, the little finger dropped off. The skin on all of the other fingers split open on the backs or tops and hung down, and the finger and thumb nails still hung to the flesh, which made my hands look as if I had eight fingers and two thumbs on each hand, and when Mrs. Lishman took the scissors and cut the skin and flesh away, I said — for God's sake don't cut my fingers off! She said — I am not cutting your fingers off; and she picked up one of them with the nail still on it.

All of the flesh that had frozen would have to be cut away, she explained, and it would be nine days before his hands and feet began to heal.

The families at Little River were on the edge of starvation. Their food consisted almost entirely of flour, cornmeal and dried codfish. They had neither milk nor eggs, cattle nor fowl. The only source of fresh meat was their dogs. Drinking water was obtained by melting ice and snow, and the common beverage was hot spruce tea. Mrs. Lishman cooked her pitiful fare in the great fireplace with iron utensils. No table was set for meals; each member of the household helped himself from the common pot into an earthen bowl or tin plate.

Four days after Blackburn's arrival some of the men succeeded in sailing their small boat around the coast to Burgeo. They went directly to the Reverend John Cunningham and told him how a badly frozen American fisherman had rowed into Little River with his dead dorymate. And they described the conditions in their homes. Mr. Cunningham immediately telegraphed the American consul at St. John's and was instructed to send the sick fisherman everything he needed. The boat was loaded with enough provisions to last one man for six months and returned to Little River.

There was rejoicing when it arrived. The supplies were packed across the ice and piled in the Lishmans' back room. Everyone crowded into the cabin to hear the account of the trip to Burgeo.

While the men were talking, the children sneaked around back and got into the sugar; it was a substance most of them had never tasted in their lives. But enough was left for Mrs. Lishman to give steaming sweet mugs of real tea to all the grownups.

The rejoicing was short-lived. The food was shared with everyone, and in a few days it was almost gone. Again the men sailed for Burgeo, but bad weather intervened and they got only as far as Ramea Island. Mr. Penney, who kept the store there, stocked their boat and sent them home.

Dry gangrene gnawed at Blackburn's fingers and toes, and every now and then one dropped off. He kept a tally: it was fifty-one days from the loss of the little finger of the right hand until the last was gone, the right thumb at the first joint. He lost all the fingers from both hands, half of each thumb, two toes from the left foot and three toes and the heel from the right. The bones of the dead fingers held the curve of the oar handles to the end.

But the new flesh grew quickly, first above the wrists and then on the palms. A black scum formed over the stumps of the lost fingers and toes. "Proud flesh," it was called, and Mrs. Lishman scraped it off every day with her scissors to keep the way open for the growth of scar tissue. A nauseating job; when she tried to show her son Frank how to do it, he fainted. So she kept on with it. Nan, her eighteen-year-old daughter, would stand behind Blackburn and drape her apron over his face during the procedure.

Mrs. Lishman dusted the sores with a powder of mussel shells gathered from the rocks and pounded with smooth beach stones. It caused the festering wounds to give off pus and was supposed to promote the healing. Sometimes a swelling came up; she would scrape it away with her scissors and extract a fragment of shell that had escaped the pounding. In five weeks his hands were nearly covered with new flesh . . . distorted and ugly, but flesh.

The early spring thaws broke up the ice in the Gulf of St. Lawrence. It drifted down the coast and packed so solid against the Newfoundland shore that the men from Little River were unable to get the boat through to Burgeo for the settlement's government allowance of provisions.

The flour and then the cornmeal gave out. One by one the

dogs disappeared into the stewpot. Blackburn couldn't bring himself to eat their meat, but he was thankful for the broth. The children wandered from room to room in the cabins, crying with hunger. His appetite was never satisfied, but after eating some of whatever was served him, he would tell Mrs. Lishman to give the rest to little Willie or one of her grandchildren.

Starvation was only a matter of time. At night he would lie on his bed of straw by the fire, tormented by the frustration of his helplessness, gazing through the window at the stars. When the storms howled around the cabin, snow sifted down the chimney and drifted across his covers. One mad night he tried to go outside, to crawl on his hands and knees over the hills for help, but he was put back to bed.

And then, one day, there was a pounding at the door. Outside stood thirty men, muffled against the cold in thick sealskin coats and caps. They were the crew of the steamer *Nimrod*, a sealer out of St. John's, trapped in the ice pack seven miles off shore. They had read newspaper accounts of the terrible experience of the Gloucester fisherman who had rowed to Little River and of the poor people there doing what they could to care for him.

The seal hunters squeezed into the cabin, a few at a time. When they had talked with the big man lying by the fire, and the Lishmans, and had seen the look of the children, they drew their lunches from their clothing and left them. The strongest in Little River took a sled and returned over the ice with the hunters to their ship. When they came back, the sled was loaded with provisions that kept the settlement alive until the ice broke up and the boat again could sail for Burgeo.

Blackburn's heart went out to the children. None of them could read, and they knew only what their parents had taught them. An ancient Bible was the only book in the household. Often Nan perched on the edge of his cot and held the Bible in front of his eyes, and he read to them. Over and over he repeated for them some of the simple prayers he had learned as a boy.

Helpless as an infant, he lay on the straw cot by the fire. His feet would not bear his weight, and there was nothing he could do for himself. The Lishmans nursed him as well as they were able. His life was in their hands, and the hours and days and weeks dragged on while the outcome remained in doubt.

Every morning for the first two months someone would come in and say — well, Skipper Frank, how is that man this morning? He would always tell them — well, the poor man will never live to see the sun go down. And in the evening when they would ask him how I was he would say — he will never see the sun rise. I got so used to it that I did not mind it.

One morning a man came in just after they had dressed my hands and feet and said — how is that man this morning? Skipper Frank answered — by God he is agoing to live. I turned to ask him why he thought so, but the other man saved me the trouble. Skipper Frank said — this is the first morning since the poor man has been with us that I have noticed any steam come from his water.

April was the messenger of spring, of life renewed. The snows melted, and the ice broke out of the cove. The men went back to fishing; the sea again gave up its food. He grew restive, then impatient, as day by day his strength returned.

The twenty-second of April came clear and full of promise. He implored his friends to prepare their little boat for the journey to Burgeo. They stepped outside and conferred among themselves. No, they said, he was not yet ready for such a voyage in an open boat.

But he would be kept down no longer. The next day the wind was fair for Burgeo, and he told them at dawn that he was determined to go, live or die in the attempt.

The Lishman cabin was only a few feet from the water. They carried him out and settled him in the boat and bundled him up in sails. It was the same boat that had carried Tom's body to Burgeo for burial ten days earlier. Everyone came to the edge of the shore to wish him good-by and Godspeed. He had counted sixteen dogs when he first arrived; now there was only one to see him off.

As the boat prepared to sail, Mrs. Lishman leaned down and handed the patient she had nursed day and night for nearly three months a small wooden box. It was shaped strangely like a casket. He asked her what it contained.

It was the custom of her people, she told him, to save amputated parts to be buried, in time, with their owner. These were his.

He took the little coffin, and after they reached Burgeo that night, he had it placed in the grave in the churchyard with the body of his dorymate.

He was taken to the home of Joseph Small, for there was no hospital in Burgeo. He received medical attention, and everything was done for his comfort. The doctor there said he could do no more for him than the Lishmans had already. After a few days he was moved to the house of James Payne and his family.

In a while he was able to limp about.

He received free passage on the steamer *Curlew* and arrived at St. Pierre on May 23. The American consul gave him a ticket to Halifax, where the consul general provided his fare to Boston on the steamer *Worcester*. He boarded a train and arrived home in Gloucester on the fourth of June.

~~~~~

Time passed at Little River. One day Willie Lishman went out with the fishermen, and the sea took him. Skipper Frank picked up his gun, walked into the woods and put a bullet through his head.

3
The Blackburns

LIKE MANY ANOTHER of his countrymen, Howard Blackburn had drifted down to the fishing mecca of Gloucester from the south coast of Nova Scotia, a land whose men knew the sea before they fairly knew themselves, a hard land of rough men born on the shore where the ocean holds back the wilderness and forces their destinies on them.

Nova Scotia and Newfoundland, its twin to the north, are tough chips on the shoulder of Canada, thrusting into the Atlantic with obstinate island independence. Tough, obstinate and independent are their people, and their steel is in the backbone of Gloucester.

The first Blackburns left nothing of themselves behind but their children and their children's children. They were in that legion of American colonists who transplanted themselves to Nova Scotia after the Revolution rather than forswear their allegiance to the Crown of England. The Patriots derided them for Tories; proudly they called themselves United Empire Loyalists and set about to build their own democracy on the wild shores of old Acadia, the land their American forefathers had helped wrest from the grip of the French.

Nova Scotia hangs off the mainland of New Brunswick, virtually an island, and its people look out to the sea. To get from Liverpool to Boston in those days meant a trek of eight hundred and fifty miles through almost solid wilderness. By water it was a straight sail of less than three hundred.

That south coast from Halifax around the bend of Cape Sable to Yarmouth was a rim of harbors — more than fifty deep-water bays boring in among the fingers of the land. The whole interior was sprinkled with lakes, feeding the brooks and streams and rivers that twisted through the forests of pine and spruce and oak down to the harbors and the sea.

The Medway River, kept alive by a dozen back country lakes, meandered through the woods, under the main south coast road past the settlement of Mill Village, and then rose and fell in conflict with the tide a mile before it finally reached an inlet of Medway Harbor and expired. Deep and long and sheltered, the harbor was as fine an anchorage as any on the coast.

Along its south shore sprang up the town of Port Medway. By the 1820's there were twenty families in the settlement, a Baptist meetinghouse and a school. Timber, floated down the river from the hinterlands, was already a portent of things to come, and a dozen lumber ships a year were sailing for England alone.

And fish! In the spring the river teemed with salmon and alewives, driven toward the headwaters by the compulsion to reproduce. The men staked weirs from bank to bank and reaped their harvest. In the summer they sailed their boats as far as Labrador for mackerel and cod. Port Medway was a boom town in the making.

Bill Blackburn was a great, rawboned fisherman of thirty-seven when he married Mary Ann Thompson on a hot August day in 1845. She was an Irish immigrant who lived up the road in Mill Village and was eleven years younger than he. They set up housekeeping in a neat clapboard cottage on a hill overlooking Dock Cove of the river, a long stone's throw back from the road to Port Medway.

The Blackburns lost no time starting a family. Their firstborn was Jim, and the rest followed with cyclical regularity, every twenty-eight months — Martha, Will, Jack and Eliza. The house was filling up.

Eliza was three and a half when the fourth strapping boy was born, in the dead of winter. Mary Ann noted the time in the fly-leaf of the family Bible, along with the others — six in the evening on Thursday, February 17, 1859. They named him Howard.

In two years the fifth brother, Tom, was born, and in two more the third sister, Bessy. That was the end of childbearing. Eight in eighteen years was enough for one woman and a five-room house, and too many for one poor man to feed and clothe for very long.

Port Medway had fulfilled its promise and by the 1860's was a boom town for fair. Millions of board feet of lumber from the apparently limitless forests, rafted down the river in the spring, sledded over the ice in the winter and hauled down the road, took over the town, and piles of it as big as houses lined the streets for a half a mile back from the wharves. Vessels slid down the ways into the harbor as fast as the shipyards could build them. The anchorage was crowded with ships, coming and going, day and night. Half of all the pine in Nova Scotia was shipped out of Port Medway, and one glorious night the whole town turned out to watch more than sixty squareriggers bend their sails to the wind and slip out of the harbor in a white-bibbed armada such as few ports have ever seen. The vessels carried lumber and dried fish up and down the Atlantic, but mostly to the West Indies, and they returned with holds full of molasses and rum.

The waterfront was aswarm with sailors on the loose, and he had to be a thin-blooded lad who could resist the sea fever of their yarns, and the smells of the fresh-sawed pine and the fish, and the sight of the ships and sails.

The first years of my life was spent swimming, rowing and sailing boats on the Medway River. The nearest school house was one mile from my home. So, often when my parents thought that I was in school, I was working in a saw mill, doing a man's work for six dollars per month. When my parents found that they could not keep me in school, they bound me out to learn a trade with a Mr. Reed. I was to remain with him until I would be 21 years old.

But I had seen a picture of Columbus landing on an island in the West Indies and thought that every place but Port Medway was just like that island, and how I longed for the time to come when I would be old enough to ship on a vessel and go sailing around the world!

Howard was ten when he quit school, and his longing for manhood and a life of adventure on the sea welled up inside him when he heard the often told story of Grandfather Blackburn's famous uncompleted voyage to Halifax.

Captain John, as everybody called him, was the owner of a small two-masted vessel of about fifteen or twenty tons known as a pinky — quite a little like a schooner, but of an earlier type, being high and sharp at both ends, decked over and steered with a tiller. Her name was *Sophia Catherine*.

For some years Captain John had been in the habit now and then of running down the coast to Halifax from Port Medway with a makeshift cargo of barrel staves, shingles, lumber and other odds and ends and returning with a load of supplies for the people of the district. Often as not, his return cargo included an assortment of kegs and jugs containing what was widely considered indispensable "for the preservation of the public health."

One February day in 1855, Captain John, his dog, and David Day and John Taylor, his crew, set sail for Halifax as usual. Besides their cargo, they had stowed aboard *Sophia Catherine* a bag of potatoes, a barrel of man-o'-war biscuits, a barrel of fresh water, a few smoked alewives and a round of pork, plenty and more for three men and a dog on an eighty-mile run.

That night a violent gale whistled in from the northeast, and by the time it had blown itself out several days later Captain John and his men found they had been driven clear out of the Gulf Stream and were somewhere in the Atlantic. The weather, they agreed, seemed warm for February. They had no navigation instruments aboard — not even a compass — but the wind was fair, and they kept on sailing. They had no fire, and after a while no water, either, except what they distilled "through an old boot leg."

When she was forty-one days out of Port Medway, *Sophia Catherine* fell in with a Boston vessel, the *Foster*, which spoke them and offered to take them aboard. But since it had rained that day and given them a new supply of fresh water, and since they learned from the *Foster* that they were only a hundred miles from land, Captain John decided not to abandon ship.

The next day they made a landfall. They ran into the harbor and found themselves in Simpson's Bay on the north side of the island of St. Martin's in the West Indies.

Sophia Catherine had wandered somewhat over two thousand miles off course on an eighty-mile coasting trip.

Captain John disposed of his boat and cargo to good advantage. The brig *Pearl* from Liverpool, Nova Scotia, chanced to be in port, bound for Boston, and the three took passage in her.

Nearly a year had passed, and the fate of *Sophia Catherine* and her crew had been dolorously accepted in Port Medway, when one fine day the checkers game in Uncle Eddie Foster's shoemaking shop was interrupted by the appearance at the door of Captain John. His account of his adventures was listened to with considerable interest.

Sometime later John Taylor drifted home. He inquired immediately for Captain John, whom he described as a first-rate man, except that he ate the biggest share of the dog during the hungriest leg of the voyage.

Two weeks before Christmas of the year that Howard was bound out to Mr. Reed, his brother Will was lost at sea.

Poor Will — he was only eighteen, a rollicking, restless giant of a lad who with Jim and Jack gave the Blackburn boys their reputations as a wild and hell-raising pack of young devils.

Election nights they would all go up to Mill Village and start a parade, Will in the lead on a big white horse. Down the dusty road to Port Medway they would come, banners flying, banging on dishpans, yelling and whooping. Their ranks would swell as they picked up more young bloods on the way. When they reached the waterfront, the sailors joined the clamor, and there was whoopee for the rest of the night.

Their bag of tricks was never empty. A querulous old woman lived up the road a piece, alone. One dark night the boys sneaked onto her roof and pitched a clatter of tin pans down the chimney.

"Ghosts!" she screamed. "Ghosts in my chimney!" and picked up her skirts and ran from the house in terror.

Bill Blackburn was a big man who always wore a tall beaver hat whatever he was doing, and his temper matched his size. Many a licking he gave his boys, but he was often at sea, and their high spirits were not of the kind that could be whipped away.

To Mary Ann fell the lot of raising the brood. She was a patient and tolerant woman — and susceptible to sentiment.

Her husband was off on a voyage, and although overdue, not enough so to set her to worrying. A neighbor lady dropped by one afternoon for tea, thinking Mrs. Blackburn might enjoy a bit of company. Mary Ann brought out a plate of her famous cakes, and as they chatted in the parlor the visitor took one, wishing to be polite, though she could have eaten the whole lot.

As the neighbor eyed the dainties, hunger sharpened her wits, and she struck upon a ruse. Making a long face, she burst out with a whimper:

"Oh, Mary Ann, think of it indeed! Here we are, setting in the parlor enjoying ourselves, while the sharks are out there yammering poor Bill's bones!"

Overcome by this horrible vision, Mary Ann buried her face in her apron, and the hungry visitor downed half a dozen cakes in a row.

Howard spent about eighteen months with Mr. Reed, but cabinetmaking was not for him — and as for being cooped up in a shop the day long, it was more than he could stand at the age of eleven.

So one night while Mr. Reed was asleep, I packed my few belongings into a towel and ran away. I hid behind a fence and waited until daylight and then started to walk to Bridgewater 20 miles away. I arrived there that afternoon and got a job in a saw mill, but it did not last long, for as soon as Mr. Reed missed me he called on my parents and they soon had me back, but when I told them that if they sent me back to that trade I would run so far the next time that they would never find me, they fixed it up some way and I was free to go where I liked.

He liked hard work and danger and excitement, and he yearned to be a man before his time. He was a big, tough kid, and the next winter he disappeared into the snow of the back woods and bent his growing strength to the work of the lumberjack with ax and saw. In the spring he emerged, riding down the swollen river on the rolling humps of the logs, a boy of thirteen with the body of a man. But summer — that was the time of year for him; he lived to get out in a boat.

A boy named Hatt and I got a boat to go fishing in from an island called Pudden Pan. To reach the island from the Medway Harbor we had to cross a shoal called the Reef of Andrews Head.

When we got about halfway across we heard something roaring just outside of us. We look and saw a wall of water fully ten feet high rushing towards us. We put the boat head to it just in time, but the sea was so high that it stood the boat on its end.

I, thinking that the boat would pitch over on top of us, jumped over board. As soon as the stern of the boat was relieved of my weight she fell back on her bottom with everything but my companion washed out of her. He clung to one of the thwarts, and the next sea carried the boat ashore and left her high and dry among the rocks. Strange to say, neither the boat or my companion was much injured.

When I came to the surface I found one oar and the mast floating near me. I got hold of them and laid across them and tried to get my boat off, but before I could do so a big breaker came rushing down on me. So I let go of the mast and oar and sank so that the sea run over me without doing any harm. As soon as the sea had passed over I came to the surface and begin swimming toward the shore.

I would swim until a sea was just about to break on me, when I would sink and let it pass over me. Then I would rise again and continue to swim towards some boats that had put out from the shore and was waiting for me just inside of the breakers.

After a hard struggle of nearly an hour I reached the nearest boat. They hauled me in and rowed me ashore. After this experience I began going to sea like a man.

Far from dampening his appetite for the sea, this escapade merely whetted it, and Howard concluded that he was ready for anything. It was 1872, and he was thirteen. He shipped out as a green hand on a squarerigger bound for Funchal, in the Madeiras. He was worked like a dog and found the men he was thrown in with just as violent and heavy-handed a lot as his father had described his own shipmates. But he loved it.

Probably he never saw the fierce man in the tall beaver hat again. In November of the following year big Bill Blackburn, almost within sight of his home, drowned in the Medway River when his boat capsized. He was sixty-five, an expert mariner, and had many good years left in him. But the sea claimed him, just as it had young Will.

Three years later tragedy cut down the Blackburns for the third and fourth times. Only five weeks apart, perhaps from contagious disease, Eliza and Jack died. She was twenty-one and he twenty-three. Mary Ann Blackburn was not yet sixty, but within seven years, she had lost her husband, two sons and a daughter. Her eldest son Jim was never to marry; he lived at home and followed the sea as a fisherman. Howard was gone, God only knew where.

He was banging up and down and across the world, on one vessel after another, squareriggers and schooners, English and

American, from the Atlantic to the Pacific, from the Arctic to the Antarctic.

Seven years before the mast, he landed in Gloucester in April of 1879, just turned twenty. Those years had made him a man in every dimension. A monkey aloft, a bear at the end of a line, an ox at the oar and a fox at the wheel, he had a genius for the sea that was sharpened to a keen edge by experience. This tough, handsome goliath, hard-drinking, fun-loving and handy with the girls, was ready for the truest test of the sailor — bank-fishing on a Gloucester schooner.

There weren't many sites open for a newcomer, but Captain Murdock MacInnis took a liking to young Blackburn and signed him up to sail on the schooner *Polar Wave*. Howard proved himself immediately, and from then on berths came easy.

For three and a half years he sailed out of Gloucester, summer and winter, in every kind of weather. It was all he wanted. He knew he was born to be a fisherman — a Gloucester fisherman.

In January of 1883 the *Grace L. Fears,* short a hand, touched at Liverpool. Home for Christmas, Howard signed up for a fresh halibut trip to Burgeo Bank.

4
Saloonkeeper

HOWARD BLACKBURN limped back from Newfoundland a legend.

All Gloucester and the world knew the epic of Burgeo and Little River, and he had not been in town twenty-four hours that June of 1883, just long enough to get settled in a waterfront boardinghouse, when he was buttonholed by the newspaper editor.

George Procter was a dedicated friend of the fishermen. He had been publishing sketchy accounts of Blackburn's saga in the weekly *Cape Ann Advertiser,* and he was eager for the details.

Howard was glad to give them to him, and four days after his return the *Advertiser* ran the stark story, with this postcript:

He is a young man and is extremely desirous of doing something for a livelihood. His feet are extremely troublesome yet, but with good care promise to do well; his great desire is to obtain artificial hands, (having full use of his wrists), whereby he may be enabled to follow some light occupation. He has no money, and we hereby call upon the kind-hearted readers of the *Advertiser* to forward such amounts as they please to this office for his benefit.

Within a week a hundred and twenty-six dollars had been received, and Procter reported:

The recipient feels very grateful to those who have thus remembered him in his time of trouble, and will make every effort toward self-maintenance. In addition to the above sum the owners of sch. *Grace L. Fears,* comprising the Atlantic Halibut Company, from

which vessel he got astray, very generously paid him the amount
which they estimated as his share of the trip, $86.

Notwithstanding the generosity of the owners in turning over
to Howard his unearned share, the *Advertiser* mounted a crusade to persuade owners and masters to supply dories with emergency stores of food and water. It was not notably successful.

Howard basked uneasily in the spring glow of adulation that
warmed his return to Gloucester. Spring would turn to summer,
summer to fall, fall to winter, and what then? His old friends
made much of him, and new ones sought him every day. Every
fisherman in port knew the story and wanted to hear it from his
own lips, to see for himself the proof of it in the stumps. Every
vessel that rounded Eastern Point brought its crew of curious,
wondering men to look him up. It was drinks on the house and
a free meal in every bar and lunchroom up and down the harbor.

But what did a man do without fingers, a man born to the sea
who knew nothing else? He might as well have had his arms cut
off for all the use they were. What was there left of life?

There was Gloucester, the only roost for such a wing-clipped
gull as Blackburn. Here, at least, he was so close to the sea he
could feel it but not touch it, stand in the wind but not move
with it, gaze at the ships but not sail them, smell the fish but
not capture them, be among the men but not with them.

Two hundred and sixty years before, men had sailed from
England to fish the banks off North America, looking for a new
life in a New World. Scudding down the New England coast,
they encountered the jutting ledges of Cape Ann. To the
southwest they sailed, past the cape's cape of Eastern Point,
and when they rounded it they looked inside; back to the northeast again lay the long calm reach of the most perfect harbor
they had seen. They heeled their ship past the red-brown rocks
a mile inside the pocket of the land to a sandy beach, and there
they settled.

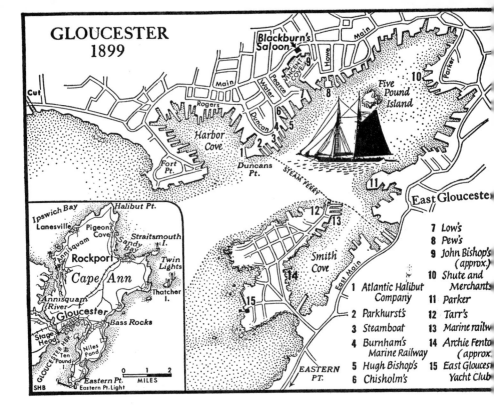

GLOUCESTER
1899

Blackburn's Saloon

Five
Pound
Island

Harbor
Cove

Fort
Pt.

Duncans
Pt.

STEAM FERRY

East Gloucester

Ipswich Bay   Halibut Pt.
Lanesville
        Pigeon
        Cove   Straitsmouth
                        I.
Rockport   Twin
                Lights
Cape Ann   Thatcher
Annisquam   I.
River
    Gloucester
        Bass Rocks
Stage
Head   Niles
    Ten   Pond
    Pound
Eastern Pt.   MILES
SHB   Eastern Pt. Light

0   1   2

Smith
Cove

EASTERN
PT.

7 Low's
8 Pew's
9 John Bishop's
     (approx.)
10 Shute and
     Merchants
11 Parker
12 Tarr's
13 Marine railw
14 Archie Fento
     (approx.
15 East Glouces
     Yacht Club

1 Atlantic Halibut
     Company
2 Parkhurst's
3 Steamboat
4 Burnham's
     Marine Railway
5 Hugh Bishop's
6 Chisholm's

What a harbor it was! America stretched out to the south and
west, and to the north and east were the virgin fishing grounds.
Southeast lay Georges Bank, treacherous and stormy but nearest
at hand. Eastward lay Brown's, off the southern cape of Nova
Scotia. And then to the northeast in succession, strung off toward
Newfoundland — Le Have, Emerald, Middle Ground, Canso,
Banquereau, Misaine, Burgeo and the Grand Banks themselves.

The ocean was gorged with fish — cod, haddock, halibut, hake,
pollock, mackerel, whiting, cusk, perch, catfish, sole and flounder.
Off the rocks of Cape Ann the bottom was alive with lobsters
and crabs, and millions of clams lurked in the sand and mud of
the beaches and flats.

At the back door were the great forests of New England,
tough oak and cedar for frames and planking, tall pine for masts

and spars. The settlement grew and spread around the harbor shore as fast as ships were built and men came to sail them — Englishmen, Nova Scotians, Newfoundlanders, Portuguese, Italians — the fishermen of the world came to Gloucester.

By 1883 two hundred and fifty-nine vessels and three thousand men were sailing out of Gloucester Harbor. Bellies full, the returning schooners nosed heavily into the wharves and discharged in one year fifty-five million pounds of cod, seventeen million, two hundred thousand pounds of herring, seven million, two hundred and fifty thousand pounds of halibut, four million, two hundred thousand pounds of haddock, hake, pollock and cusk, and one hundred and eight thousand barrels of mackerel.

The majestic curtains of canvas and the busy sheets of sail glided and scuttled over a plain of water quilled with masts. To and fro, in and out, pausing, swinging, up sail, down sail, turning with the tide, playing with the breeze, they came, rested and departed — the bankers, seiners, salt barks, squareriggers, lumber coasters, colliers, pinkies, sloop boats, catboats, sidewheelers, tugs, water carriers, yachts, launches, dories and skiffs.

Back in the recesses of the harbor, behind Ten Pound Island and Rocky Neck and Five Pound Island, by the Fort and Duncan Point, along Smith Cove and Vincent Cove and Harbor Cove, the shore sagged with wharves and shipyards, marine railways, chandleries and sail lofts, riggers, rope walks, net and twine factories, smithies, coopers and boxmakers, icehouses, warehouses, gashouses, paint shops, machine shops, sheds, stables, smokehouses, flake yards, oilskin makers, glue factories, fish dealers, salt dealers, outfitters, teamsters, brokers, agents, saloons, grogshops, poolrooms, barbershops, lunchrooms and boardinghouses.

The coarse redolence of flaked fish baking by the acre in the sun and the tang of tarred rope and nets and the pungency of fresh paint and the stink of the flats at low water and the iodine smell of the seaweed all mingled with the fresh salt air in an ambrosia of the sea. Floating arcs of snow, the gulls soared and wheeled and screamed, scavengers immaculate.

The schooners wedged in the wharves, stall after stall, like patient horses. They nudged and creaked against the pilings. The wavelets patted their sides and traded dancing shimmers of reflection with the mirrors of their sterns. The rigging sighed, and a block squeaked; a halyard slapped along a mast, and the drying sails rippled in the breeze.

Suddenly boys chased and yelled from deck to deck, scrambled panting up the shrouds, dove into the dark water, swam laughing to a hanging rope — underfoot, asking questions, watching, feeling the sea.

Men shouted and called, laughed, cursed, whistled. Iron rims rattled over cobblestones. Hammers argued with echoes of staccato. Steam hissed up into a fluff of cotton. A mallet clumped against a trunnel. A barrel clattered over a drum roll of loose boards. A crate thumped, a hatch slammed, chain clanked off a winch. And over it all the crying chorus of the gulls.

Late that summer Howard rented a vacant store on Main Street, a wooden cubbyhouse so close to the harbor that high tide crept almost to the back stoop. The subscription fund had reached five hundred dollars, including the proceeds of the Athletic Club's Blackburn benefit ball. It was enough to get started in business. He laid in a stock of cigars and tobacco and other such sundries as a fisherman might buy with his loose change.

A local artist named Paul Collins painted three scenes for him, stark and wild. The first depicted the dorymates busy at the trawl in driving snow and mounting seas; then the dory lying to the drag, with Blackburn bailing for his life, the frozen body in the stern; finally a gaunt figure rowing up Little River under cliffs reaching high toward a frosty moon.

"He couldn't have come nearer the mark had he seen the whole!" exclaimed the subject when he viewed the finished work.

The artist's brother, Captain Joseph W. Collins, did him a similar good turn. Once a highlining Gloucester skipper, he had become an international authority on fishing and was employed as an expert by the United States Commission of Fish and Fisheries. A facile and prolific writer, Captain Collins was so moved by the Blackburn story that he wrote it up for him, and Howard had it published privately as a booklet entitled *Fearful Experience of a Gloucester Halibut Fisherman, Astray in a Dory in a Gale off the Newfoundland Coast in Midwinter*.

Reproductions were made of the paintings, and Howard offered them for sale along with the booklet.

He opened for business on the sixteenth of October. The very same day he took the train to Boston with a couple of friends, Mike Keefe and Jim Corbiey. They stood witness while he swore before the Circuit Court to uphold the Constitution of the United States of America. He was an American citizen.

A week later he inserted an advertisement in the *Advertiser*:

CARD OF THANKS

The subscriber hereby returns his heartfelt thanks to the many kind friends who have assisted him by their contributions and words of sympathy. Having now established a cigar and tobacco store on Main Street, and engaged in the selling of photographs representing the terrible incidents of my life, I hope to be able in the future to be self-supporting.

HOWARD BLACKBURN

There was in the man a curious mixture of ingenuous willingness to exploit himself, genuine modesty, simple warmth and hard, fierce pride.

As a tobacconist he was a success. It was not a line to get rich in, but he had business sense. His hands made a clumsy job of it with the customers, but it was his feet that bothered him the most. Standing on them, walking on them — all day behind the counter — they were embers of pain at the ends of his legs.

Just before Christmas he received word that his mother had died in Port Medway. He was thankful that he had visited her the year before, but the blow made him the more wretched.

His feet finally drove him to a doctor, who amputated what was left of the toes. It was good riddance. When the stubs had healed, special shoes were fitted, and some of the spring returned to his step. As for the hands, the doctor ordered steel hooks for him, strapped them on where the fingers had been and sent him on his way.

All the while he was selling cigars and tobacco, Howard had his eye on a more potent and infinitely more profitable commodity.

Liquor was a hot issue in Gloucester. At election every December its dispensation was put to the vote. If the ayes had it, the saloonkeepers the next April applied to the City Council for licenses, effective the first of May; if the nays prevailed, the barroom doors swung shut on May Day. The trouble was that Gloucester couldn't make up its mind. The indecision of the voters put the saloon business cycle on an annual and completely unpredictable basis.

Temperance was on the march. The issue seesawed back and forth, one year to the drys, the next to the wets. The rallies increased in tempo and spirit as election day approached. The clergy harangued from the pulpit, the Anti-Saloon League marshaled its forces and the fire-eating circuit riders descended on the city.

The decent people of Gloucester (and the businessmen with a vested interest in the sobriety of their workers) annually responded to the call with a rising fever of moral excitement. The saloons were a cancer in the body politic, and their keepers were the vanguard of Satan's army, degraders of the public morals, panderers to the baseness in men, corrupters of the fishermen and mechanics, contributors to delinquency and enemies of the hearth and home. It was not thought safe for a respectable woman of any age to go abroad alone after dark, so infested was the seaport said to be with rough, drunken men carousing through the streets, singing, shouting and cursing.

Nevertheless, the spring tides ran with the wets. Morality, in spite of temporary victories, was inevitably driven to take shelter by the heat of the parched throat and a thirst fired by seven months of official virtue and rendered irresistible by the prospect of at least five more after election day.

When Howard opened his cigar store, the city happened to be wet, but in two months it turned dry, until December 1884, when it switched back to wet.

Having spent enough time on the drinking side of a bar to know that it was a lucrative business, the following April he applied for a liquor license and a victualer's permit along with it so he could serve the salt fish, smoked halibut, pickles and crackers that blunt the hunger and sharpen the thirst.

But he had not reckoned on politics. The City Council tabled all the liquor applications and granted the victualer's licenses. Here was a fine fix: what good to a saloonkeeper was food without drink?

The aldermen were actually trying to make it appear that the new mayor, with whom they were already in a brawl, was really responsible for obstructing the mandate of the voters, for they longed to put him on the griddle where it hurt the most.

An alderman himself for three years, John Parsons was a rough village Cromwell type, a self-made man in the business of wrecking buildings. He was stocky and humorless. His massive bald head was fringed with luxuriant curls, and he had all the stubbornness of a billygoat and the chin whiskers to match.

Having allied himself with the forces of decency and temperance during the campaign, Parsons immediately upon his election as mayor mounted an attack on Marshal Joseph A. Moore, the chief of police. The marshal, he claimed, was soft on prostitution, and while Moore was otherwise engaged in court Parsons took out warrants and personally led the police in a series of red light raids. After three months of harassment the marshal resigned, and Parsons replaced him with the man of his choice, Captain

Robert Tarr. Marshal Tarr went after the illegal liquor sellers, and when he found they had locked their supplies in their safes, hired a locksmith and cracked them for his evidence.

The Council having decided to sidestep the license responsibility, the mayor flooded his former colleagues with nominations for liquor commissioners, but they rejected them all as unsatisfactory, and the applications remained on the table. By July, Parsons was accusing his own man of laxity and demanding his resignation. Marshal Tarr held out until December, when the frustrated wets again had their day but unaccountably re-elected the mayor. Then Tarr gave in, declaring that nothing could induce him to serve any longer under Mayor Parsons in an office which he had accepted at the first against his better judgment.

Two days before Christmas, with a fine sense of timing, Howard dropped by the *Advertiser* office on a matter of business which the flabbergasted editor rushed into his holiday edition:

Mr. Blackburn came into our office on Wednesday, stating that he now wished to donate the $500 raised for him in his time of need, for the benefit of the fishermen's widows and fatherless children, here in Gloucester, and he wished us to take charge of it, having the fullest confidence that from our experience in this work the money would be faithfully distributed. He furthermore said that at the time he looked upon the donation, not as a gift, but merely to help tide him over a time of great need. He had done fairly well in business and was able to take care of himself, and wished to assist those who were poorer off in the world than he was. To say that we were surprised at the noble generosity of this crippled fisherman does not express our feelings in the least, and we endeavored to persuade him not to give up the whole sum at this time, but divide it, as he might greatly need it himself. But he would not listen to it, as his mind had been made up for some time, and he wanted the widowed and fatherless to have the whole of it.

This money comes in good time. Already this season we have had repeated applications for aid which we could not meet, as the funds placed in our charge have been expended. We shall place a goodly share of it with the Gloucester Female Charitable Association, and under their administration this money will do the good which the donor is so anxious it should. Many a poor family in this city will partake of Christmas cheer out of this fund today, as it came just in time for that.

Mr. Blackburn wishes us to thank the friends who contributed this money to him, and feels assured that they will be pleased with the disposal which he has made of it.

He was the talk of the town.

As the opening gun of his second term in January of 1886 the mayor appointed George Douglass, one of his ardent campaigners, as the new marshal; Parsons' Purge, as it had come to be called, was renewed with zeal.

Marshal Douglass went on the warpath for firewater, and on April 8 he found some — in Howard's store. A batch of bottles had been carelessly concealed in the back room, and the offender paid a trifling fine in court.

The raid on the popular Blackburn was not widely applauded; there was feeling among the wets that the saloonkeepers' right to pour and theirs to quaff was being subverted by this feud among a pack of political mules.

Nothing daunted by his brush with the law, Howard resubmitted his request for a license. Again the Council tabled the applications.

But he was not inclined to let it bother him. Something else was on his mind.

There was a girl in Gloucester, a quiet Irish girl, and she was pretty as a picture, tiny and full of grace. Her level eyes were steady and warm, and there was just enough thrust to her chin to hint that she had a mind of her own. Her black hair swept up in ringlets from her forehead to the pert little bun that was the fashion of the day.

Theresa Lally was twenty-four, three years younger than Howard, and she worked as a dressmaker. He towered head and shoulders above her, like a protective giant.

The manner of their meeting is their secret, but they traveled to Boston — perhaps because he was Church of England, though he rarely if ever attended services, and her Catholic faith frowned on the alliance — and were married on the twenty-fourth of June, 1886. When they returned to Gloucester man and wife, they set up housekeeping in a flat a few doors up the street from the store.

That December (he was still waiting for the liquor license to which he believed himself entitled) the inscrutable electorate voted dry, threw out Mayor Parsons and elected David I. Robinson, a hell-or-high-water temperance man.

Frustrated to the limit of his short temper, Howard had by now convinced himself that he had a right to sell liquor that transcended the whims of the voters. Less than two weeks after the election Marshal Douglass and Officer Eben Clark entered the store, pushed into the back room and surprised the clerk, Steve Spidell, in the act of trying to hide several flasks of whiskey he had just filled from a jug. The law walked out with two and a half gallons of bootleg, and for the second time the offender paid his penalty in court.

In a month, on January 14, 1887, the suspicious cops paid Howard a return visit and seized some more. The man was incorrigible.

Six days later Theresa had a baby boy, and they named him Howard. His father was wildly happy. He yearned for children, lots of them — the more sons the better — and here was a fine start. He fussed over his diminutive wife and her infant like a solicitous genie.

They had a nurse for their baby. When he was six weeks old he caught a cold, and the doctor left medicine for him. The nurse

Annie Forbes

The Blackburn homestead at Port Medway, Nova Scotia.

Addie Dolloff

Annie Forbes

Theresa and Howard

misunderstood the instructions and gave the infant a large over-
dose. She confessed her mistake to Theresa, but it was too late.
The baby died in convulsions.

The poor woman begged the brokenhearted mother not to tell
Howard what had happened. Theresa carried the terrible secret
to her grave, convinced that had he known the truth he would
have killed the nurse.

Howard was beside himself with grief. He ranted and cursed
and demanded of God why He had done such a thing to him.
But to the end of his life he believed his son had been carried
away by illness.

Then Theresa was taken to the hospital. The pregnancy apparently had been too much for her. There was an operation;
she would never bear him another child.

His grief turned to bitterness, an abiding rancor which he
turned against his wife.

The voters kicked the traces again in December, to no one's
surprise, cast their ballots for the saloons and re-elected their
temperance mayor. In April of 1888 Howard applied for a license
for the third time. The City Council approved the applications,
but Mayor Robinson refused to sign them, declaring that under
no circumstances would he be a party to the legalized sale of
liquor. A dealer took him into the Massachusetts Supreme Court
and got an order compelling His Honor to sign his name. The
mayor called a meeting of the Council and resigned.

The city was in an uproar. The aldermen elected William W.
French, a dapper lawyer with side whiskers and a boutonniere
in his lapel, to succeed their departed leader.

Mayor French immediately and without ceremony signed the
licenses. Howard was finally and legally in business as a saloonkeeper — until December, when the city voted dry.

A less obstinate man might have been discouraged, but the
saloonkeepers of Gloucester were an optimistic and resourceful
lot, and they had unbounded faith in human nature. They played

a waiting game. They knew the city was wet at the core, and they knew they could count on those pivotal citizens, the damp drys, to vote for their pocketbooks whenever the deprivation of license fees threatened to increase the tax rate.

In this forward-looking spirit Howard in August of 1889 bought the waterfront property where he had been renting his store. The deal included a house and a blacksmith shop. He paid twenty-five hundred dollars cash and took over a three-thousand-dollar mortgage which he discharged fourteen months later. He was prospering.

The Gay Nineties were launched from the ballot box in December with a vote so wet that it dripped for six wonderful years.

Among nautical men Blackburn's was one of the best-known saloons on the North Atlantic seaboard, and it was a favorite hangout for fishermen from Newfoundland to New York whenever they touched at Gloucester.

The proprietor was generally behind the bar from the hour it opened in the morning until closing time late at night. Business would increase as the day wore on, and by the late afternoon and evening the saloon presented a picture that has remained one of the nostalgic symbols of the era — the long mahogany bar crowded elbow to elbow with roughly dressed fishermen, shifting their feet in the fresh sawdust on the floor; the glistening brass spittoons; the famous paintings on the wall darkly ominous beyond the smoke-dimmed glow of the gas lights — all of it omnisciently presided over by the commanding figure of the owner with his neatly parted hair and handlebar mustache.

There he stood behind the bar, cigar clenched in the thumb stub of one hand, the other crooked on his hip. After he had filled one of the big pot-bellied beer glasses from the tap, he squeezed the stem between the thumb creases of both hands, set it on the bar and gave it a flourishing shove down the length, to be intercepted by the waiting hand of the consignee.

Men came and went, in from fishing trips with tales of hardship and heroism that left their barmates shaking their heads. But always in front of them was the one who went to sea no more but whose hands told more than any words.

Howard had learned to use those useless hands with an ingenuity that was shocking in its effect. The steel hooks were all but forgotten. He had mastered the ability to grasp any number of objects, including pen and pencil, with the remnants of his thumbs. He could pick up a coin lying flat on the bar with the folds in his palms, and the muscles of his arm rippled up to the shoulder with the effort. It was a tour de force, and citizens of ordinary sobriety came in for a short beer just to see him do it. To top this off, he developed the trick of balancing a coin on edge, an idle habit to while away the time and entertain the house.

Roast beef and steak were his staff of life. He dined on one or the other — with all the fixings — almost every night, and since he had the appetite of two men and a thirst to match, the results were evident by the time he was thirty-five. The rough bones of his face retreated behind a blanket of flesh, his neck came out to meet his chin, and he nourished an impressive paunch.

Portliness merely made him the more imposing. He let his hair grow longer and curlier and sported a raffish spiral at the ends of his mustache, which he was in the habit of twisting absentmindedly. When he dressed up, he wore a natty frock coat of the latest cut, a starched white shirt, an enormously knotted four-in-hand or bow tie and sometimes striped or checkered trousers. He had worked out a trick of doing up his collar by passing a looped string through the hole and around the button and pulling it to draw one through the other. His waistcoat alone was worth the price of a drink to admire. One that he favored was adorned with silver buttons, invariably draped across with his heavy gold watch chain strung with charms, and banked with tiers of change pockets that he worked deftly with his stubby thumbs; it was a sartorial cash register.

Photo by George Bacon Wood

Gloucester was the world's busiest fishing port around the turn of the century. Looking out the harbor.

Gordon W. Thomas

With a mighty splash another schooner slides into Vincent Cove from Tom Irving's shipyard, just west of Blackburn's saloon, 1890's. Rogers Street runs through here today.

Blackburn's was a workingmen's club, like most of the saloons of the day, and that was the way he kept it. Fighting, frivolity and loud talk were not allowed. Rarely did he have to raise his voice to maintain order, but when he did the glasses vibrated and silence fell on the place like a curtain. If he were powerfully provoked, as happened on a few occasions, he swung into action and more than once knocked a man down with a blow of his stumpy fist.

Inevitably he was a boxing fan. These were the years when a degree of respectability was being pounded into prizefighting by the big mitts of John L. Sullivan, Gentleman Jim Corbett, Bob Fitzsimmons and Jim Jeffries. Somewhere along the line he had met the great John L., and they got to be good friends, naturally enough, for the two had much in common. The Boston Strong Boy was only four months older than the Fearless Fisherman of Gloucester; they looked alike, and both were physical giants, supremely courageous and given to hard drinking, although Blackburn never let his taste for whiskey — which was the bare-knuckle champion's downfall — get the better of him.

Howard had company and friends enough, but he was a man alone. Day and night his old life walked into the saloon with its talk of fishing and fares, of schooners and skippers and weather, but it stopped across the bar from him. That gleaming expanse of mahogany was a million miles and a decade across. Every year it widened and pushed him back farther into the past.

He was the slave of his own legend. How sick of it he was, and how doggedly he clung to it! After a few years he exhausted his supply of the booklet Captain Collins had written for him, and in 1895 he asked his friend Dr. William Hale to write a new one, revised and enlarged. Dr. Hale was an occasional poet, romanticizer of the fisherman's hard life and an old Blackburn admirer. *A Fearless Fisherman* was privately printed by Howard, full-blown and adulatory to a degree that should have been embarrassing but probably wasn't; false modesty was not among his weaknesses.

The experience of '83 evoked another equally compulsive side of his nature which first revealed itself that Christmas when he turned over to charity every penny of the subscription fund. Once he had discharged this debt, as he regarded it, he threw his energies and resources into philanthropy with such a vengeance that he came to be regarded as possibly the most consistently devoted and generally least flamboyant friend of the poor in the history of his adopted city. Within ten years he had already repaid the kindness of his fellow citizens three times over.

The memory of those three months on the Newfoundland coast, lying like an infant in the Lishmans' hut, sharing in the cruelest poverty he had ever seen and owing his life to them withal, haunted him all his days and was the wellspring of his benefactions.

Year after year he sent a special order of clothing and food to the Lishmans, and nearly every fall, as the Gloucester herring fleet prepared to sail for Newfoundland, he rounded up supplies from all over town and had them put aboard the schooners to lighten the winter of the poor people along the coast.

In November of 1895 a wire came into the office of the *Cape Ann Advertiser*, and George Procter hastened with it to his composing room:

A despatch from Halifax, N.S., says that a day or two ago a stranger visited a number of wholesale houses in that city and purchased a quantity of flour, meat, molasses, tea, clothing, etc., to be shipped. He picked out what he desired, and then asked if they took Canadian silver; they said, yes, of course; and he went to the hotel and brought a large bag full, with which he paid $500.

He explained that he had been a Gloucester fisherman nine or ten years ago and was lost adrift. He got to Burgeo, Newfoundland, but his fingers and toes were frozen so that most of them had to be amputated. He was nursed and cared for by two families there. Finally he got back to Gloucester, started business, was successful, and all Canadian silver that came in he threw in a box by itself. Hearing of the destitution in Burgeo, and that his kind friends would likely share in it, and having some other business that way, he went to Halifax, bringing his Canadian silver, and bought as related.

The gentleman did not want his name divulged, but the mysterious donor is said to be Mr. Howard Blackburn of this city.

Howard's traditional Christmas largesse was astonishing. That portion of his seasonal dispensation in 1893 that came to the attention of the newspapers, for example, consisted of ten barrels of flour, ten bushels of potatoes, a hundred pounds of sugar, eighteen turkeys, twenty-five dollars' worth of tea, coffee and other supplies and five tons of coal for the poor of Gloucester.

Throughout the year he would give away so much that he never knew himself what it amounted to. Shoes, suits, dresses, coats, barrels of flour, tons of coal would unaccountably be delivered at the door of some family in distress, and the source would forever remain a mystery, although it could be guessed at. He always carried large amounts of cash with him, and unworthy indeed was the suppliant he refused. Every cause or subscription that came along could count on him for one of the largest donations, for he was known as a man who reached down deep. Many a customer at the bar paid twice over and told the proprietor to keep the change, knowing how he would use it.

But there was more to this than simple charity. His own self-sufficiency was an obsession with him. He couldn't stand the thought of being in any man's debt. Thus he paid back the money that had been raised for him out of his first savings and likewise cleared his mortgage in fourteen months. If a bill arrived in the morning, it had to be paid by noon.

It was as if his charities were coin in the bank of his self-esteem, a savings account of gratitude, always kept well ahead to insure that his side of the ledger of his human relations would remain in the black.

Perhaps there was something about the nature of his business that caused him to be uneasy and resentful. His background and skimpy education placed him beyond the pale of Gloucester's "decent" society, and the saloon clinched it. Yet his charities were the means of raising him to a position of moral pre-eminence over those who ostracized him, and he had the satisfaction of knowing that he — not the leaders of the community — was first in the hearts of his countrymen.

And perhaps something else, something that compelled him to return in his own way his tithe of the poor man's money that crossed the bar.

Although his motives were complex, it is a simple fact that poverty and suffering touched him deeply. He had a big heart and an uncomplicated view of his fellow man; he liked to feel that all was well with the world, and he did what he could in his straightforward fashion to make it that way.

When the six wet years ran dry in December of 1895, Howard turned the saloon over to a friend for a fishermen's outfit store (presumably) and left on a trip out West.

He was gone for several months. The nature of this jaunt is obscure, but the following May he was in Hot Springs, Arkansas, taking the baths in the hope that they would relieve the pain of the recurrent arthritis in his legs and feet. Years later he enjoyed telling how he joshed the boy stationed at the entrance; every day this youngster held out his hand and asked for the "ciftick" of admission, and every day he pretended not to understand; the lad never did learn how to pronounce "certificate."

Only one other vignette remains of this excursion — a photograph of Howard (his vanity bloomed at the sight of a camera) in company with five other dudes taken by McLeod, the Wild West Photographer, who billed himself as the owner and operator of "Happy Hollow for outdoor amusements. Free entertainment every pleasant day. Cages open all the time. Donkeys and ponies for mountain rides and phuny fotos."

It is an odd group. His companions are of various sizes and shapes, all clad in suits and derby hats, all astride donkeys, their feet barely brushing the ground.

All except Blackburn. His pants and coat bursting at the seams, he is bending the back of a careworn longhorn steer. A broad-brimmed Western hat is pushed back on his steaming forehead, and he is eyeing the photographer with the look of a stout sheriff bent on the pursuit of some fleeing desperado, wherever it may take him and by whatever mode of transport.

Meanwhile, back at the saloon, the police brought the fishermen's outfitter into court but were unable to satisfy the judge that the men they had observed emerging from the rear room were actually intoxicated. The "store," however, was turned over to another friend.

Five weeks later, in July, the marshal (who else but old John Parsons) crashed in at the head of five officers. They found a trapdoor in the floor and were rewarded with the discovery of two and a half gallons of whiskey, forty-six bottles of beer, five hundred and forty-four empty flasks, thirteen glasses, two tubs, a pitcher, funnel, corkscrew and four baskets. Not a large operation, but certainly well equipped.

For the rest of the year Howard and his tenants managed to keep clear of the law. Or maybe old Parsons just let them alone. Anyway, there were no more encounters, and in December the invitation to engage in illegal activities was extended for another year when the city voted narrowly to remain dry. Again he rented out the saloon as a store.

On the evening of June 14, 1897, Dennis McNary, a young Nova Scotian working for a fish company, went on a binge. Thoroughly drunk, he reeled over to the depot and boarded the Boston train, intending to get off in the Magnolia section of Gloucester, where he lived. He was ugly and insulting and refused to pay his fare, and the conductor threw him off at the next stop, West Gloucester.

Alone in the night, Dennis stumbled along the roadbed toward Magnolia. Another train suddenly puffed around the bend and

Annie Forbes

The saloonkeeper...   ...and his saloon

Annie Forbes

Aboard a longhorn, Dude Blackburn poses with a posse of sitters for McLeod, the Wild West Photographer, at Hot Springs, Arkansas, in 1896.

slammed into him. He was taken to the hospital, horribly mangled; his left hand had been severed from his arm.

Later he was asked where, in a dry city, he had been able to drink himself into such a stupor.

At Howard Blackburn's, he said.

The details of the accident were reported fully in the newspapers — with one exception: neither Howard's nor his tenant's name was mentioned. And the police took no action.

It was a bad business.

5

Gold Crazy

THE STEAMER *Portland*, a month out of the miserable little Alaskan port of St. Michael, bumped into her berth at Schwabacher's Dock in Seattle. It was July 17, 1897. The hour was six in the morning. Five thousand people jammed the wharves, waiting tensely. The rest of the world waited with them.

The lines were made fast, and the gangplank thumped onto the pier. Every eye swept over the passengers crowding the rail. The gate opened. The moment had come.

A ragged sourdough tottered down the gangplank with his battered grip. Suddenly the handle broke, and the crowd gasped; it had been snapped off by the sheer weight of its contents — gold!

Down struggled another bearded prospector, bent by the burden of a hundred thousand dollars in gold dust wrapped in a blanket; when he reached the wharf he hired two men to help him carry it away. A third staggered off the ship; two years earlier he had borrowed three hundred dollars for a stake to Alaska; he lugged one hundred and twelve thousand dollars from the *Portland* in three bags.

And still they came — sixty-five more of them — dragging their fortunes back from the wilderness of Seward's Folly to the civilization they hadn't seen in years.

Two days earlier the *Excelsior* had docked at San Francisco with a tattered vanguard of miners carrying such riches in suitcases and bags and bottles that the world could only gasp in disbelief. But out of the *Portland* poured the proof. It was the biggest strike since '49.

The Klondike! That's where it was — nuggets on the ground as big as pebbles, sand glittering with dust. One reporter figured they hauled more than thirty-two thousand ounces off the *Portland* — a ton of gold (he was wrong; it was two). *A ton of gold!* The words were electric.

Howard Blackburn, age thirty-eight, retired mariner, crippled hero of a day gone by, paunchy slave of a life ashore, read them and was electrified. His time had come at last . . . the redemption of his manhood.

"Alaska or Bust!" headlined the Procters' new daily, the *Gloucester Times,* and reported that hundreds were already preparing to sail for Alaska within hours of the *Portland*'s arrival.

It was the American dream all over. Everywhere men were throwing over their jobs and heading for the Coast — bank clerks, farmers, doctors, carpenters, lawyers, storekeepers. The glint returned to the eyes of old frontiersmen and Forty-niners, and once again they fled from the civilization that had overtaken them. Off went the unemployed and the dreamers and the schemers, the gamblers and the confidence men; here was the sure-fire chance they'd been waiting for. America had grown fat and bored and uneasy, even as Howard Blackburn had, and suddenly the dream came true again. The old optimism was back. Nothing was impossible, after all. Three cheers for the Klondike, boys! Hurrah!

Howard was aflame to join the rush, but not as a stampeder. He read all the papers, got maps and charts, studied every scrap of information the steamers had brought back from Alaska and talked with sailor friends who'd been there. He conceived and laid his plans with reborn self-confidence. If gold was indeed to be had for the taking, it lay at the end of a long, hard trail. Everything he knew of hardship told him hundreds would fail for every man who made it. He intended to get there.

The quickest way to reach San Francisco or Seattle was overland by train. But once on the Coast, a mining outfit and provisions for a year or two or three had to be purchased, doubtless at sharper's prices. Passage to Alaska would have to be found for a man and tons of supplies. It was a month's voyage of three thousand miles across the North Pacific, through the Aleutians at Dutch Harbor and up the length of the Bering Sea to St. Michael, the port at the delta of the Yukon River, three hundred miles from Siberia. Here the worst of the journey would begin. The Yukon snaked seventeen hundred miles across the whole of the Alaskan wilderness before it reached the Klondike, just over the border in Canada. Two little steamers, the *Alice* and the *Portus B. Weare,* plied the river, and then only during the brief summer; the rest of the year the Yukon was frozen solid and the Klondike was a limbo.

Howard quickly concluded it was no use trying to reach the gold fields this summer. The thing to do was to get there as soon as the ice broke next spring and have a full season of prospecting. If he could go by water all the way from Gloucester to St. Michael, and get up the Yukon on his own hook . . . it sounded fantastic, but maybe there was a way.

Back in '49 five Gloucester schooners had sailed around the Horn at the height of the California gold rush and carried expeditions to the very back door of the mining fields.

Why not?

The whole plan fell into place. This was no venture for a man alone. It was a job for an expedition. Bring together the skills and courage of many men for a common goal. Make it one for all and all for one — share and share alike — the old code of the dorymates.

Organize a cooperative mining company. Have each member ante up an equal share and take out an equal slice of the pie. Buy a fishing schooner, fit her out and load her with supplies. Build a small steamer, shallow enough to navigate the Yukon, and put her aboard the schooner. Sail in the fall around the Horn, twelve thousand and five hundred miles to San Francisco. Refit, stock the vessel for two or three years in the Klondike and sail the thirty-seven hundred miles to St. Michael, arriving at the Yukon just before the ice breaks up in the spring. Sell the schooner, assemble the launch and put it in the water and steam another seventeen hundred miles up the river to the Klondike.

This way, the pot of gold would be at the end of a rainbow eighteen thousand miles long. But what a slick rainbow! A bridge you built as you crossed it!

Howard moved swiftly and surely. Within a week of the *Portland*'s arrival his plans were roughed out. He named the expedition the Gloucester Mining Company, drew up articles of agreement for a company of twenty men and began negotiations with two vessel owners. He had already interviewed a batch of applicants for membership when word of his scheme reached the *Times*.

Yes, he told the reporter who came down to the store, he had a plan to go to the Klondike, and it was far enough along to be a virtual certainty.

The members of the company must be healthy, able-bodied men, willing to work, courageous and convinced of its ultimate success. Each was to put up two hundred and fifty dollars as his share, of which fifty dollars must be paid by September and the balance by October. An eighteen-thousand mile ticket to fortune for two hundred and fifty dollars!

They'd buy a schooner for about three thousand dollars. Already Loring Haskell had offered to sell them the *Helen F. Whitten* and take a share, and Captain Charley Lawson had likewise proposed to sell the *Dora A. Lawson*, take a share and go along as navigator. The schooner would be loaded with coal or whatever else they could sell on the Coast at a profit and sail around the tenth of November with the steam launch in her hold.

When they arrived in 'Frisco, they would dispose of their cargo, take on provisions, probably pick up a few paying passengers and head for Alaska. From St. Michael they would navigate the Yukon as far as possible, sell the schooner and complete the voyage in the launch.

"Already I have had many applications from parties who wish to go," he told the newsman, "but none but the very best men will be selected. You see, we will start in November so as to reach the gold fields in May and have the benefit of the whole summer. I have been many degrees further north than the gold fields, when I was in Greenland, and the summers were very mild although there was snow on top of the mountains."

The paper published the interview on July 28, eleven days after the news of the Klondike strike hit the world, and it created a sensation. Others picked it up, and the details of the plan and the background of its author, with columns of comment, were featured all over the country. It struck readers as the more remarkable in view of the headlines that were coming out of California.

'FRISCO GOLD CRAZY

ONLY LIMITED TRANSPORTATION
FACILITIES PREVENTS ITS DEPOPULATION

Many Women in the Mad Throng

EVERY DAY BRINGS NEW SCHEME
TO REACH KLONDYKE

Now Howard was swamped with inquiries. The metals firm of Houghton and Richards in Boston offered to back him financially and send along two of its own men, both of them tough and rugged. An old salt from Boston who had been mate on square-riggers wanted to know what kind of vessel he planned to buy and if she would be sailed by a competent crew. A retired miner in Rhode Island wrote that he had prospected for gold from Tombstone to British Columbia, made and lost two fortunes and was all set to try for a third.

He answered each letter with a printed copy of the articles of agreement and slowly screened the avalanche of applicants by personal interviews.

Every contingency seemed to be covered in the six articles or by common understanding and Blackburn's word. It was even provided that if they were unable to sell the vessel at St. Michael, a crew from the company would sail her between the Coast and Alaska with passengers and freight while the rest went on to the gold fields. If a member got sick, he would be cared for and continue to receive his share; if he died, his share would go to his heirs.

"Each and every member of the said party," stated the final article, "further agrees that all money or moneys or other products of the expedition, in whole or in part, either in the gold fields or as receipts from the sale or traffic in which the vessel may engage, shall be equally and fairly divided, share and share alike, among the members of the said company."

Share and share alike — there it was, the dorymates' code.

By early August, Howard had signed on nine men, and his plan was being copied. Captain William Swain of Nantucket announced he had purchased the Boston packet schooner *William O. Nettleton* and planned to form a company of twenty on five-hundred-dollar shares; he would reach Alaska next April and take along a nest of dories that could be rowed up the rivers and carried around the rapids. The idea intrigued Howard, and he, in turn, borrowed it from the Nantucket skipper. Dories it would be — Gloucester dories on the rivers of Alaska!

In two more weeks all nineteen of his comrades-to-be had signed the articles, and although there would be changes in the company before it sailed, five disappointed applicants stood ready to fill the place of every man that dropped out. Furthermore, twelve others hoped to make the overland trip, meet up with the expedition at San Francisco and take passage to Alaska.

Howard dropped down to John Bishop's shipyard on Vincent Cove and told him what he had in mind. The Yukon from all accounts was fraught with shallows, sand bars and wild currents. To buck the river, a stout steamer with plenty of capacity but of slight draft was needed. Bishop set to work and designed a flat-bottomed launch, fifty feet long, sixteen wide, five feet eight inches deep, with a capacity of thirty-five tons but drawing only three feet of water. It would be built in frames, so it could be stowed away in the schooner and assembled at St. Michael. Over at Stoddart's shop he got them started on the engine and machinery. Its name would be *Eclipse*.

On the twenty-first of August, Blackburn took the train to Boston and bought the schooner *Hattie I. Phillips* cash on the line for twenty-five hundred dollars. Two days later she was towed the twenty-five miles to Gloucester and tied up at Chisholm's Wharf. The *Phillips* was a big, black fisherman built at Essex in 1885, able and sound. She was registered at ninety-six tons and was about a hundred and ten feet long, rather larger than the *Grace L. Fears,* but with the same clipper lines.

The schooner was winched up on Burnham Brothers' marine railway, overhauled from stem to stern and painted inside and out. Back in the water, she took on a load of blacksmith's coal as a deep-hold ballast cargo and was moved to the wharf of the Gloucester Electric Company, where the fitting-out was completed.

Meanwhile, the stampede for the Klondike was in full frenzy. Few paid any attention to the warning of Secretary of the Interior Cornelius N. Bliss, who tried to call the attention of the public to the exposure, suffering and danger that lurked on every side of the Klondike trail, noting that three thousand men and two thousand tons of freight and baggage were already jammed up at White Pass in British Columbia, futilely waiting to cross the Coast Mountains, still hundreds of miles from their destination. By the first of September, nine thousand men and women and thirty-six thousand tons of luggage had left Seattle, although there wasn't a ghost of a chance of their reaching the

Klondike until next summer, if ever. They would have been smarter to heed the newspaper ads of a household cleaning powder manufacturer:

Don't Go to Alaska for GOLD DUST
ALL GROCERS SELL IT

The dire reports from the West seemed only to bear out the good sense of the Blackburn brainstorm, and its imitators proliferated. By the end of September, the plans of the Gloucester Mining Company were so far along that Howard advanced the date of departure three weeks.

It was all his idea, and he was bound to be the first to leave, but he had better hurry. A group in the nearby shoe manufacturing city of Lynn had organized the Lynn Mining Company on almost the precise lines of his plan and was getting ready to sail in the *Abbie M. Deering;* next door, in old Salem, the Witch City Gold Mining Company bought the *Reuben L. Richardson* and prepared for the long voyage; Loring Haskell, who had offered to sell Howard the *Helen F. Whitten,* set up his own company instead; one group from the Boston area purchased the *Stowell Sherman* of Provincetown, another outfitted the *Abbie F. Morris* and a third the *Carrie and Annie;* the Chelsea Mining Company was formed and bought the *Julia A. Whalen;* Llewellyn Lothrop, the Gloucester ship chandler, caught the fever, created the Cape Ann Mining and Trading Company and prepared to send an expedition off in the *Charles Levi Woodbury;* and a party from Portsmouth, New Hampshire, began fitting out the *Concord.*

In all, more than a dozen schooners would follow the Blackburn expedition out of New England ports by the end of the year.

Time was getting short. Howard signed an experienced skipper as his navigator and first mate. Captain John Harris was forty-five and in the '80's had sailed schooners around the Horn twice. Blackburn hadn't the experience to navigate the *Phillips* on his own hook, and Harris would be his good right arm. Peter Rice, another seasoned fisherman and mariner, signed as second mate, and Jim Nelson, one of the best galley men in the port, was welcomed into the company as cook.

The final week was hectic with excitement and last-minute preparations. The disjointed skeleton of the *Eclipse* and her machinery were stowed in on top of the coal, and the members of the company came on with their luggage and picked their berths. Captain Blackburn was everywhere, supervising everything, and roaring exuberantly to newspapermen that he wouldn't sell his chance to go for twenty-five thousand dollars.

He made a great hit with the reporters and told them they treated him "finely." He loved the publicity, and they loved him. He was a newsman's ideal — colorful and salty, affable, always ready to stop and talk, and he had a flair for the dramatic; he seemed to know instinctively what made good newspaper copy and was never without some tidbit to spice up an interview.

On Saturday, October 16, he closed the store, fourteen years to the day after he had opened it. Then he briefed the man from the *Cape Ann Breeze* on his latest plans:

When they arrived in 'Frisco they would sell most of their coal, purchase mining equipment and take on provisions for thirty-two months. They would dispose of the *Phillips* at St. Michael, assemble the *Eclipse* and steam up the Yukon, towing six dories astern. Instead of heading straight for the Klondike, they would divide up into squads and, in the dories, explore the lower tributaries of the river, where he was sure there was gold, before proceeding on to the headwaters. They were prepared to be away three years.

Commented the *Breeze:* "Members of the party are greatly obliged to Howard Blackburn for the indefatigable manner in which he has arranged every detail of preparation for the long voyage, something which in the beginning he had not expected to do, but to which he has given almost his entire time and attention the past two months."

Monday the eighteenth dawned crisp and clear, a perfect October day, New England at its best. The *Hattie I. Phillips*, shining in her coat of black, lay at the Atlantic Wharf near the ferry landing, a huge American flag flapping from her maintopmasthead. The wharf and the deck of the schooner were united in a criss-crossing bustle of activity; the excited crew ran back and forth between ship and dock on final errands, double-checking their sailing instructions and getting set for the afternoon departure.

The sun climbed and warmed the morning. As Howard stood on the wharf, an eye on everything, giving directions, sending messages, conferring with his lieutenants and answering the questions of the reporters, a man crossed over to him, and there was a brief, heated conference.

It was Deputy Sheriff William Cronin. He told Howard he had no taste for what he had to do, but no alternative, either. He handed him some papers and announced stiffly that he, Howard Blackburn, was being sued for three thousand dollars by Mr. and Mrs. John McNary of Canso, Nova Scotia, on behalf of their son Dennis, under a statute permitting parents to recover damages from a liquor dealer who sells to a minor. The McNarys claimed their maimed son had been their chief support.

Blackburn exploded. He denied vehemently that he had sold liquor to the youth, and vowed he had witnesses to prove it. The whole thing was blackmail, so blatant that no lawyer in Gloucester would take their case, and they had been forced to go to Salem to find one. He refused to discuss it further and turned back to giving orders.

By noon everything was on board and shipshape, and he had cooled off. The suit couldn't go to court until his return from Alaska, and that was three years away; he put it out of his mind.

The noon train was crowded with friends and relatives of out-of-town members who hurried from the depot to the waterfront to join the crowd that by one o'clock was gathering on the wharf in a holiday spirit. At two Howard boarded the *Phillips*, and the excitement rose as Captain Bill Smith worked the tug *Joe Call* alongside with a party of forty enthusiastic friends of the gold-seekers who scrambled over the rail and spread around the decks of the schooner.

By two-thirty the crowd on the docks had reached a thousand and was still growing. A long tow line was bent from the *Joe Call* to the *Phillips*, and the tug idled in the harbor off her bow, waiting.

The hearts of the sixteen fortune hunters who were leaving their homes and families for they knew not how long (the others were to travel overland later and meet them in 'Frisco) were swept by contrasting emotions. Howard was bursting with excitement and anticipation; at last he was returning to sea, master of a vessel this time, leading his men on an unprecedented adventure into the unknown; he strained to be off. Harris, Rice and Nelson, Charley Strandberg and Eldridge Wolfe were all Gloucester fishermen, tough men of the sea, and on their shoulders weighed the responsibility for sailing the schooner on her great voyage, with help from young Fred Head, who was only twenty-one but had shipped often with his father. With them and their captain resided the safety of the expedition, and they could afford scant sentiment in parting.

Charley Clark and Les Cavanaugh came from Manchester and were carpenters; they knew ships and would keep the *Phillips* in repair during the months ahead, assemble the *Eclipse* in Alaska and erect the company's buildings and mining structures in the wilderness.

But the others knew little of the sea; their usefulness lay in the future, and anxiety vied with the gold fever as the hour drew nigh when there would be no turning back. Will Murray was fifty-two and the oldest man aboard, a stonecutter skilled from labor in the Rockport granite quarries, the nearest Howard was able to come to a mining expert. Clem Pelly of South Boston was a machinist, Otis Rowell of Stoneham a shoemaker, Steve Sponagle of Gloucester a barber, and Clarence Towle, down from Buxton, Maine, a brick mason. Lew Berry of Boston was a store clerk, and so was Fred Story of Gloucester. Fred was nineteen, the baby of the expedition. What had he let himself in for, he wondered. But it was too late for second thoughts.

At three-thirty the waterfront was aswarm with spectators. They packed up to the very edges of the wharves, overflowed onto the salt stages, covered the roofs of the buildings and leaned from every window.

Messrs. Houghton and Richards of Boston, the partners themselves, properly dressed in black suits and stiff collars, shook hands with Captain Blackburn. Two of their men were on board, and they expressed unbounded faith in the leader, instructing him expansively to draw on their account should he need funds.

A matron stepped from the crowd and presented him with a pair of barometers. Collector of Customs Frank C. Richardson ceremoniously gave him a book, and as the multitude hushed he declared in his best speech-making voice: "Mr. Blackburn, I wish you favoring winds and fortune as fair as this beautiful day!" Howard returned the compliment with a box of cigars.

A little girl was nudged from the crowd, walked shyly up and gave him a bouquet with an awkward curtsy.

At the very last minute there was a flare-up of activity and a hurried conference. Jack Harris had forgotten a nautical almanac for 1898 and refused to sail without this indispensable guide. But Howard was equally as stubborn in his refusal to disappoint the crowd, and it was agreed that one of the men should go to Boston for the book and rejoin the ship at Provincetown.

And now the moment was at hand. Arthur Millett of the *Gloucester Times,* one of a dozen intimate friends of Blackburn invited aboard the schooner, watched and wrote:

> The sightseers maintained a respectful silence, while fathers and mothers parted from sons, and wives and children said their goodbyes

to husbands and fathers. All strove to be brave, but it was a trying moment and the tears would come as the thoughts of parting filled the hearts of these little family groups. It was a scene never to be forgotten.

At quarter of four came the order, "All ashore, cast off the bow line!" There were hurried clasps of hands, the murmured "God bless you," the last kiss of love and affection and then the cries of "Good luck, Howard; take care of yourself, Steve; goodbye, Peter; best of luck, Eldridge; drive her, Jack Harris; be good, Fred." Once more came the order, "Cast off the stern line, loose the mainsail!" Now she is clear from the wharf and other goodbyes lost in the cheers of encouragement.

If Theresa was there, the newspapers — meticulous in their detail — failed to note it.

The men jumped to the halyards. The great mainsail lifted clear of the boom and spread up in a flapping sweep of canvas. Then the foresail, and the jumbo and the jib.

Roar after roar rose from the crowds. Hats soared, and hand-kerchiefs fluttered. The whistles of factories and tugs and light-ers and ferries exploded in a shrieking din as the schooner, re-porter Millett himself at the wheel, moved with slapping sails down the harbor behind the chugging, churning little tug.

In mid-channel the *Joe Call* drifted to a stop. The tow line was cast off; it splashed in the water and was pulled back aboard the tug. Millett turned the wheel over to Jack Harris. The tug circled and came alongside. Hands were shaken all around, and with shouts of farewell the send-off party jumped over into the tug and she pulled away.

The helmsman hove the wheel hard over. The schooner's bow fell off, her sheets were started and her sails filled to the west wind.

They were off.

And who among the crowds that watched the schooner scud by Eastern Point and out to sea could help but share the wistful parting sentiments of the *Times:* "Good fortune to them all, who, like Jason and the Argonauts of old, go boldly forth to unknown lands to dig from mother earth the Golden Fleece of shining treasure."

6

Around the Horn

WITH A COOL SOUTHWEST WIND off her starboard beam, the *Hattie I. Phillips* reached across Massachusetts Bay during the night, ducked inside the curled fingertips of Cape Cod and dropped anchor in Provincetown Harbor.

Bright and early at eight the next morning, a dory was put over and rowed to the town landing, where the man with Jack Harris's almanac was already waiting. He jumped in and was brought back to the schooner. She was ready now for the open sea.

The anchor was hove up, and the *Phillips* bore away from the harbor. She slipped around Race Point and slid past the bright beaches and dunes of the outer Cape shore. Soon the low-lying peninsula was lost behind the horizon, and Harris set the helmsman on a south southeast course for Bermuda.

The brisk October breeze held fair from the southwest all day, and when the greenhorns turned in that night they had decided that nothing could be finer than an ocean voyage, the way the ship cut steadily through the azure waters under a towering acre of smooth canvas. A day on shipboard and they fancied themselves sailors.

On Wednesday, however, they began to have their doubts.

The schooner had passed by Georges Bank, and as it entered the Gulf Stream the wind hauled around from the eastward. The *Phillips* came about and bowled along on the port tack, smashing geysers of spray from her bows. Unexpected gusts bent her over until her decks tipped at a crazy angle, and white water poured through the lee scuppers. Now a man had to hang on for dear life to whatever was handy, and stomachs, once landlocked, turned somersaults. Gray clouds galloped low across the sky, and the sun was gone. Captain Blackburn and his old hands kept their eyes on the glass. It was falling. A storm was making up.

The wind increased and by evening was blowing a moderate gale. One of the gusts was too much for the mainsail and snapped the main throat hook; the mast end of the gaff dropped, breaking the even contour of the sail, and the peak slapped violently. There was too much wind for the main, and Blackburn ordered it taken in and the jib furled as well. For the rest of the night the schooner lay head to the storm under foresail only.

The landlubbers hugged their bunks and wished they were ashore.

The night was black and wild. The seas mounted higher under the force of the rising wind. Sheets of rain and spume drove across the ocean so thick and biting that a man couldn't turn his face to windward and keep his eyes open. Dawn labored through the rushing clouds, and still the storm increased. The wind worked around to the northeast and registered gale force.

Early Thursday morning the jib lashing parted, and the sail unfurled with a noise like a shot. In a split second it spread and stretched tight as a drumhead under the full blast of the wind. Instantly the schooner's bow swung off to leeward. If she fell away broadside to the seas she would be at their mercy, might even be knocked down on her side.

"Cut away the jib!" roared Blackburn above the scream of the gale, waving his arm forward violently. A man heard him and began to creep along the deck, clutching rails, ropes — anything to save himself from being carried overboard. He reached the bow, took out his knife and waited. The next time the schooner heaved herself up on top of a sea, he slashed the leech line. It was taut as a piano string, and when it parted the sail whipped away from him and spilled the wind; it gave one final slat, tore from the stay and disappeared in the murk like a frightened ghost.

With her jib gone, the *Phillips* worked her bow laboriously back into the eye of the wind. All hands sighed with relief.

Still the storm increased. By noon the wind was clocked at eighty miles an hour.

They were in a hurricane.

The seas were rolling hills of water, their summits higher than the topmasts. Now the schooner is at the bottom of a windless canyon, ten thousand tons of ocean towering over her. Then she begins to struggle up the sheer wall — up and up until she seems to be standing on her stern. Up and up she pulls herself, and after an eternity she makes it and hovers on the peak. The wind strikes and fills her slack foresail with the blast of a cannon shot. For a crazy instant she is the mistress of all around her. And then her bow topples over the brink, and she dives headlong down the slope, thrown over on her side almost, wallowing in the trough, her sail soaking and aslat. The water engulfs her, an avalanche of it, filling her decks from bulwark to bulwark, and spilling over the rails.

As each huge wave bore down on her, it appeared to Howard that "she would shake herself like a thing of life and prepare to meet it." He felt like patting her side and saying, "Well done, old girl!"

But his crew did not wholly share his elation.

One great sea boarded the plunging schooner and washed two men over the rail; they were saved by the quick action of their companions. Another carried a man overboard, then lifted him up and dumped him back on deck. Although the foresail had been shortened with a double reef, Howard was incredulous to see the boom "bent like a hoop." A sea caught poor Otis Rowell, the shoemaker, and slammed him against the boom, raising a knot on his head that "even a phrenologist," he said as he ruefully fingered it later, "would find it hard to account for."

Rowell was so sick he thought he would die, as indeed everyone else was. As for his sea legs — "I got into my bunk, but soon found myself on the dinner table, but as those quarters did not suit me, I soon found myself on the floor."

Late in the afternoon the worst of the hurricane was over. Although the seas continued to thunder down on the schooner, the wind fell off. It was another black night, and nothing could be seen but solid water streaming across the decks.

Friday morning the wind backed into the north. The seas were dying but still rolling by in long, mighty swells. Captain Blackburn remarked to his men that in eleven years at sea he had ridden out gales in everything from a twenty-two-hundred-ton ship to a dory, but this was the worst he ever encountered. For him it had been an appropriate reunion with his old adversary after fourteen years on the beach. His judgment in buying the *Phillips* had been proven; she was a fine sea boat. He reflected on the men he had assembled: whatever their thoughts may have been, not a murmur of dissatisfaction or despair had escaped them. If they could take this, they could take anything.

He ordered the jumbo and storm trysail swayed up. The helm was swung off to the south southeast, and the *Phillips* careened away from the quartering seas. The voyage was resumed.

The dying storm left a strong easterly as a reminder of itself for three more days. Rain squalls appeared from nowhere and were gone as abruptly, and the schooner pushed on toward the warmer latitudes with the foresail reefed and the jumbo flying. Late Friday the company rushed to the rail for the happy sight of the first ship they had encountered since leaving Gloucester. She was a steamer banging eastward through the swells. Another was sighted the next day. The first Sunday at sea found the *Phillips* a hundred miles north of Bermuda, and as an omen of better days to come, the men saw a flying fish.

At last the sun broke through. The scattered clouds blew away, and the wind abated to a warm breeze. Bermuda was left astern. Some of the men set to repairing sails. Others made thrum mats, weaving lengths of rope yarn into pads which they sewed to the rigging to prevent the chafing of the sails. By evening there was not a breath of wind, and the schooner lay motionless on the glassy Sargasso Sea, her sails drooping and boom jaws creaking.

She was becalmed in the horse latitudes, an airless no man's land between the edge of the westerlies and the northern extent of the tropical trade winds. The region is said to have drawn its name from the plight of mariners bound from New England for the West Indies with deckloads of horses; trapped in the calm, sometimes for days, they threw some of the poor animals into the sea for lack of fresh water to keep them alive.

A heavy thunderstorm came by and dispelled the heat. The breeze returned, and for the next few days they bowled along under full sail. The late afternoon hours of the dogwatches were whiled away on deck with singing and banjo playing.

On the first of November they entered the northeast trade winds, sweeping fresh in from the west coast of Africa. Captain Blackburn ordered all sail set, and the schooner reached across the wind under fair skies with joyous contagion. The event called for celebration; Jim Nelson mixed up a barrel of root beer, and the men swore they wouldn't go near it until it had "worked."

For ten days the trades blew on, hot as a furnace blast. The men lounged on deck, barefoot and undershirted, their sunburned faces shadowed under broadbrimmed straw hats. Night and day the *Hattie I. Phillips* cut cleanly through the sea, the helmsman barely moving the wheel. Occasionally she crossed paths with another sailing vessel, purposefully pursuing its course across the ocean, and once she passed an ancient sea turtle that lazily ignored attempts to capture it.

The barrel of beer, safe from predatory marshals, fermented to the bursting point under the tropical sun; the watchful cook announced that it was ready, and there was a high-spirited party. The schooner drove on toward the Equator, and some of the men tried to escape the heat by slinging their hammocks under overturned dories.

The weather wore a threatening look on the tenth of November. The mainsail was taken in for safety's sake, but in a few hours the skies cleared and the sail was hoisted again. But a violent squall tore across the water with unexpected suddenness, shook the *Phillips* like a toy boat and disappeared. It came so fast there had been no time to drop the main, and it was ripped two-thirds of its height from gaff to the second reef points. For the next few days the vessel limped along under the trysail while the canvas was laid out on deck and repaired.

St. Peter and St. Paul Rocks, a cluster of mountain peaks that barely break the surface six hundred miles off the Brazilian coast, were passed on the seventeenth of November; the following day, exactly a month out of Gloucester, the adventurers crossed the Equator.

The remainder of the voyage toward Cape Horn was uneventful. Jack Harris followed a course that kept the *Phillips* about five hundred miles off South America. One day they spoke the British bark *Ladstock*, forty-two days out of Liverpool, bound for Arica, Chile.   A few hours later they exchanged salutes with another Englishman. The last three days of the month the weather soured, and one sloppy sea tossed a luckless squid on deck.

December brought a fine breeze and an albatross, riding effortlessly above the vessel on a snowy spread of wings. Unmindful of Coleridge's dark warning, someone brought the bird of good omen down with his gun.

Soon a gale arose. The schooner was hove to under double-reefed foresail, but the vengeance of the albatross was fleeting; the weather faired for a week and fickled for another, and at one in the morning on December 19 the mariners sighted Cape Virgin on the north side of the Strait of Magellan. The landfall called for three cheers. They were weary of the sea; it was their first glimpse of a solid shoreline in two months to the day.

It was blowing a gale as the *Phillips* bore around the Cape and into the Strait. Since the nights were only four hours long, Howard ordered her hove to until daylight, when the wind subsided.

It was so gentle, in fact, and the tide was so strong on the flow that the schooner was carried against a sand bar near the south shore, where she stuck fast. Howard directed his men to drop the kedge anchor off the bow; then they ran the line to the windlass and hove it taut. Thus she was held from beating harder on the bar.

When the tide turned, it came with a rush. The tidal wave charged down on them through the Strait, and as it struck the grounded vessel they bent their backs to the windlass. The bore lifted her clear of the bar, and she hauled herself back into the channel to her anchor.

The Yankees were struck by the appearance of the land on either side of them. Cape Virgin to the starboard and Tierra del Fuego to port reminded them of Cape Cod. Far-stretching plains, bereft of trees or habitation, reached back as far as the eye could see from the abrupt banks of the shore. Here and there an isolated peak broke the monotony of the plateaus.

Tuesday, December 21, was the first day of the southern summer, and the sun smiled. Early in the morning the *Phillips* passed through the first narrows, following the course of the Portuguese navigator who charted the first path through the Strait three hundred and seventy-seven years earlier. Only twenty-two months ago Captain Joshua Slocum, the lone around-the-world sailor, had found the tides and winds of the Strait not to his liking or to *Spray*'s.

Just after noon they entered the second narrows and ran into an oncoming tide the like of which they had never seen before. Squeezed through the constriction of the land, it rushed by the vessel like a river on the flood. Although the wind drove the schooner on at nine knots, she was held at bay until the tide slacked off. When it turned, however, it teamed up with the wind to carry the *Phillips* on to the town of Punta Arenas in jigtime, and the anchor was dropped in the harbor early that evening.

Punta Arenas (Sandy Point) was the southernmost city in the world, an outpost of civilization established on the wasteland tip of the continent by Chile in 1849 to demonstrate her claims of sovereignty over the Strait. The land here was higher than the eastern plateau. The town, with its helter-skelter population of a few thousand Chileans, Patagonian and Fuegian Indians, American, English and French merchants, was largely a refueling station for the trade passing through the Strait. It squatted on the north shore against a backdrop of snow-capped mountains.

Captain Slocum had found it a dreary spot and the natives as squalid and corrupted by civilization as contact with unscrupulous traders and their liquor could make them. Eldridge Wolfe, the Gloucester fisherman who was one of Howard's trusted stalwarts, reported in his log of the voyage that the scenery was very wild and beautiful. When they anchored, a customs officer came aboard, and they found that English was the principal language of the place. Wolfe saw a steamer, a Chilean man-of-war and fifteen whalers in the harbor.

Otis Rowell, the shoemaker, took the opportunity to post a letter home. He was not happy about the venture. Since crossing the Equator, he wrote, they had not had five days of dry decks — "there are some things about this life that I like, but more that I don't." The people, "if you call them such," were engaged in sheep-raising and some mining, and as for the natives, "I have seen some Patagonian Indians, though not plenty, but if we went back into the mountains we would be converted into pot pie."

Howard wandered around the town and viewed all he saw with interest. He learned that the Chilean government was sending emigrants to Punta Arenas, and while he arranged for repairs to the schooner, eleven hundred of them arrived on a steamer; they were quartered in old sheds and open fields and were to go up into the country to work on the sheep ranches. He found he could obtain the best beefsteak for two cents a pound. The port was still free, and anything could be bought or sold without duty. A German artist painted the *Hattie I. Phillips* on an ostrich egg for him, but he thought it looked more like a St. John's wood boat. When they reached San Francisco he sent it home by Wells Fargo Express.

To make room below decks for water barrels, he sold a few tons of coal at twelve dollars and fifty cents, for a profit of nine dollars a ton. Several men wanted to take passage for Alaska on the schooner, but there were no quarters for them; the gold fever had hit the Strait, and large numbers were prospecting the area with indifferent success.

Two days after the *Phillips* arrived, a sudden gale swooped down on the harbor, and she rode it out with both anchors down. Friday all hands were mustered for repair work. Saturday was Christmas, and Jim Nelson served up a feast of roast beef and lamb.

Monday the Gloucester Mining Company bid good-by to Punta Arenas. The Pacific lay ahead — but to reach it, they would have to beat their way through one of the world's most fearsome passages, a labyrinthian channel that twisted treacherously through mountain islands and sand bars. The Strait was a funnel for the westerly winds of the Pacific, and every sailing vessel passing to the west had to fight them every foot of the way. Sneaky tides ripped through the channels. Violent squalls called williwaws exploded out of nowhere and struck without warning, furious whirlwinds of hurricane strength; in minutes they could whip up monstrous waves, strip a vessel of her sails and stand her on end. The passage was a mariner's hell and the curse of every navigator, sail or steam.

The crew of the *Phillips* saw stark evidence of the williwaw's work as she tacked through. The bones of uncounted sailing vessels and at least three steamers were strewn along the shores.

But luck was with the Gloucestermen. Cautiously, they anchored every night and enjoyed many a good gunning trip ashore, for birds were plentiful. They rounded the Turn, the wide bend at the bottom of the Strait where the channel changes direction from southwest to northwest. It was here that Josh Slocum, having passed through the Strait only to be beaten back by Pacific gales, anchored for his second try after re-entering through Cockburn Channel. He had sprinkled carpet tacks on deck before retiring for the night, and when the barefoot savages he awaited sneaked aboard, they got the point. The Fuegians, with painful memories of Yankee ships still in mind, kept clear of the *Phillips*, and on December 29 she put in to Cape Gallant and filled the water casks, her last chance before the long ocean leg ahead. Two days of foul weather kept her at anchor, but on New Year's Day of 1898 she again set sail.

The next day the Klondikers dropped anchor in Borja Bay, and all rowed ashore. Nailed to the trees and bushes were signs with the names of vessels that had paused on their passage through, "a sort of nautical autograph album," as Eldridge Wolfe described it. Modestly inscribed at the bottom of one of the weatherbeaten signs were the words *Sloop Spray, March 1896*, Slocum's calling card left on his second run by. The crew put up a board for the *Hattie I. Phillips* with the date and all their names and then departed. Two days later they passed Cape Pilar, left the Strait of Magellan behind and entered the Pacific.

After a tough beat against head winds, the schooner cleared the swirl of air from the northwest that had carried Slocum back toward Cape Horn. On the eleventh of January the upper bobstay from the stem to the bowsprit snapped, and two days were spent repairing it.

For another week she reached across the westerlies, heeling hard to starboard all the way, and good time was made. Then she coasted into the doldrums. The sun was fierce and the sea flat, and as an antidote for the creeping listlessness the men broke out the hammocks and slung them again under the dories. The banjos reappeared, voices were tuned up and the hours were whiled away with singing and nostalgia. On the twenty-first the wind picked up.

We were in the South Pacific, in latitude 31 degrees 40 minutes, longitude 95 degrees 21 minutes. We were going about nine miles an hour, the wind being fair for the first time since leaving the Strait. It was a dreary day. Black clouds rose to windward and passed over us very rapidly.

One very black cloud passed over unusually low. When it got a short way to leeward of us, I noticed that the water all around us began to boil like a pot. The watch below had not turned in. They were lying around expecting every minute to be called to take in sail. It was about 2:30 P.M.

I was watching the black cloud which passed over us so low, when suddenly I saw the water go up into the air and take a circle covering a large area. I called all hands to see the waterspout. In a few seconds everyone was on deck, and just then the waterspout, which was going around at a tremendous rate, suddenly came toward us with great speed. The course it was taking would have brought it right across our wake very close to our stern. It was coming from about abreast the lee main rigging.

We hauled the vessel to three point so as to bring it farther from us, and some of the men got their guns ready to fire into it, when suddenly it changed its course and disappeared in the blackness to leeward of us. When I last saw it, it was the most frightful thing I ever saw, rushing and dragging the water for miles around toward it and sending thousands of tons of it up into the air.

We had to run three or four points to windward of our course all the rest of the afternoon, in order to keep to windward of what looked to be other waterspouts making. There were hundreds of them all around us. We all dreaded the coming of the night, for we thought we would surely run into some of them, but as night came on the clouds disappeared, and we had a fine night.

Two more days and the *Phillips* moved into the hot southeast trade winds. Again the flying fish fluttered and flopped on deck, and the broad straw hats were broken out. They were nearly two thousand miles off the Chilean coast, and though the schooner slipped through the blue Pacific at her top speed, the heat increased with every mile. An awning was stretched over the deck. But even this was not enough, for they seemed to be rushing into the bowels of a furnace. On the second of February a dory was filled with cool sea water, and all hands had a bath. At midnight they crossed the Equator.

A great sea bird flapped in from across the endless ocean one day and came to rest on the bowsprit. It hung around for two days, so trusting it allowed the men to stroke it; then it rose from its perch and soared away.

The weather held fair, and they angled in toward the North American coast, past Mexico and Southern California. On February 16, San Francisco bore north by east six hundred miles, and numerous vessels were sighted nearly every day.

The Gloucester schooner plowed on. At daybreak on the twenty-second, up went the cry — Land ho! It was the cliffs of Monterey, dark against the dawn, ninety miles from their destination. The *Phillips* stood up the coast and on the morning of the twenty-third sailed through the Golden Gate and into San Francisco Bay.

As she approached her anchorage a pilot came on board and told the news-hungry New Englanders that the battleship *Maine* had blown up in Havana Harbor a week before, and war with Spain was expected any day.

At eleven the anchor was dropped, and the sails were let fall to the decks in smothering billows of canvas. With high excitement the members of the Gloucester Mining Company secured their ship and got ready to go ashore. Bad news, unfortunately, awaited young Fred Head; he would learn that his father had gone down with the schooner *Annie and Mary* on Georges Bank during the same hurricane that had nearly taken the *Phillips* four months ago.

Four months to travel from the east coast of the United States to the west! But the distance was equivalent to sailing halfway around the world, and it had been an exceptionally fast passage, as Howard learned when he was interviewed by a reporter from the *San Francisco Call*. About two weeks before the *Phillips* sailed from Gloucester, two fast clipper ships had filled away from Philadelphia on the same course. Their owners had a wager and a race. One reached 'Frisco in a hundred and thirty-eight days, the other in a hundred and forty. The schooner, sailing a greater distance and lying for six days at Punta Arenas, made the voyage in a hundred and twenty-nine.

He concluded that he had not had a finer time in fifteen years.

7

Klondike Trail

SAN FRANCISCO that winter of early 1898 was in a turmoil of frustration. The city was gorged with thousands of men who had dropped everything and rushed there from every part of the world, expecting they could push on with hardly a pause to the Klondike, where nuggets as big as apples lay on the ground for the taking. To their dismay, they discovered their journey had barely begun.

Far to the north, the Klondike lay utterly isolated in Alaska's deep winter freeze. It might have been a million miles away. The lucky prospectors who got there first toiled all the while, setting wood fires and burning shafts through the frozen earth fifteen feet down to the gold in the bedrock. They piled up their fortunes, with nothing to spend them on. For nine months of that winter the rich couldn't get out and the greedy couldn't get in. Dawson City, swept by scurvy, was on the edge of starvation.

Eighteen hundred prospectors had left Seattle by the water route the previous fall. Only forty-three reached the Klondike before winter, and thirty-five of these had to turn back because there were no supplies for them in Dawson City. The stampeders had converged on the Klondike from every direction, but winter stopped them in their tracks. Of twenty-five hundred who were stranded on the Yukon, not one reached Dawson until July. Not a man who left the States after the first of August reached his objective that winter by the all-water route.

Expeditions came to the West Coast from Norway, Australia,

England, Scotland, Italy. They came with every sort of outfit and with every sort of expectation. A million people around the world made plans to leave for the Klondike that winter; at least a hundred thousand actually set out.

And so San Francisco, like Seattle, was chaotic and explosive with frustrated greed. Every man had a scheme to get to Alaska in the spring — but he had to wait, wait, wait. And for every gold-crazy dude there were a dozen shadowy figures fleecing him of all he had in the world — or what might be his if he were lucky.

The adventurous argonauts of the Gloucester Mining Company sailed into this den of lambs and lions from the dream world of the sea and were bewildered.

Their leader, the confident planner of their destinies, was momentarily set back by what he saw and heard. The outlook was not entirely as he had foreseen four months ago in Gloucester. It appeared that his expedition was merely a well-organized platoon in an army of anarchy.

Captain Blackburn expressed his feelings after three days of San Francisco in a letter to his friend Dr. William Hale in Gloucester:

Things here are a little different from what I expected, but I believe we will come out on top yet. I see by the San Francisco papers that a large number of vessels are on their way here. It is an undertaking that requires patience and perseverance. People here say that not over one per cent of the men who go to Alaska will ever get any gold. It looks like a slim chance, but we will take it . . . I will be obliged to you if you will send me a paper with the names of the men who were lost in the last twelve months.

The best Howard could get for the blacksmith's coal was nine dollars and fifty cents a ton, and he wished he'd sold the lot at Punta Arenas for the higher price.

Then he learned to his dismay that instead of being able to

reach the Klondike in May they couldn't even get to St. Michael until June 20, and it would be late summer at least before they arrived in the gold fields. After breaking this bad news to the company, he set a sailing date of May 10 and looked around for some means of turning the next two months to a profit and keeping his restless men busy.

A deal to carry lumber from Gray's Harbor in Washington to Alaskan ports fell through. He considered selling the schooner in San Francisco and taking the expedition to Alaska by steamer but couldn't find a buyer. No one seemed interested in purchasing the *Phillips* for delivery at St. Michael, and he was told the chances of disposing of her in Alaska were worse still.

So he dreamed up another scheme: they would kill time until May and then take with them thirty seal hunters, charge them seventy-five dollars each for passage and allow them a ton of freight apiece. This plan fell through when he learned that the government had banned sealing.

He called another meeting of the men. Would they be willing to make a trip up the coast for the sake of something to do and the chance of a few extra dollars? They were. So he went into the city and bargained to sail the schooner up to Astoria, Oregon, load her with lumber and return to 'Frisco.

Hustling back aboard, he reported the good news. The trip would be a lark, a regular cruise. Astoria was only seven hundred and fifty miles to the north, snuggled in the big mouth of the Columbia River, and they could get there in a week at the most.

But once outside the Golden Gate they all wished they were back at anchor. One gale after another rolled down on them along the coastal currents like balls in a bowling alley. The *Hattie I. Phillips* beat and tacked and drove and labored on, and it took her all of sixteen days to reach the shelter of the Columbia basin — at sea all the way because there wasn't a port to put in to the whole distance.

They arrived on March 23. The Astorians went wild; Blackburn and his Gloucestermen were heaven-sent.

Sandy Bay Historical Society

Klondike-bound, the schooner *Hattie I. Phillips* clears Gloucester Harbor with the Blackburn Expedition, October 18, 1897.

Estate of Charles Swinson

The bitter end for the Gloucester goldseekers and their steam launch *Eclipse* — frozen in for the Alaskan winter of 1898 at the fork of the Koyukuk and Allan-kakat rivers.

It seems that lumber from the vast forests of the Pacific Northwest wasn't the only commodity to put cash in the coffers of the businessmen of Astoria. There was fish — the great salmon of the Columbia, right at the back door; the salmon fisheries were as good as gold mines — better, in fact, because the supply was unlimited. Furthermore, the ocean floor off the coast was said to be teeming with cod and halibut. Whenever the businessmen of Astoria thought of this hidden treasure they trembled with cupidity. Already the railroad had been pushed through to the city; now fish could be shipped East faster than from any other port in the Northwest. A rich new deep-sea fishery was ripe for exploitation. Only the know-how was missing.

Into Astoria sailed the Gloucester fishing schooner *Hattie I. Phillips,* eighteen thousand miles from home, manned by a crew of the world's best bank fishermen, intent on picking up a load of lumber and mesmerized by the glitter of gold in the Arctic wilderness.

The Astorians leaped on the nonplussed members of the Gloucester Mining Company and showered them with solicitude. Forget about this ill-advised and hazardous venture to the Klondike! Forget about the lumber! Here are the keys to the city! Be our guests!

They offered to stake Blackburn and his men to ice, gear and outfits for bank fishing. They offered them five thousand dollars cash to bring their friends from Gloucester to start a complete fishery from catching to dealing. They talked of sending a representative to Cape Ann to look over the ground and see what could be done to establish Astoria as the Gloucester of the Pacific. The local newspaper devoted columns of enthusiastic type to the matter, and the citizens tried every device they could think of to persuade their visitors to settle with them.

But all to no avail. The fever of the gold was a passionate sickness. The *Hattie I. Phillips* had not sailed around the Horn on a fishing trip! When the lumber was loaded, she weighed anchor and left.

Riding the tail of the head winds that had lashed her on the trip up, she sped back to San Francisco with a bone in her teeth. This time she covered the distance in only four days, one of the fastest runs between the two ports under sail ever recorded.

The freight from the lumber, thrown in with the profits from the coal, paid all the company's bills and refitted the *Phillips*. When the men had finished repairing and painting her, Howard proudly exclaimed that she looked like a yacht. But already it was April, and their scheduled departure for Alaska was only a month away.

He wired the three men in Gloucester who had planned to join the company by the overland route and told them to get started. Charles Swinson was a carpenter who would help assemble the *Eclipse*; John Wennerberg would be her engineer. The third was an older man named W. N. Grant, a contractor from Lynn.

After more inquiries, Howard concluded he would have to find a buyer for the schooner in 'Frisco after all and take passage for the company on another vessel, a disquieting prospect since some of the boats that were planning to make the voyage to Alaska weren't fit to go outside the Golden Gate.

His men wanted him to ask six thousand dollars for the *Phillips*, a price he told them was out of all reason; but since he had insisted on majority rule, he renewed his search for a buyer.

When an older miner named Thomas Adams wrote him from Riverside, California, requesting that he and four miner friends be admitted to the expedition, Howard called another meeting. They were all for it and directed him to write Adams immediately and offer to take the five in for four hundred dollars each. He balked; it was a hundred dollars more than their own shares, and the Riverside men were experienced miners to boot. The issue was argued heatedly, the majority claiming any new men should be required to buy in at a premium since the original members had brought the schooner all the way around the Horn.

In the end he bowed to the majority again, but the crack in the solidarity of the Gloucester Mining Company was widening.

I soon saw they were inclined to block every move I made. When I saw I could not sell the vessel at San Francisco, I wrote to Seattle and offered the vessel for $4500, and while waiting to hear from there I went to the firm of Cassidy and Snow, outfitters, on California Street, and asked them that in case I failed to sell the vessel, if they would take her at St. Michael for a grubstake, and they promised they would do the best they could to get some one to take her on that lay. I agreed to carry five men to St. Michael to bring the vessel back for them.

I knew by the way the company were acting that some were trying to get charge, while others were trying to get a man by the name of Merriman to put in $2000 and take the vessel for security. They claim he agreed to do so, providing he could have the leadership of the company. They asked me if I was willing, and I told them yes. So I left them in disgust, and so did several other members of the company.

They notified Captain Merriman through Mr. Grant, and he promised, so Grant says, to come down the next day, but instead sent a boy saying he would have nothing to do with it.

When Captain Merriman went back on them, several of the party wanted to know who authorized anyone to ask me to give up the leadership. They held a meeting when some of them said — now Blackburn got up this scheme and carried it through successfully until we began to interfere with his plans. They came to the conclusion that they had better send a man to ask me to carry it through to suit myself. I told the man that he could go to a hotter place than Alaska and that I was through. I sold out my interest to a San Francisco man who afterwards died in Alaska.

When they found I would not come back into the company, they flew from one scheme to another like a lot of children. They wrote to Mr. Adams saying that they would be pleased to have them join the company for $300 each and tried to make it appear that it was me that wanted to charge them $400 each.

I went to Cassidy and Snow and asked them if they would give the men a grubstake for the vessel and told them I would see that they got a clean bill of sale. They agreed to do so, and the company traded the vessel for $1400 worth of provisions. I had a hard job to give the firm a clean bill of sale, as some of the members who did not want to go to

Alaska entered a protest in the custom house against the sale of the vessel for $1400. One of these sold out his interest to another man and went away owing me about $30, and failed to withdraw his objections to the sale at the custom house.

When Mr. Cassidy came on board and asked me what went with the vessel, among other things which belonged to me which I agreed to leave in the vessel was a barometer, which was given to me by a friend before leaving Gloucester. When I thought of it, I told the new leaders that I was going to send it back to Gloucester by express. We agreed to buy a second-hand one to put in its place, as we knew where to get one for $2.50. After I had sent mine away by express, they refused to help pay for the other, so I bought a new one and put it on board.

There are some very good fellows among the crew, but they are not the leaders. I have been told that several more of the crew left the vessel before she sailed. They have a fair outfit and a good crew of hard workers and a good steam launch, and if they fail to get any gold in Alaska, they will lose the least money of any similar expedition going to that country. I am more convinced than ever that a crowd of men going with such an outfit as a steam launch and dories ought to do well. Let us hope they will.

Howard didn't hang around San Francisco long. He considered going to Dawson City on his own and setting up a business, maybe a saloon. But he injured his knee somehow, and this convinced him to call it quits. With a heavy heart, he took a train as soon as he was able and arrived home in Gloucester on crutches in June.

After a squabbling reorganization of the Gloucester Mining Company, those who were left loaded the *Hattie I. Phillips* with the supplies Blackburn had provided for them and sailed out of the Golden Gate on the thirteenth of May, just three days behind their former leader's schedule.

Immediately they ran into a storm, and by nightfall they were all seasick. But the gale passed, and they had fine weather for the rest of the voyage. On the fifth of June the schooner slipped through Unimak Pass in the Aleutian Islands. The next day they dropped hand lines into the Bering Sea; the cod bit furiously, and all hands had that familiar fish for dinner.

Two days later they encountered scattered field ice drifting down on them from the north. The ice got thick and dangerous as the schooner worked her way toward the Arctic, but she passed through it safely. The days were like those in the Strait of Magellan at the other end of the earth; the sun set at eleven at night and rose again three hours later.

Early on the morning of June 13 the *Phillips* entered the harbor of St. Michael, and the men who had been with her from the first prepared to say good-by to the stanch old schooner, their home for eight months. It had been a quick passage from 'Frisco, and they were amazed to learn that theirs was the first ship of any kind to reach the port that year.

Prospectors from the Klondike, their fortunes made, thronged the dock. They had heard nothing from the outside world for nine months and only then learned from the newspapers the Gloucestermen brought with them that their country was at war with Spain.

The supplies and the prefabricated parts of the *Eclipse* were put ashore, and in five days the schooner set sail on the return trip to San Francisco. On board were forty Klondikers and eight hundred thousand dollars in gold dust. Some of them offered the captain a five-hundred-dollar bonus if he could get them to 'Frisco by the Fourth of July; they wanted to reach the States in advance of the main body of prospectors so they could unload their poor claims on the suckers.

Fred Story, the baby of the expedition, wrote his mother in Gloucester that he and Eldridge Wolfe had rowed three miles in a dory for fresh water. St. Michael was a queer place, with a population of three or four hundred white men and about as many Indians. "They are a funny race. The men go hunting for a living, and the women do all the rest of the work. When one of their tribe dies, they break his back, double him up and put him in a box, put the box on top of the ground, and cover it with wood. The people here have tried to make them bury their dead, but they will not do it."

When the *Eclipse* had been assembled, her steam engine was installed and she was launched and loaded with supplies and mining tools. The dories were strung out in tow, and she chugged across Pastol Bay and into the Yukon delta. The current was swift and the going hard. Ice cakes slammed by, and one broke the propeller. They replaced it with their spare and pushed on. Then they got a tow as far as the settlement of Nulato.

Blackburn had figured there might be gold in the hills that give birth to the lower tributaries of the Yukon. The expedition had already come over five hundred miles. The Klondike was still a thousand miles upstream. It was late summer by now, and soon the river would freeze. They would never get to the gold fields until next year. So they decided to stick to his plan.

Bucking the ever swifter current, they slowly moved on a few miles to the junction where the serpentine Koyukuk River, fed by a centipede of streams back in the Endicott Mountains, disgorges into the Yukon. The current ran so fast now that much of the time the *Eclipse* could make no headway at all. Whenever she groaned to a standstill, the men would carry a line from the bow upstream and run it around a tree on the bank. Sweating, straining and cursing Blackburn, they would haul against the tree while the steam engine was gunned until her boiler threatened to blow up; slowly the launch would creep on past the banks to a place where the current was easier.

It took them sixty days to labor nearly four hundred miles up the Koyukuk, and when they reached the bend where the Allenkakat (Alatna) River tumbles in — a spot precisely on the Arctic Circle — they struck another chunk of ice and broke their second and last propeller.

The brief Alaskan summer had come and gone. The Gloucester Mining Company was low on food, had no tents and had lost some of its mining tools. It was too late to turn back. They anchored the *Eclipse* and left her as their supply base. They made two small boats, stowed what supplies they could in them and the dories and set out to row and pole their way up the Allenkakat.

Hardly had they started when the river froze solid. They made sleds and dragged them over the ice and snow. When they had hauled themselves a hundred and twenty miles up the river, they made camp. At last they were ready to look for gold.

The snow mounted and the temperature fell, hitting bottom, finally, at fifty-five below.

One bitter day in November, Charley Strandberg, one of Blackburn's fisherman stalwarts, left his cabin a few minutes ahead of his partner to trek back to the *Eclipse* for provisions. His friends found him a week later, frozen to death.

They held on, staked a few claims and hoped for the best.

News of the Blackburn Expedition, as it continued to be called, was sketchy back in Gloucester. Fred Story turned up at home, then departed by rail for Seattle in June of 1899. He told the *Gloucester Times* that he planned to rejoin the company and was taking with him a new propeller for the disabled *Eclipse*. He would have to travel the hundred and twenty miles from the launch to camp on foot and alone, since the men didn't know when he was arriving and wouldn't be there to meet him.

Nothing further was heard until Charley Swinson appeared in Gloucester the following October. Swinson wrote the epitaph of the Gloucester Mining Company, two years after it had sailed down the harbor with high hopes and a wild send-off.

The Argonauts had sought the Golden Fleece of shining treasure all winter with scant success, he told the *Times*. Worn out, down to the last of their supplies, half dead from the cold and utterly discouraged, they finally gave up, packed their gear, sledded down the river to the *Eclipse* in deep snow and disbanded.

But it still wasn't cold enough to kill Swinson's fever. He got back to St. Michael just as another stampede headed for Nome, where the sandy beaches were rumored to be yellow with gold. He was able to sift out four thousand dollars in dust and planned to return in the spring for more.

As for the *Eclipse*, Swinson had nothing good to say about her. Blackburn's idea was to use her to break the ice of the Yukon, he said, "but I should have liked to see Blackburn bucking up against the ice of the Alaskan rivers in that old tub."

Later Howard rebutted him with asperity. He hadn't designed her to break the ice but to take twenty men up the river. With the ice in mind he had ordered protectors made for each side of the propeller. The men who took over the expedition after he left didn't know what they were for and didn't install them, and that was why the propellers had been sheared off.

The *Hattie I. Phillips* eventually ended up in the Mexican trade. Four of the other schooners from New England were sold on the Coast after disagreements shattered the parties that sailed them around the Horn.

Of the hundred thousand stampeders who were estimated to have started out on the Klondike trail, thirty or forty thousand reached their goal, and perhaps four thousand found some gold; a few hundred gained wealth, and a meager handful kept it.

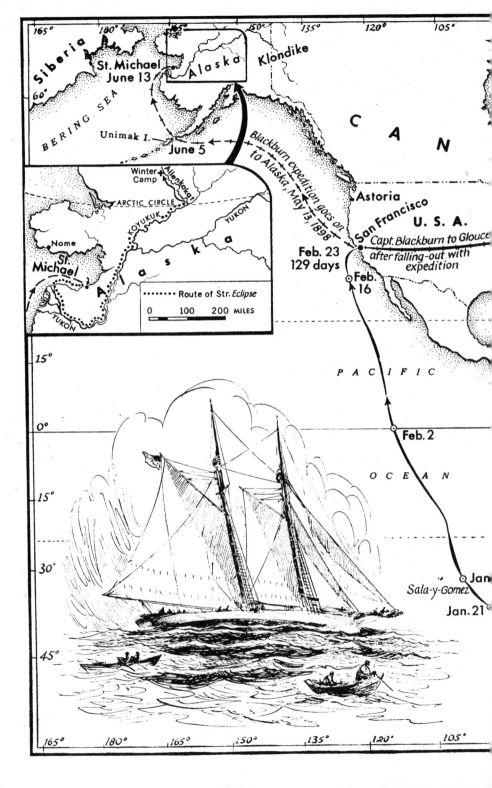

Siberia

St. Michael
June 13

Alaska

Klondike

165° 180° 165° 150° 135° 120° 105°

60°

BERING SEA

Unimak I.
June 5

Blackburn expedition goes on to Alaska, May 13, 1898

C

N

A

Astoria

San Francisco **U.S.A.**
Capt. Blackburn to Gloucester after falling-out with expedition

Feb. 23
129 days

Feb.
16

Winter
Camp

Allenkokat

ARCTIC CIRCLE

KOYUKUK

YUKON

Nome

St.
Michael

Alaska

Route of Str. *Eclipse*

0   100   200 MILES

YUKON

15°

P A C I F I C

0°

Feb. 2

15°

O C E A N

30°

Jan

Sala-y-Gomez

Jan. 21

45°

165° 180° 165° 150° 135° 120° 105°

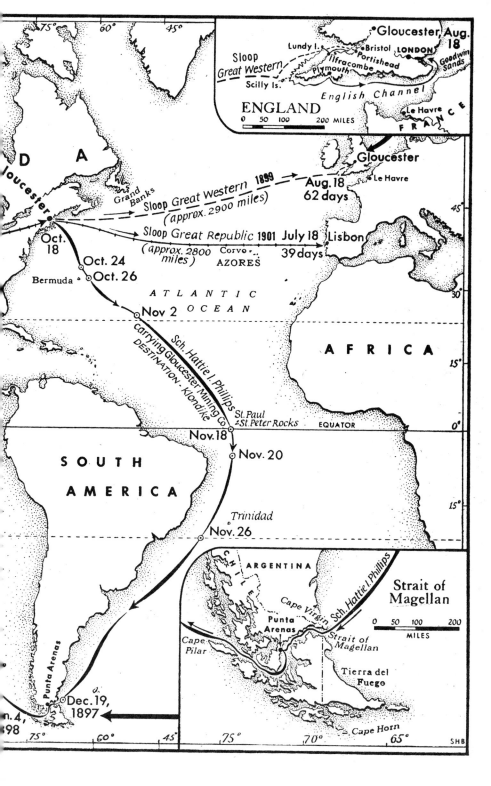

8

Singlehanded Fever

THERE WERE no newspaper interviews when Howard Blackburn limped despondently off the train at Gloucester in June 1898. He hobbled straight home to nurse his injured knee and pride.

Before leaving San Francisco he had sent the Gloucester papers his own version of the events that led to his downfall as the leader of the Blackburn Expedition, and there is no reason to doubt that he set them down as he saw them.

His former comrades were silent on the point, but it is hard to believe that the blame lay entirely with a handful of dissidents. Howard was at the head of a crew he had picked himself; when the chips were down, he failed to hold them together, and when they asked him back, his pride and temper got in the way of a reconciliation.

The whole business strengthened his conviction that he was better off when he didn't have to depend on anyone but himself to carry through his plans.

There was something else about the Klondike affair that stuck with him in a different way. It had to do with the voyage on the *Hattie I. Phillips*, with being back at sea again, discovering that he could pull his weight aboard ship in spite of his handicap.

It was as if fifteen years of his life had been given back to him — as if he were back in the dory. The memory of those days and nights burned inside him. There had been a kind of fierce exhilaration about them, like having his living in the dory and his dying all around him and rowing his life through an ocean of death.

He was obsessed with a feeling that he had to return to the sea, not in company with other men on board a ship, but for a private rendezvous, to settle a personal score.

How would it be to go back to sea again the way it had been in the dory, to prove that what had happened the first time was not just an act of fate or stroke of luck? How would it be to do it all over again, but a hundred times harder, this time deliberately, announcing his intentions to the world so that the world could watch, conquering the sea with the very hands the sea itself had mutilated?

During those months when he clumped around Gloucester on crutches, trying to mend his injured knee, he thought about such a rendezvous, sometimes with elation and sometimes with a morbid longing; for when the old frostbite agony came back in spasms and twisted its knives in his legs, he swore he would do it and die in the act. But more often it was with high anticipation, because he knew he loved life if he could only get at it.

It was thus that in the winter and early spring of 1899 Howard Blackburn settled on the idea of sailing across the North Atlantic Ocean alone in a small boat.

There was an element of strange logic to it, since five lone men in history had already embarked on that most terrible of the seas and lived to reach the other side.

This logic took an almost imperative twist, however, when he considered that the very first of the five, the prototype of the single-handed mariner, was at that moment very much alive and sailing out of Gloucester as master of a fishing schooner.

His name was Captain Alfred Johnson, but the world knew him as "Centennial" after the twenty-foot dory he sailed on a dare from Gloucester to Liverpool, England, to celebrate the hundredth anniversary of American independence in 1876. It took him sixty-six days, and he nearly lost his life in the attempt.

When he got back to Gloucester he returned to fishing like a sensible man, and to anyone who asked about the voyage thereafter he growled that he'd been a damned young fool.

Nevertheless, it was a contagious kind of foolishness. Johnson had hardly returned from England when two young brothers from nearby Beverly, William and Asa Andrews, went down to Gloucester and bought a nineteen-foot dory which they named *Nautilus* and sailed to Cornwall in the summer of 1878 in forty-nine days.

It took ten more years for William Andrews to make up his mind to try it alone. The man was a born promoter, though at first not much of a sailor, and he built a fourteen-footer named *Dark Secret* for a theatrical show in New York and got the *New York World* to sponsor him. *Dark Secret* was a leaky boat, and after two months at sea he gave it up in mid-Atlantic and was plucked from his tub by a passing bark.

In three more years the incredible Andrews tried again, in the fifteen-foot *Mermaid*. This time he had company, of a sort. An expert sailor from Chelsea named Si Lawlor had sailed *Neversink* the year before from New York to Le Havre and now proposed an ocean race in his new boat, *Sea Serpent*. They sailed out of Boston Harbor in June of 1891. Lawlor reached England in forty-five days. Capsized during a gale and completely done in, Andrews was rescued by a steamer after sixty-one days at sea — only six hundred miles from Europe.

But Captain Bill Andrews (he never commanded a crew of more than one) wouldn't give up. He built a fourteen-and-a-half-foot canvas-covered folding boat, *Sapolio*, and set out from Atlantic City, New Jersey, in July of 1892. Eighty-four days later, he landed on the south coast of Portugal. He had sailed the smallest boat ever to cross the Atlantic — as an advertising stunt for a soap manufacturer.

In 1894 Rudolph Frietsch, a Finn, sailed his forty-foot schooner *Nina* from New York to Ireland.

And on April 24, 1895, Captain Joshua Slocum, a fifty-one-year-old Nova Scotian who had run away to sea at the age of twelve, nosed his sloop *Spray* out of Boston Harbor toward Gloucester, a stiff southwester at his back. He spent two weeks fitting out there and then started across the Atlantic. Three years and two months later, having sailed forty-six thousand miles around the world, he dropped his hook in the harbor of Newport, Rhode Island.

Such were the only men to have ever sailed alone across the three thousand miles of gale-swept waste called the North Atlantic. Others had done it in twos and threes, navigating every kind of craft from a lifesaving float with sails to a twenty-six-foot square-rigged boat; two brave men had sailed from Gloucester to England one summer and back to Halifax the next; another pair had even rowed across from New York.

But Johnson, Lawlor, Andrews, Frietsch and Slocum — they were the single-handers. Theirs was the way of unrelieved alone-ness, of willful self-reliance.

The stage was set.

In late March of 1899 Captain Andrews announced that in mid-June he would embark alone in a seventeen-foot boat from Atlantic City on his fifth attempt to cross the Atlantic.

Less than a week later, Captain Thomas Crapo, who twenty-two years earlier had sailed to England in a twenty-footer with his wife, departed from New Bedford with the intention of launching his nine-foot dory, perhaps from the Carolina coast, and sailing it alone to Cuba.

Two days later, on the evening of April 6, Captain Slocum — bald, bearded and jaunty as ever — delivered a well-publicized lecture on his voyage around the world before a packed house at the Chapel Street Baptist Church in East Gloucester.

Inside of two weeks certain rumors were abroad in Gloucester. A reporter tracked Blackburn down: Was it true that he was planning to build a small boat and sail her across the Atlantic?

Well, it was half of the truth, said Howard. He was having a boat built, all right. Hugh Bishop, whose brother had designed the *Eclipse* for the Blackburn Expedition, was already making the model, and the boat itself would be finished by June. But he had no intention of crossing the ocean in her; he was just figuring to do a little coastal cruising for his health.

Ten days passed. His partner, Prady Nunes, renewed the license for the saloon. Did this mean Blackburn had other things in mind?

Five more days went by. The newspapers reported the fate of Captain Crapo. He had sailed from Providence, Rhode Island. A gale arose. His dory, bottom up, was washed onto the beach a few miles down the coast.

On the twenty-sixth of May, Howard invited the papers to send over their representatives, as he had an announcement to make which he thought might be of interest. They met in the billiard room at the rear of the saloon. When everyone was there, he called for quiet. Then, in his matter-of-fact way, he tossed his bomb.

His sloop would be launched within a few days. In three weeks he would set sail alone for England.

The reporters stared at the big man and their eyes dropped to his fingerless hands.

Was he *serious?*

Certainly. His plans were all made. The sloop was thirty feet long, and he would christen her *Great Western* in whimsical succession to the famous British four-masted sailing steamer of fifty years before. He would sail on the seventeenth or eighteenth of June with a letter of introduction from Mayor French to the Lord Mayor of Gloucester, England, his destination. During the first leg of the voyage, until he made the Grand Banks, he would remain at the helm all night and through each morning, sleeping from noon until six in the evening. For the remainder of the crossing until he reached the Irish Channel, he would sail from dawn until dark, lying to and sleeping every night. The passage would take about fifty days. He would visit the principal ports of the

British Isles, cruise down along the coast of France, winter at various Mediterranean ports, and the following summer visit the Paris Exposition before returning home by steamer.

That was it. The incredulous reporters went back to their papers. A man would have to be queer enough to want to do such a thing. But for Blackburn to try it — in his condition — he must have gone mad. Still, there was something about him that made the wildest scheme seem possible . . . They wrote straight-faced accounts of the interview, and the news went around the world.

The *Cape Ann Breeze* headlined:

LONE VOYAGER

HOWARD BLACKBURN TO CROSS THE BROAD ATLANTIC

The Man of Iron to Engage in Another Hazardous Enterprise. Going to Gloucester, England

And it commented blandly that "he has gained the reputation of having an iron constitution and possessed of energy equalled by few."

What did Theresa think of all this? Her adoration of a husband she couldn't understand must have been exceeded only by the fear that she was about to lose him forever.

One evening a week later the Man of Iron took time out from his preparations for the voyage to be the guest of honor of the Acoriana Society, a Portuguese-American club in Gloucester. Howard and the Portuguese fishermen had been mutual admirers for years; his saloon was a favorite hangout of theirs, and he enjoyed selling them wine by the barrel for what it cost him. After dinner his friends presented him with a giant American flag nine feet long and a burgee all of thirteen feet in length with the name *Great Western* spelled out in huge letters.

"I value the flags fully as much as I do the boat," he told them; and as for the latter — "if she should prove otherwise than a good sea boat and good sailor, the fault will not be with the builders but with myself, as she was built according to my own ideas."

He had good reason for his confidence. *Great Western* was no fancy yacht design, untried at sea, but the little sister of a small fishing vessel, well proven for twenty years and the darling of the independent fishermen, the "Gloucester sloop boat."

Averaging forty to fifty feet in length, their hulls similar to those of the clipper schooners, they became popular during one of the periods of temporary decline in the fishing industry when schooner building suffered from scarce money. They were in a direct line of descent, though sharply modified in some particulars, from the Boston cutter, or Irish boat, built in Boston for generations by the Irish immigrant fishermen somewhat after the fashion of the Galway hookers they had sailed off the shores of the old country. The Gloucestermen adapted the Boston design to their own tastes, and the sloop boat, in turn, showed up in the lines of the famous Friendship sloops built by the Morse family at Friendship, Maine.

The sloop boat was a compromise of three qualities not easily compatible — speed, seaworthiness and capacity — with a bit of beauty besides. For many years most of them were built by the Bishop brothers and by Tom Irving, another famous local shipwright and designer. Their customers were Gloucestermen who wanted a boat in which two or three or four men could fish offshore for days at a time, ride out the nastiest weather the New England coast could dish up, and run home or to Boston in jigtime with a full hold while the catch was fresh and the prices high.

Great Western slid off the ways at Bishop's on the sixth of June. A big crowd was on hand to watch the launching, jamming the wharves at the foot of Water Street. No sooner was she overboard than the men went to work installing her spars and rigging.

She aroused a buzz of comment among the old hands along the

waterfront, for although a yacht, strictly speaking, she was an entirely novel one, and everybody was intensely curious to see what Captain Blackburn had devised to take him across.

No question about it, *Great Western* was a small Gloucester sloop boat, thirty feet from stem to stern, eight and a half feet wide and four feet four inches deep, displacing 4.77 tons. She had the same fine clipper bow, graceful sheer, broad beam and buoyant stern, and she gripped the water with her deep bottom.

Not wanting to carry more sail than he could conveniently and safely handle, Howard had adapted the sloop boat rig by shortening both the bowsprit and boom proportionately and eliminating the forestaysail. He had, however, retained the topmast for jib and gaff topsails. The big gaff mainsail had two rows of reef points so he could reduce its area in a blow, and these lines were extra long for easier tying by a man with no fingers. The jib was made for shortening by a different method: it was put together with a detachable lower section called a bonnet; this separate piece of canvas forming the foot could be unlaced and taken off, giving the same effect as a reef.

Great Western's deck was smooth and uncluttered, and the planks themselves formed the cabin top; when the seas swept over her, there would be nothing to batter or carry away. She steered with a wheel. Her shallow cockpit was watertight and bare except for the binnacle. Under the cockpit was a sixty-five-gallon water tank. The cabin was roomy and lined with lockers and drawers. Bars of pig iron were stowed beneath the floor for ballast. There was a little galley with a three-burner oil stove. The interior was finished in natural cypress except for the overhead, which was painted white with blue trim. Way up forward in the forepeak was her master's bunk.

Even the staid East Gloucester Yacht Club on Rocky Neck was swept by the popular excitement over Blackburn's impending departure. The night of the launching it voted him in as a member.

By now he had made up his mind to sail on Sunday, June 18,

the same day Captain Andrews would be heading out to sea from Atlantic City. The two would not be racing officially, but each hoped to reach Europe first.

Time was getting short. With ten days left for *Great Western*'s shakedown trials, Howard had to familiarize himself with her sailing ability, tune her up to her best form, and stock her with everything he might conceivably need for an ocean voyage the like of which he had never taken before.

He crammed provisions into every nook and cranny to last for ninety days. His choice suggests that he had a steady seagoing stomach:

Eleven loaves of bread	One bushel of potatoes
Ten cans of salmon	Half-bushel of onions
Six cans of baked beans	Eighteen pounds of salt pork
Six cans of peas	Thirty-five pounds of corned shoulder
Six cans of kidney beans	Fifteen pounds of corned beef
Eighteen cans of clams	Five pounds of pressed ham
Thirty cans of condensed milk	Eight pounds of cottage ham
Six cans of tomatoes	Ten pounds of fresh pork
Two cans of cocoa	Twenty pounds of butter
Twelve bottles of pickles	Nine pounds of lard
Two bottles of ketchup	Four pounds of coffee
Eight packages of rolled oats	Two and a half pounds of tea
Two bags of salt	Twenty pounds of sugar
Two packages of pepper	Two pounds of saleratus
Two boxes of mustard	One quart of vinegar
Crackers	One bottle of pepper sauce

His old friend Dr. Hale supplied him with a medicine chest and several bottles of a new concentrated nutritive food called "malted milk," which he recommended highly. The good doctor also handed him a letter to be opened after thirty days at sea, doubtless containing a few morale-boosting sentiments and perhaps a verse or two.

He was well stocked with thick clothing, oilskins and boots, a chronometer, barometer, sextant and taffrail log. Two items of equipment were to be carried as a precaution against heavy weather. One was a drag to serve the same purpose as the keg buoy he had kicked in to keep the dory head to the wind on Burgeo Bank. The other consisted of several canvas bags filled with rags; should he find himself running before the wind, with breaking seas overtaking him astern, he would saturate these with oil and trail them alongside; there was nothing like oil to calm the troubled waters.

Besides these necessities, Howard laid in plenty of cigars, tobacco and matches and a stock of strong drink to keep his spirits up and circulation moving when the cold easterlies blew.

Two days before departure, *Great Western*, having been hauled out for a final inspection of her bottom, was returned to the water and moved to Lane's Wharf, a cable length from the back door of the saloon, where the public was invited to inspect her. Later in the day Howard went over to the Yacht Club and was cheered roundly by the members as Commodore Alex McCurdy presented him its burgee to fly at his masthead. He thanked the assemblage, talked informally about his plans and departed to another round of cheers.

On the eve of departure the traditional exchange of gifts took place. He received solemn tokens of affection and good luck — a history of the city, a mirror, a barometer and a pair of binoculars, a box of candy, a silver spoon, and that characteristic nugget of the '90's and mark of a gent, a gold toothpick.

With his usual flair for the dramatic, he presented twenty-five dollars to the Addison Gilbert Hospital and a hundred dollars to a friend to be used for the poor.

Sunday came in a perfect June day, bearing out the partiality of lone mariners for the nautical blessings of that sweet month. Gloucester was in a holiday spirit, and by noon thousands had already strolled down to the harbor in search of the best vantage points. *Great Western* lay at Lane's Wharf, nudging at her dock lines as if to be free. Everything was on board but her master, and she was ready for the sea.

Shortly before two Howard left home and strode down Main Street toward the wharf, accompanied by a crowd of cronies. Accounts of the events of that afternoon carry not a word about Theresa. Perhaps she could not bear to stand there and watch him sail away.

Wearing a cap and a blue serge suit, cigar stuck behind his thumb, he shoved through the dense crowds. Wave after wave of cheers marked his progress as he laughed and joked with well-wishers who fought through to him to pump his hand and thump him on the back.

Every wharf around the loop of the inner harbor was packed with people. All along the shore they thronged, and back into the streets. The rooftops were black with them. They perched on rocks and pilings and scrambled high in the shrouds of schooners and leaned out windows and climbed trees — anything that would get them a glimpse of this man without fingers as he headed into the Atlantic.

There were ten thousand of them.

On the wharf a path opened up for him and closed as he passed. He went directly to *Great Western* and stepped aboard. Thirteen close friends and reporters swarmed over with him, and she settled uneasily with their weight. At the stroke of two from the City Hall clock, he ordered the mainsail and jib swayed up. One friend cast off the stern line, while an old shipmate from the *Grace L. Fears*, which eighteen months earlier had carried all hands to the bottom in a gale off Newfoundland, was given the honor of letting go the bow. Captain Joe Merchant, who had been chosen by the Yacht Club for the privilege, took over the wheel. Aloft the flag and pennants flapped lazily in colorful array.

The wind was fair and light from the south, skittering patches of ripples across the flat water. The sun shone down warmly out

of the brilliant blue sky, and the mewling gulls wheeled overhead, dispossessed of their usual roosts by the swarm of hu-
manity.

Burdened by her passengers, *Great Western* made a short
starboard hitch to Five Pound Island, came about and moved
slowly on a close-hauled tack down the harbor.

The roar of the crowds echoed from shore to shore as the black
sloop sailed by in the middle of a flotilla of boats so thick that at
times she could barely be seen. It was one continuous deep-
throated ovation that she floated through, punctuated by the boom
of guns and the blasts and shrills of horns and whistles. *Great
Western* dipped her colors in response, and her master — perched
easily on the wheelbox with his cigar — waved his cap and grinned
as boats passed in close and admirers leaned over the side to shout
to him "God bless you, Howard!" and "Good luck, Captain!"

Precisely as *Great Western* was working out of Gloucester Harbor, almost adrift in the dying breeze, Captain Andrews was sailing from Atlantic City in his twelve-foot *Doree.*

As he bore off for the open sea, a rowboat with four veiled
women as passengers pulled away from a yacht, overhauled Andrews and came alongside. Each girl, in turn, lifted up her veil,
leaned far over the gunwale, threw her arms around the astonished
sailor and kissed him heartily. He was so shaken that he jibed,
and his boom nearly knocked his admirers overboard.

But just as they turned back, a second rowboat came after him
in hot pursuit. In it was a young lady whom he had agreed to
take as crew but later had rejected. Throwing a line over his tiller,
she screamed: "I have my valise here all packed. Do take me with
you, Captain dear!"

But Andrews cast her off remorselessly and continued out to
sea.

Meanwhile, in Gloucester Harbor, the breeze dropped to a flat
calm, and it was five in the afternoon when *Great Western,* her

sails slatting in the sun, lazed past Eastern Point and into the Atlantic. Most of the boats in the flotilla now turned back after a last look at her and a bon voyage, and she continued on, hardly moving, by the lighthouse, where Keeper George Bailey clanged the fog bell, blasted the whistle and shouted "Godspeed!" through his megaphone.

Then the wind came up again, fresh from the southwest. The flying jib and topsail were set, and *Great Western* bowled along smartly in company with five sloops from the Yacht Club and a little fishing boat. Howard entertained his guests with talk of the voyage and a drop or two of cheer. Shortly they were overtaken by an excursion steamer with a gay farewell party aboard, including Alderman Roderick McDonald, who exuberantly tossed his hat so high in the air that he lost it in the sea.

At six o'clock *Great Western* was abreast of Thatcher Island, a half-mile off the easterly tip of Cape Ann. Blackburn ordered her hove to and took over the wheel. The yachts luffed up alongside, and one by one his friends, with firm handshakes and many a wet eye, said their good-bys and stepped off.

The yachts filled away for home. He threw the helm over and pointed his bow to the sea. He waved his cap and then watched them until the white sails disappeared around the Cape.

9

The Fingerless Navigator

THE OBLIGING BREEZE which permitted him to part company with his friends waited until they were long out of sight before it died. By nightfall *Great Western* lay almost motionless on the glassy sea, a few miles to the eastward of Cape Ann.

Her sails hung limp; the gaff at the head of her main creaked idly against the mast when she rolled a little with the swell. He lit the riding lamps and hung them in the shrouds, red to port and green to starboard, and settled back in the cockpit, hardly laying a hand on the wheel, his cigar glowing in the darkness.

The beam from the twin minarets of granite on Thatcher Island swung overhead with tireless regularity. Once or twice a Mother Carey's chicken — the sailor's name for the stormy petrel — skimmed close by, satisfied its twittering curiosity and fluttered off in the night.

At two in the morning a schooner drifted up on him. They exchanged clear hails across the water; she was the *Judique*, out of Gloucester. In a while she was gone, leaving her wishes for his good luck.

As he stood his first watch that night, scarcely yet out of the lee of the land, he knew that something was already wrong. Half aware of what it was, still unwilling to admit the whole of it, he found himself rubbing his right leg — the knee, the muscles of the thigh — and then he took off his boot and massaged the thick, deformed foot.

Fog was closing in. The cold, clammy dampness of the sea penetrated his clothing and his skin and soaked into the flesh and the marrow of the bone. By dawn both the foot and the knee were starting to swell, and the throbbing pain worked up the leg and filled his body.

All through the day the swelling and the pain increased. He dragged himself forward and took in the flying jib and top-sail. A little wind was blowing the fog past him in a swirling, dripping cloud of gray, but he was too sick to keep all sail on.

It was the same for eight days. The sloop limped along under mainsail and jib, brushing through the dense, intermittent banks of fog. He was so ill that he couldn't bring himself to cook, and during the whole time he consumed nothing but the contents of one bottle of Dr. Hale's malted milk. Ashake with the wet cold, or burning with fever, he gulped down his quota of water for days to come.

He applied what remedies he had from the medicine chest. He could get neither boot nor slipper over the monstrously swollen foot. But he gritted his teeth and bore on, steering well to the southward of his intended course to avoid meeting homebound vessels that would raise anxieties by reporting his condition.

Finally it got to be more than he could stand — not just the pain, but the crippling. How could he ever handle the boat when the weather kicked up?

The last fiber of his morale broke, and he gave up.

By now he was to the south of Nova Scotia, and the fog had thinned out slightly. He swung the helm northward for Shelburne and a doctor and ran straight into a wall of fog so thick that it closed in astern like a door on the night. The danger of colliding with another vessel or of running his boat up on the coast in this soup was imminent; he hauled back to the southward again, trapped.

No sooner was he on course, however, than he felt better. The swelling and the pain began to subside. His appetite returned, and with hot food in his starved stomach, his spirits rose. There was a light westerly wind on his tail, and he set all sail and drove hard to make up for lost time.

For another twenty-four days he pushed toward the Grand Banks. He was never especially aware of loneliness, out alone on the empty ocean, for the daily routine of taking care of himself and his boat, watching the weather and keeping to his course, commanded all his attention. Yet the going was so slow that there were twenty-four-hour stretches when *Great Western* logged as little as six, eight or fourteen miles.

His plan was to take the shortest route to England — the northern track followed by the transatlantic steamers — but to stand off to the southward far enough to keep clear of the traffic. He had plotted a course that by midsummer should avoid stray icebergs drifting south with the Labrador Current but that skirted to the north of the storm-brewing Gulf Stream. The prevailing winds of the North Atlantic are westerly. The westerlies and the Gulf Stream current should carry him east of the Grand Banks to mid-Atlantic, where he would be lifted along by the North Atlantic Current that swings up and by the British Isles. For it is said that given time enough, anything that floats will be borne by the sea and wind from North America to Europe.

Though the westerlies were logy with fog and rain, they held for the first thirty-two days. As his health mended, he settled into the planned routine of the first leg of the voyage. The passage between the Grand Banks, Nova Scotia, Gloucester and Boston was the fog-swept path of the fishing schooners; so he stood his trick at the wheel from six in the evening until noon of the next day, keeping a sharp lookout for lights and dark forms in the murk of night and fog. At noon he hove to and trimmed his sails, for *Great Western*, to his disappointment, turned out to be too quick on her helm to steer herself when the wind was abaft her beam. Having towed the log for an hour in the morning to determine his speed, he would break out the sextant and shoot the sun — if it happened to be visible — and figure his position; if he could see neither sun nor stars, he plotted it by dead reckoning. After marking his estimated location on the chart and eating lunch, he would crawl into his bunk and sleep until five in the afternoon, letting *Great Western* tend herself. On awakening, he would cook up his dinner — and next day's breakfast and lunch if it wasn't too rough — set sail and resume his course with another eighteen-hour stint at the helm.

Before he sailed out of Gloucester Harbor he had practiced handling the lines aboard ship, and neither rigging nor sails thereafter gave him any trouble he was willing to admit.

The halyards were rove through fairleads on the deck at the foot of the mast and led back to the cockpit. Though there was great strength in his hands, the gripping power of his half-thumbs was limited. Consequently, to sway up a sail he would run the halyard around his waist, lean away, take up the slack in the pinch of his thumbs and lean away again, repeating this procedure until the sail was up and the halyard taut. Stooping over and maintaining the strain on the line with the turn around his waist until the halyard lay across the cockpit coaming, he would press one hand hard on the halyard against the coaming and with the other secure the free end around the cleat.

When he needed to trim the main sheet to haul the sail in closer to the wind, he would make one turn of it around the cleat and lean against the taut length of line leading to the sheet block on the boom, gripping it near the block with his thumbs and hauling up the slack around the cleat with his teeth. This procedure, too, was repeated until the set of the sail satisfied him, when he cleated the sheet down securely.

As for handling sail and performing a thousand other essential tasks at sea, he managed well enough and never thought them worth mentioning.

One night *Great Western* was dawdling in the fog, immobilized by a flat calm east of Sable Island, the long and narrow jut of rock and shoals seventy-five miles off the coast of Nova Scotia known darkly as the Graveyard of the Atlantic.

As the boat could make no headway, I thought that instead of setting on deck all night with the fog horn in my hand, watching for steamers, I would turn in.

About 2 A.M. a steamer blew her whistle which woke me up. I grabbed the fog horn to rush on deck, struck my head against a beam, fell on the floor with my knee on the fog horn, which injured it so badly that when I got on deck I could not make a sound with it.

It made no difference, as the steamer was just passing my boat. The night was so black that I could not see her, but the waves from her bow washed over my boat.

The westerlies carried *Great Western* over the fog-shrouded Grand Banks and about five hundred miles east of Newfoundland before they blew themselves out. Her sails drooped, and she lay listless in mid-ocean, becalmed halfway to England. Not a breath disturbed the endless flat of the water for three days.

Time hung heavy as the sloop drifted in the vicinity of the fortieth meridian. On the fourth day (it was about the twentieth of July), the undulating mirror stirred with dancing ripples, and he felt the strange coolness of a breeze in his face. The stretch of canvas above him came to life, and elatedly he swung the helm over so the sails would catch the moving air. His boat heeled happily away from the freshening wind. Again the bubbles gurgled along her bottom, and she flung the spray aside. It was a great moment for all hands, and a fresh cigar was lit and a drop was had in celebration.

Now the wind blew from the east, from dead ahead, and as it freshened the sloop skipped on smartly. He sheeted the sails in flat and tacked zigzag back and forth across his course. He would plow along for a few hours on one hitch, towing the log for a while to gauge his speed and tracking his direction with the compass; checking the time and estimating the distance he had traveled, he would mark his position on the chart by dead reckoning and throw over the helm. As *Great Western*'s bow swung into the wind, her sails rattled momentarily and then fell silent again as she leaned off on the other tack; her windward shrouds tightened from the strain of the canvas on her mast, while her leeward rigging dangled loose from the sudden relaxation.

Thus he beat onward, crossing and recrossing his true course, ever alert at the wheel and the sheets to keep the best advantage of the wind and maintain the fullest driving force of his sails.

It was the keenest brand of sailing and called for a new turn of life aboard *Great Western*. She was making spanking good way, and he was determined to recoup the lost time of the first month at sea and hold the passage to fifty days.

Reversing his schedule, he took the helm from four in the morning until eight at night, squeezing every minute out of the daylight. He had already discovered to his irritation that his sloop was not the self-sailer he had hoped she would be, but he found he could coax her into a course just to the east of southeast or northeast if the wind was between them. Under these conditions, and if the wind and sea were moderate, he would furl the mainsail at the end of his watch, replace it with the little trysail and reef the jib by taking off the bonnet. Then he would lash the wheel close to amidships, and *Great Western* would jog along at her own pace while he hung the riding lights in the shrouds and went below to fish around in the lockers for his supper.

After cooking up a meal to his taste, he would turn in for the night, lulled to sleep by the splashing rush of water past the bow a few inches from his head. An hour before dawn he would be rattling around in the cabin, cooking a hot breakfast if it wasn't too rough to use the stove, or if the weather was foul, contenting himself with a mess of oatmeal stirred into a bowl of cold water.

During thick weather he kept to the south of the steamers. If it was clear, and he felt a twinge of loneliness, he stood up into their track, where he might sight as many as five of them during the course of a day, lumbering along on the horizon, trailing wisps of smoke. Time, like the steamers, slipped by at a distance, and his very aloneness left him alone. He was content to be relieved of the demands of human relationship. Busy enough sailing and navigating and running the microcosmic world of his own making, he was alone but not lonely.

One morning while taking down the sidelights I lost the port light overboard. After that I had to put a white light in its place. One morning just before daylight while I was sound asleep, a steamer came along and blew her whistle. I, thinking it had set in thick fog during the night, grabbed the fog horn which I had repaired and rushed on deck. I found the weather was clear and fine. They hailed me and asked me if I needed anything. I answered that I was all right. They blew their whistle three times and passed on.

I was glad when they left me, for as I had not heard the sound of a human voice for about thirty days, my own voice sounded so disagreeable when answering them that I made up my mind that I would never let an hour go by without saying something.

So after that, whenever anything had to be done, I would give orders to do so and so and then go and do it myself.

The apparition of a thirty-foot sloop in mid-Atlantic, displaying a white light where her red port lantern should be, would excite the curiosity of any passing vessel. But a few nights later he compounded this transgression of the rules of the road and by so doing saved *Great Western* from a quick trip to the bottom.

It was stormy and rough, and he had fought his way along deck to hang the green lantern in the starboard rigging. The confounded wick refused to stay lit, and in a burst of temper he flung the lamp into the sea, stomped below for another white lantern and hung it in its place.

A few nights later *Great Western* was bouncing along in the chop, steering herself as best she could. It was raining torrentially, and her master was below, fighting to keep his balance while he tried to wheedle a hot supper out of the stove. Suddenly the drumming of the rain on the deck overhead was split by the deep-throated blast of a steamer whistle. It sounded on top of him.

His heart pounding and his ears ringing, he burst up on deck.

The black, hulking bow of a steamer loomed up out of the driving rain, twice as high as *Great Western*'s mast, pointed straight at her, only a few yards away. It was motionless. The helmsman had seen the white lights under his bow just in time, signaled the engine room and brought the ship to a dead stop.

He clambered forward and stood near the lights, soaking in the rain, so that he could be seen. As soon as the sloop had meandered out of its way, the steamer's great screw began again to thrash the sea, and it bore off to the westward. Not a word had been exchanged during this eerie encounter, and he returned to his supper.

Mile after mile he drove on in the teeth of the easterly, begrudging every minute that the need for rest and food took him away from the wheel. Twice he stood watches of thirty-four solid hours without leaving the cockpit except to grab a bite, mark the chart and light his pipe; once he was at the wheel for thirty-five hours, once for thirty-eight. But the beating he gave himself paid off; his best day's run across that expanse of the Atlantic was a hundred and twenty-two miles.

He was not, strictly speaking, alone the whole time.

One morning when I turned out at daylight and was getting ready to go on deck, I heard a noise in the stew pan which I had left on the cabin floor, the cover of it being about half ways off.

I reached over without looking and hauled the cover into its place, thinking that the rocking of the boat made the cover of the pot make the noise.

But to my surprise the noise increased. I gave the pot a kick which upset it, and out hopped one of Mother Carey's chickens. It was covered with stew that I had left in the pot.

I took it in my hands, went on deck and threw it up into the air. It flew a short distance and then fell into the water, where I hoped after freeing itself from the stew it would be able to fly again.

When clouds and fog shut him in, as they did during much of the voyage, navigation was a problem, and the only way he could check his logged position was to sneak a shot at the sun whenever it peeked momentarily through a break in the skies. Once he was eight days without being able to make an observation, and he wasn't at all sure exactly where in the vastness of the ocean he was. It was toward the end of July, and he decided to stand up into the steamer track, hoping he would cross paths with a vessel and obtain from her his position. He was in luck that day. The *Carlton* of Newcastle, England, homebound from the States, sighted him and steamed alongside.

She hailed me and asked me where I was from. I told them that I was thirty-eight days out from Gloucester, Massachusetts, and bound for Gloucester, England. They asked me if I needed any assistance. I told them no, but asked him what his longitude was. But he did not have it worked up at the time, so he answered — I will let you know in a few minutes.

As his ship was going three miles to my one, by the time he would have it worked up he would be several miles away. But he hove his wheel hard astarboard, turned his great ship around and came and passed me again, gave me his position and passed on.

I felt sorry for putting him to so much trouble. I made up my mind that I would never again ask a man for his position.

After all, there was no need to be beholden to anyone, or to put anyone to any trouble. A man shouldn't sail across the ocean alone in the first place if he had to rely on passing vessels for his longitude.

One day a very heavy black cloud passed over. A long sharp point shot gradually down towards the water. All at once the water around the boat began to leap and jump in all directions. In a few minutes I saw one of the largest water spouts that I had ever seen. But it was a good ways to leeward and did not trouble me.

By dint of beating diagonally against the easterlies, *Great Western* had made a good eight hundred miles since they first blew in, although she had to cover half again the distance to do it. But at the twenty-first meridian, with nine hundred miles still to go, the wind exhausted itself. He was becalmed for four days.

Then, as abruptly as it died, it revived with redoubled energy, blustering back in from the east, surly and morose with squalls and rain, raising the hackles on the back of the sea. He was impatient with the voyage, and cursing the weather, he kicked his heels into the flank of his boat. But like any steed, she had her limits. She could run no faster than she had been built to run, and with every drenching, pitching tack he grew more sick of the whole thing.

Day after day they fought through the gray seas and against the screeching wind and the pelting rain, and the line of his pencil inched erratically across the chart, laboring its jagged way toward the English coast.

At nine-thirty on the morning of August 16, the sixtieth day at sea, the Scilly Islands — western guardians of Cornwall's bluff coast — rose up on the horizon dead ahead.

What a wonderful clump of rocks and isles they were! When he beat past and dropped them in his lee he saw the thin gray line of Land's End, shimmering in the sun so far away — good old England!

All day he sailed up the Cornwall coast, bursting with excitement. His eyes — asquint from the sight of sky and water — feasted on the thread of distant land.

At noon the next day, twenty-five miles to the westward of Lundy Isle, he spoke the tug *Thistle* as she plied across his course, her crew crowding the rail in surprise. Driving on past Lundy, he shaped around Ilfracombe and at eight in the evening entered Bristol Channel. He was so keyed up that he kept sailing right through the night. At two in the morning, full of restless energy, he broke out the anchors and chain and hauled them up on the forward deck, ready for the landing.

The wind was brisk and fair at dawn. *Great Western* skipped gaily up the channel and ticked off a good run to King Road.

Gloucester lay ahead, up the broad reach of the Severn and inland where the river narrows.

A pilot boat swung at her anchor in King Road off the resort town of Portishead, and he came up to her smartly. It was four-thirty in the afternoon. The men aboard could not have been more astounded if he had dropped out of the sky.

They took his lines and made *Great Western* fast, hustled him into their skiff and rowed him ashore. He went straight to the telegraph office and cabled Commodore Alex McCurdy of the East Gloucester Yacht Club that he had crossed the Atlantic Ocean and arrived safely in England after a passage of sixty-two days.

10
England

Having dispatched his cable home, Blackburn relaxed. While the news was being flashed around an astonished world, he took a hot bath and ate a hearty dinner and then held court for the Gloucester newspaper reporters and a crowd of curious Englishmen.

Captain Andrews, he learned, hadn't made it. Battered by winds and heavy seas, exhausted trying to keep afloat, he was picked out of the ocean more dead than alive by the steamer *Holbein* on July 11 and taken to Liverpool. His twelve-foot boat was left adrift, only seven hundred miles from Ireland.

Howard picked up a pilot at Portishead, and at two the following afternoon they cast off from the pilot boat and filled away for the Severn basin.

It was a glorious day. With all her canvas spread, and her fine pennants flapping in the breeze, what a sight *Great Western* must be from shore, he thought, as she leaned up the broad expanse of the estuary! What a credit to America!

Four hours later his pilot swung the sloop into the dock at Sharpness, the entrance to the sixteen-mile river canal that would take him to Gloucester. Captain Field, the dockmaster, had strung a rainbow flutter of signal pennants at the pier head; the code read WELCOME TO GLOUCESTER. The sails were dropped, and *Great Western* was made fast. The crowd cheered and clapped as Captain Blackburn stepped ashore, and a delegation of officials strode forward to greet him.

Nearby at the pier lay the steam yacht *Sabrina* with a party

aboard, chartered to brothers John and James Fielding. The Field-
ings introduced themselves and informed him that it would be
their privilege to tow *Great Western* up the canal to Gloucester.
In fact they would like to have a tea for him in *Sabrina*'s saloon
after they got under way. Might they have the pleasure of his
company during the short trip?

He was delighted and accompanied his hosts aboard their yacht.
A line was put astern to *Great Western*, and *Sabrina* steamed
away from the pier. He was escorted to the saloon and introduced
around to the guests. The British were fascinated by this giant,
deeply tanned American, salty and still rolling from sixty-two
days at sea; and of course he was pressed to relate how he had
come to lose his fingers as the prelude to his account of the voyage.

Looking back on it, the passage had not been difficult, though
it was disappointingly long. To tell the truth, an open dory could
have made it, with the possible exception of six or seven especially rough days. His health had been the greatest hazard, and
that only during the first eight days. Everything considered, he
believed he had made the crossing as fast as it could be done under the conditions — the fogs, the calms, the light westerlies, and
then a month of beating against the easterlies. All told he had
sighted seventy or eighty sailing vessels and forty or fifty steam-
ships, and spoke several of them, but it was well for a singlehander to keep clear of the steamer track in foul weather and at
night. To be frank about it, however, he regretted that he hadn't
sailed down the American coast to a warmer climate; it would
have been easier on his health to have departed from a southern
port and taken a more southerly route across.

As for *Great Western*, she was a good sea boat, no doubt of it.
He managed her better than he had expected, but if he were ever
to plan another such Atlantic voyage he would want a smaller
boat with a lighter rig. She was too heavy and carried too much
sail. He had rarely set the gaff topsail and flying jib; it was a

tricky piece of work for one man in the middle of the ocean, and they weren't good for much except to help push her along in light winds. More than that, she was an erratic self-steerer except when close-hauled, and she demanded too much attention from her master. But she had carried him across, and that was enough.

Early in the evening *Sabrina* puffed into the dock basin at Gloucester, her tow sliding up to the pier behind her. The wharf was packed with citizens who had rushed down to the waterfront as word of Blackburn's approach spread through the city. Notified only a few hours earlier of his scheduled departure from Sharpness, the officials had been making hasty plans for a reception and were particularly harried in the absence of Mayor H. R. J. Braine, who was away on a holiday in Jersey.

The crowd cheered lustily as Howard stepped ashore, and the constable and a troop of police had all they could do to prevent the spectators at the edge of the pilings from being pushed into the harbor by the pressure of those who surged from behind in their frantic efforts to shake the mariner's hand.

Deputy Mayor Frank Treasure, High Sheriff A. V. Hatton, Councilor C. G. Clark, Clerk G. Sheffield Blakeway and a contingent of prominent citizens extended the congratulations and welcome of the city. Then they escorted Captain Blackburn to an open carriage which rattled through the streets to the Guildhall past sidewalks lined with shouting and clapping Gloucestermen. An even bigger throng jammed the area around the municipal building to catch a glimpse of the famous sailor as he passed and went on into the mayor's parlor for the reception.

In the course of his welcoming speech, Deputy Mayor Treasure commented that "at one time of your journey we were in fear that some accident might have befallen you, in consequence of it having been reported that when sighted and signalled by a passing steamer you took no heed of the signals."

Howard then recalled that two weeks earlier he had observed a vessel signaling from a considerable distance but had not both-

The GREAT WESTERN
Capt. HOWARD BLACKBURN.
DIMENSIONS: Length over all 30 feet. Breadth of Beam 8 ft. 6 in. Depth of Hold 4 ft. 6 in.
Sailed from Gloucester, Mass., June 18th, 1899. Arrived at Gloucester, Eng., August 19th, 1899. Time of voyage 62 days.

Great Western lies off the docks at Gloucester, England, in large captioned photograph distributed by her skipper to friends back home.

This view of *Great Western* and the intrepid mariner on their triumphant arrival appeared in *The Illustrated London News* of September 2, 1899.

ered to respond because he assumed she was communicating with another ship that was also passing by.

Councilor Clark drew a round of laughter when he remarked that during the evening the Australians, who had been playing cricket against the Gloucester team, had left, only to be speedily replaced by an American guest. They had given the Aussies a warm welcome — in fact, they had tried to make it as hot as they could for them — and they were glad to extend to Captain Blackburn an equally hearty reception. They were all admirers of pluck and recognized the spirit of adventure with which he had undertaken so perilous a journey, now brought to so happy an ending. Indeed, he had forged an additional link in the ever-strengthening chain of mutual esteem and regard between the two nations.

Deputy Mayor Treasure read the letter of introduction from Mayor French which its subject had delivered across the sea: "This will introduce to you Mr. Howard Blackburn, a well known and respected citizen of our city of Gloucester. Any favor or attention you could render him will be appreciated."

The guest of honor replied briefly (he hated speaking in public) and expressed his delight with the favors and attentions he had already received. The party forthwith adjourned to the Wellington Hotel for light refreshments and a second reception, and late that night he was driven back to the docks and his bunk aboard *Great Western*, most probably in a state of high spirits.

The next five days were filled with activity and excitement as Gloucester took the lone voyager to its heart. Mayor Braine returned from Jersey and impressed the visitor — mindful of his old license troubles — as just his kind of man, and he couldn't refrain from writing the papers back home that His Honor, "being a man who believes in live and let live, has won the admiration of the citizens, and they made him their mayor."

Great Western was entered at the customs free, and all her dock and canal charges were waived. Thousands came down to the pier to see her every day, including the venerable Senator George Frisbie Hoar of Massachusetts, who happened to be traveling in England; her master was not on board, unfortunately, and the Senator left his card.

One evening Howard was the guest of honor at the Gloucester Theatre. The Stars and Stripes were draped above his box, and the audience arose and cheered as the band played *Yankee Doodle*.

He was still troubled with arthritis and visited a doctor, who prescribed a remedy impossible for his patient — rest.

Having in mind, as always, his newspaper friends, he visited the offices of the *Gloucester Citizen* and obliged them with an account of the voyage. The man from the *Illustrated London News* came down to photograph him and his sloop at the dock, and the magazine presented the picture to the British public with the following caption:

Captain Howard Blackburn of Gloucester, Massachusetts, has come to our English Gloucester in a manner that lacks all precedent. By himself he has crossed the Atlantic in a cutter-rigged boat, the *Great Western*. After sixty days afloat, without any particular adventure where all was so adventurous, he anchored in King Road, and delivered (with a hand from which the fingers had long before been frostbitten) a letter of recommendation to the Mayor of Gloucester from the civic authorities of its namesake town across the uniquely traversed tract of water.

Like any other tourist, he did some sight-seeing; he wrote back to the papers:

Gloucester is one of the most interesting cities in all England. It was here about three hundred years ago that Bishop Hooper was burned at the stake, and a fine monument now marks the spot. The first Sunday school in the world was opened there by Richard Raikes, and the house in which he lived is still standing. A fine monument also marks the birthplace of William Tyndale, who translated the Bible into the English language. The cathedral itself is worth a journey across the ocean to see. The town is surrounded with farms, handsome trees, and as fine roads as can be found in any part of the world, and its best citizens, like everywhere else in England, have a way of making you feel as if you had known them all your life.

Howard's next port of call was London, and at noon on August 24, to a farewell ovation from the good people of Gloucester, he cast off his lines and with pennants flying was pulled away from the dock in tow of the *Violet*.

This time his passage had been thoroughly heralded, and hundreds of women and children tossed flowers and fruit down on his deck from the drawbridges above the canal. As he neared Sharpness, the stevedores left their work unloading timber from the ships in the docks and gathered at the edge of the river to cheer and sing "For He's a Jolly Good Fellow" and "Auld Lang Syne." He dipped Old Glory in salute, and the lumpers burst out with as much as they could remember of "The Star-Spangled Banner."

He arrived at Sharpness in the afternoon and was delighted to find himself the center of attention of a bevy of pretty schoolteachers who were there on a picnic with their pupils.

Signing on a Captain Adams of Gloucester as his pilot, he swung *Great Western* into the outgoing tide the next morning and beat down the Severn basin into Bristol Channel. Again the wind was against him, and when he was about thirty miles past Lundy Isle, it blew up so stiff from the southwest that he thought it wise to put back to the eastern lee of the island, where he anchored and went ashore.

Lundy was a wild and craggy block of rock three miles long, its precipitous cliffs climbing out of the sea to a prairie tabletop of stubbly grass. On one promontory were the Norman ruins of Marisco Castle. The island's lee for centuries had given refuge to passing vessels caught in the gales that swept the channel. Lloyd's of London maintained an agent there, a man with a spyglass who signaled to the mainland the identity of each ship that took shelter in the cove. Howard spent the day with him and tramped about the island, inspecting the ruins and the lighthouses at either end.

On the thirtieth of August he sailed again, determined to beat around Land's End and into the English Channel. But the southwester still piled hard against him, and he was further exasperated by Captain Adams, who "considered every black cloud the forerunner of a cyclone." So again he put back, this time all the way to Ilfracombe on the coast twenty-five miles east of Lundy.

It seemed that he was getting nowhere fast. But he had a gay time at England's Coney Island, which was overrun with pleasure-seekers, thousands of whom came down to the dock to see *Great Western* after the town crier had gone through the streets announcing the arrival of the famous Captain Blackburn. A delegation of charitable ladies asked him if they might place a contribution box on board for the benefit of the hospital, and several pounds were collected.

Three days later he made his third attempt to beat around Land's End. It was a hard drive all the way, but he finally left the bluffs on his port quarter and sailed into Plymouth on September 8. The bad knee was chronically painful, and he consulted a doctor for treatment. At the same time, he paid off Captain Adams and sent him home. Then he hired an oldster he picked up on the waterfront and filled away for the English Channel.

After sailing from Plymouth we encountered strong easterly winds. I did not leave the deck for fifty-two hours. At the end of that time we hove to off North Foreland [twenty miles beyond the Strait of Dover]. Night was coming on and it was blowing and raining quite hard. I told the old gent to keep the boat close into the land where the water was smoother while I turned in to get a few hours sleep.

But instead of doing so he allowed her to drift nearly over to the Goodwin Sands [a treacherous line of shoals about six miles off the Kent coast]. He then called me, saying — come on deck quick, there is breakers under our lee! I rushed on deck without hat or shoes. It was raining and blowing hard.

I looked to leeward and saw the other line of breakers only a few boat lengths away. She could not carry the mainsail, and the storm trysail was in the cabin. I hollowed to him to pass me the sail from the cabin, but the poor old feller was laying in the cockpit as helpless as a child. I got the sail on deck and set it. The breakers was then just under our stern.

As soon as the sail was hoisted up, it threw the boat down on her side, so far that she could not gather headway. I grabbed the anchor and chain and threw it from the deck into the cabin. I then got the old gent down into the cabin. As he weighed about two hundred and seventy pounds, the boat then righted and began to gather headway.

I kept her on that tack until I could no longer see or hear the breakers. I then hauled down the storm trysail, hove the wheel hard up and she came around like a top. Then I set the storm trysail again and let her drag in toward the shore, which we reached just before daylight.

The Goodwin Sands are about eight miles long, nearly four miles wide, and lay east of Deal Beach. There has been more vessels and lives lost on the Goodwin Sands than any other spot of its size in the world. They claim that if all the treasure that lies buried in them treachous sands could be recovered it would pay the National debt of England. The life savers of Deal Beach are famous all over the world. Scarcely a day, never a week, passes without those brave men being called upon to risk their lives to save others.

After daylight, as it was still blowing hard, we run back to Ramsgate, where I paid the old gent off and remained two weeks.

I shipped another man and sailed for London. Had a fine run up as far as Gravesend where we met a strong head tide. We made fast to one of the many buoys that are anchored in the river and waited for the tide to turn.

Just as we were getting ready to start a tug boat came along and seeing the American flag asked us if this was the boat that had acrossed the Atlantic. When we answered yes, he said — I will tow you to London for ten shillings; the distance is about twenty miles. I told him to take ahold, which he did, and *Great Western* never covered a quarter of that distance in so short a time before.

While towing up the river we were saluted by people along the shore and passing steamers. The tug boat put us alongside of the St. Catherine's Dock. The dock master advised us to put our boat in the

London Dock, which we did, where hundreds of some of the best people in London visited her.

Howard arrived in London on September 28 and remained there for about six weeks, "seeing everything worth seeing in that Great City." Then he crossed the Channel to France, but not in *Great Western;* his arthritis plagued him and he was not happy with her; he sold her, with some regret at the parting, to R. K. Braine, the brother of Gloucester's mayor.

Once in France, he went directly to Paris, where he was taken in hand by a group of Americans and Englishmen, among them the correspondent for the *New York Journal,* who showed him "about everything worth seeing in that beautiful city," including the Exposition, which was under construction. After a month, his legs still bothering him, he decided to cut short his European tour and crossed back to Liverpool, where he booked passage on the Cunard liner *Umbria* for New York.

When the *Umbria* was edged into her berth at New York on Saturday night, December 2, reporters were waiting to interview the remarkable and notoriously colorful Captain Blackburn. For some reason the men from the *Times* and the *Herald* couldn't get it out of their heads that the name of his boat was *Great Eastern,* and so it appeared in their stories next morning. Howard was in an expansive mood, and the reporter from the *Herald* outdid himself to catch it:

Did I get off my course? Well, I reckon not. I kept a dead reckoning all the time. When it began to blow I fastened the cabin door, locked my legs around the binnacle and puffed smoke into the eye of the wind so that it made him wink.

But one time I thought I heard the archangel's trumpet. I was down the hatchway when I heard a blast of steam. Do you know I was on deck quicker than any fellow with fingers? I didn't need fingers, I simply bounded.

Well, sir, there was a steamer dead ahead. Coming my way? I reckon it was. I grabbed my fog horn, but it slipped and I fell down on it. Just then the steamship went grazing by so close that I could al-most have touched it with my forefinger if I had had one.

The story was getting better already.

In a week he was home, and the writer for the *Gloucester Times* went down to the billiard room to interview him.

He looked thinner but claimed he had gained weight. His leg had become a serious problem, and he planned to remain in Gloucester for the winter and doctor it. After that he was un-decided what he would do. As for his reception in old Gloucester — "it was most too much for me, and I should have enjoyed it fully as much if I could have seen some old dorymate who would have slapped me on the back and said 'How are you, Blackburn, old boy!' "

His modesty, however, did not get the better of his pleasure when he read what the *Fishing Gazette* had to say about his voy-age:

"There must be a great deal of backbone about this hardy sailor. He deserves to be pensioned for life for what he has done. The Government should reward such heroism."

Here, after all, was the judgment of his peers.

11
Great Republic

THE BUSINESS OF A SALOONKEEPER is good will, in high places and low, and as soon as the Fingerless Navigator, as the newspapers were calling him, got home he set about repairing his fences.

First he went down to the police station and during a ceremony in the office of Marshal Edward J. Horton presented the force with a token of his affection. It was a large framed photograph of *Great Western*. Superimposed like a benign ghost on the mainsail was a portrait of her skipper, signed just below the lapel in his laborious hand — *Yours Respectfully, Howard Blackburn.*

Then he sent around his customary dispensation of Christmas dinners to the poor families of Gloucester.

Another ten days and it was the final year of the old century. Nineteen hundred . . . the words had a clean and portentous ring to them. America was on the march. She had whipped the Spaniard and extended her influence southward into the Caribbean and westward across the Pacific. A new world was riding the stream of inventions that poured forth from the laboratory of Thomas Alva Edison. Motor-driven carriages were skittering horses off dirt roads everywhere, and some men were even fooling around with flying machines. An Italian named Marconi was conducting some interesting experiments with a system of communication called wireless telegraphy. In the belief that she was divinely appointed to destroy the saloon, Miss Carry A. Nation was beginning her crusade in Kansas, hatchet in hand. A Gloucester saloonkeeper had just sailed across the Atlantic, alone and without fingers. Anything was possible, and the times called for great deeds and grand gestures.

Although Howard had been away as much as he'd been home the last two years, the coins had kept on crossing the bar. Liquor sent him to San Francisco, built *Great Western* and financed his voyage to England. And still the money flowed in.

That winter he buried himself in plans, grand plans for the new century. One was a set of drawings for a splendid brick building to replace the old wooden saloon. The other was a dream from which the lines of a boat were emerging.

By late spring the building was finished. It was the most impressive structure in the neighborhood. He had supervised every detail himself. The new saloon was on the street floor, and there was a fine apartment for the Blackburns on the second two stories. It was said that it cost him thirty-two thousand dollars, and there was no mistaking who had built it.

The city named the alleys on either side of the building Blackburn Court and Blackburn Place. Over the second story, chiseled in bold relief in the facing stone and nearly a foot high, was the legend 1900 BLACKBURN 1900. Right above the saloon his name was spelled out in electric lights — eighteen or twenty feet wide. And every patron stepped across the name in mosaic on the entry floor. The two large plate-glass windows, protected from the lurches of the clientele by shining brass rails, displayed pictures and mementos representing episodes of the owner's adventurous life. The interior of the saloon was furnished in the substantial style of the day, the long mahogany bar extending toward the rear along the mirrored wall at the right, a tier of tables on the left, a poolroom in back, the whole place charged with an atmosphere that was a combination of the waterfront and the dominant personality of the proprietor.

Meanwhile, the boat was abuilding in Archie Fenton's yard over at the head of Smith Cove. Howard enjoyed being mysterious; this only increased the general curiosity along the waterfront, which watched the progress of her construction with growing interest and conjecture. He said the same thing about her that he did about *Great Western* at the beginning — that he had a little coastal cruising in mind. But as the lines of the new boat took shape with her framing and planking, it was obvious that he had designed her for heavy weather and comfort.

She slid off the ways on a high tide one day in late June of 1900, and the kibitzers were impressed. A fellow member of the East Gloucester Yacht Club and an accomplished yacht designer and builder, Archie Fenton had retained the general appearance of *Great Western* but had sweetened the lines. She had less of the fisherman's work boat in her and was smaller — still a trifle heavy to show much speed in Gloucester's usual light winds, but plainly she would prove a windjammer when it blew. There was some talk that Blackburn meant to sail her to the Mediterranean, but he looked bland and said nothing.

Twenty-five feet long, seven wide and three and a half deep, she had the same fine clipper bow, flush deck and wide, high-riding stern as her predecessor. But when her spar was stepped it proved to be a pole mast, minus the topmast, and her bowsprit was longer. Her sail plan resembled that of the larger local yachts; she carried proportionately less canvas than *Great Western*, no gaff topsail at all, and a reef-pointed jib from which the bonnet — which had been difficult to lace and unlace — had been eliminated.

Her keel was relatively longer than *Great Western*'s and carried fourteen hundred pounds of iron; this length would keep her straighter on course and make her a better self-sailer. Her snug cabin was large enough for comfortable sitting room, though not for standing. Her frames, wood keel and deadwood were of oak and her floor timbers of black ironwood; above the waterline she was planked with yellow pine, below with cedar; her topsides were black, her deck and furnishings white and her spars varnished.

Altogether she was a sturdy girl, built to show speed in a seaway, ride nicely when hove to in a gale and do what her master told her to.

With his customary whimsy, Howard christened her *Great Republic* after the largest wooden sailing ship ever built, Donald McKay's enormous clipper that had burned in New York forty-seven years earlier on the eve of her maiden voyage. He had brought his old burgee back from England and sewed *Republic* on in place of *Western*.

One evening in July he entered her in the Yacht Club's weekly race around the harbor. Although the wind was fresh from the west, he got off to a slow start, and the three fast sloops he was up against showed him their sterns. Rather than acknowledge defeat, he dropped out before the finish. *Great Republic* wasn't meant for such frivolity; she was a sea boat, not a rich man's toy.

He sailed her around on his own for the rest of the summer, getting to know her, and in the fall he hauled her out of water and canvased her over for the winter.

For three years his day of reckoning in the McNary accident suit had been postponed, whether by the slow machinery of the courts or his protracted absences. But the wheels of justice were inexorable, and on the seventeenth of December it came up for trial in Salem before Superior Court Judge Albert Mason and a jury.

Howard had gone straight to City Hall for the best legal talent he could find; his co-counsel were Mayor-elect William W. French and John Burke, the brilliant city solicitor. The McNarys were represented by a third smart Gloucester lawyer and politician, Michael McNeirny.

Howard flatly denied the allegations of the plaintiffs that he had sold liquor to their son and that he was responsible for the young man's horrible encounter with the train. When court recessed that afternoon the reporters crowded around and tried to

The Fearless Navigator

Captain Blackburn takes *Great Republic* and a party of friends for a sail after her launching.

get him to comment on the suit. He replied with a few anecdotes about his adventures.

Next day the jury awarded the McNarys six hundred of the three thousand dollars they had sued Howard for. Presumably it concluded that liquor was being sold illegally at his place at the time of the accident, that it was sold to a minor as well, and that as owner and lessor he was ultimately responsible for the boy's drunken condition. Angry and chagrined, he announced he would appeal the verdict.

His next move was characteristic. Conceivably it was a spur-of-the-moment reaction to the tribulation of his trial, even as the launching of the Klondike adventure had followed so closely the tragedy which gave rise to the suit. Or he may have had it in mind for some time, so that it was merely a coincidence with his defeat in court.

Whatever lay behind it, two weeks later he invited the reporters to his rooms to hear an announcement. It was New Year's Day, 1901, the first day of the twentieth century.

He then publicly challenged any man in the world to race him single-handed from America to Portugal.

His gauntlet was flung specifically at the redoubtable Captain Andrews and a certain Charles Bigney, who were said to be talking about a contest themselves. But anyone who dared could pick it up, and if there were no takers he would sail in mid-June for Lisbon regardless.

The voyage would be undertaken partly for his health, in the hope that the sun and sea air would help his arthritis, and partly to celebrate the new century, by the end of which, he predicted, men would be crossing the Atlantic in flying machines. (The Wright brothers, incidentally, were not to get off the ground at Kitty Hawk for another three years.)

To spice up the challenge, he proposed that the contenders race for a stake of a hundred dollars each, or more if they wanted, and to show his good faith he had already posted half that amount with the commodore of the East Gloucester Yacht Club, the money to be covered by the first of March and the balance by May. It would suit him fine if yachtsmen anywhere in the world should take his dare, and he hoped that one of the great yacht clubs or newspapers would offer a trophy to the winner.

He wasn't interested in fudging the challenge with a lot of conditions. Boats could be designed and rigged according to the ideas of the contestants so long as they didn't exceed thirty feet in length and were sailed alone. If illness or accident prevented a contestant from starting, and if he couldn't find a substitute, his stake would be divided among those reaching the other side.

Blackburn's dramatic proposal caught the public imagination and was picked up by newspapers around the world. There was an undercurrent of skepticism, however, about his chances of getting any genuine takers for such a daring race.

His first response came within five days and tended to bear out the cynics.

A Miss Albena Carpenter of Nashua, New Hampshire, was reported to have signified her intention of accepting the challenge in the role of Captain Andrews's crew. Nothing more had been heard from the man Bigney, Andrews's presumed rival. Andrews was down in Atlantic City building his sixth boat, a thirteen-footer named *Dark Secret* after one of her predecessors; he had agreed to take along the attractive young lady, who was not yet eighteen.

Howard told the newspapers he had no objection to the arrangement, for Andrews was full of grit; but he had heard nothing from either of them and put little stock in the report.

A reporter tracked Albena down and found her working in a cracker factory near Boston. She had never been on the ocean in a boat, she said, but she had nerve enough to try anything. She had "helped the boys with their boats" on the Mystic River and was exceedingly fond of the water, having won two swimming prizes.

That was the last ever heard from her, and Howard called the whole business a fake.

A few days later a fellow member of the East Gloucester Yacht Club told the papers he might fit out his twenty-one-foot sloop for an ocean voyage and take Brother Blackburn on, bringing his dog along for company. Unfortunately he didn't have the money right at hand to stake himself, but if someone were to offer a purse of, say, a thousand dollars, it would be worth his while. No one did.

Two weeks after his challenge Howard received a letter from a Captain Nat Martin of East Boston:

Mr. Blackburn:

As you are desirous to have an ocean race across the Atlantic next summer in a small boat, and as I am desirous to learn the conditions of the race and what you are racing for, I will accept your challenge, providing we can agree on the conditions of the race.

I would be pleased to hear from you to learn the kind of boat you wish to race in. I should say let the boat not be over 30 feet overall, let her be any kind of a boat you like; let her be a sloop or a schooner, just as you like; ballast or trim her as you like; but she must not be over 30 feet bottom, nor 30 feet overall, and without topmast. Neither steam nor any motive power, but sail to be by the four winds of heaven; must not be taken in tow of any vessel, either steam or sailing craft, for the purpose of defrauding the other out of the race.

You see, captain, I would say south water line, but that is out of the question, for the longer the passage, the lighter the ship. I am well aware to whom I am writing. I know you crossed in a little boat not long since, and you are a hard man to buck against, but somebody must lose and anything for excitement.

Aha! This sounded like the real thing! Howard replied and received another letter, in the course of which Martin stated:

In regard to the race, I am anxious to have one, but I am not in favor of racing for notoriety. Neither do I propose to furnish stakes to race for, but if a substantial purse is offered for an ocean race, let it be open to all. Let each and every contestant deposit a sum of money with the sporting editor of one of our Boston papers as a guarantee of good faith. I have practically finished my plans for the boat that I think I will sail in and am ready to let them go to the builder.

A conference to iron out the details was arranged, and on January 30, Martin, in company with a friend, J. A. Fosque, and O. W. Brown of the *Boston Post*, came down to Gloucester on the afternoon train. They went directly to Blackburn's place, which was already crowded with reporters.

The Boston newspaperman started it off by reading aloud the articles of agreement proposed by Martin, a short, slight man who hardly looked the part of an intrepid ocean voyager. They were all right with Howard, all except the second — and here was the hooker: each contestant should rig and *man* his boat as he pleased.

What the devil kind of an idea was this, he wanted to know. Wasn't Martin aware that he had clearly stated it was to be a single-handed race?

The point was argued back and forth, Martin and Fosque claiming that the account in the Boston papers failed to specify. But Blackburn showed them copies of the Gloucester papers substantiating his position.

Blackburn: "That was the chief idea of my challenge — to have it a one-man affair, which would have been a test of courage and endurance."

Martin: "I want to have a race, not a drifting match."

Blackburn: "Why do you think one man to a boat would be a drifting match?"

Martin: "Because one man has got to sleep, and he can't sail and sleep too. There would be a big difference in the time."

Blackburn: "How much difference in the time do you think there'd be?"

Martin: "One man alone couldn't do it in much short of sixty days. With two men it ought to be done in forty-five easy."

Blackburn: "Well, will you give me a fifteen days' start, me to sail alone and you to take someone with you?"

Martin: "No."

Fosque broke in and said to Martin: "Give him eight."

Martin would have none of it, and Fosque, by now apparently disgusted with his friend, commented wryly: "Martin will never go across the ocean unless I go with him. Why, that man would not go outside of Boston Light alone!"

At this, Howard lost his temper and roared: "It's no use for you two to talk any more. I intend to go alone anyway, whether I race or not. The challenge that I originally sent out stated that fact explicitly, and I won't race any man unless he will sail alone. I will take no companion, not even a dog, on any account. I have no more time to fool with such men as you."

With that he turned on his heel in disgust and stomped out of the room.

The ever-loyal *Gloucester Times* commented that "Mr. Blackburn and the newspapermen present were convinced that Martin had no idea of racing, but appeared to be simply looking for notoriety, gained through free newspaper advertising."

And, indeed, nothing further was heard from the man.

Howard was by no means discouraged. In fact, he was enjoying himself immensely and soon afterward confided to the *Boston Journal*:

I do not take these trips for the notoriety that I gain but for the pleasure I derive from such. And then it does me lots of good. Why, do you know I believe that I shall gain a great deal in avoirdupois from this trip.

You have no idea what a pleasure it is to get about four hundred miles out to sea with not a thing in sight except water and sky. I take my time about sailing, and when I reach land I look around and see the sights instead of coming right home. I am going to take this next trip wholly for my health.

If I am successful in getting anyone to accept my challenge, I will have a much better chance to make a record-breaking voyage, for you know competition does wonders. I intend to take practically the same course, if I race, that I shall take if I go alone. Of course, I shall shift a little and try to be about a hundred miles away from my opponent. If he starts in on a southern course and the wind blows with him, I shall take the eastward tack and get right away from him.

Oh, I have lots of plans up my sleeve if any adventurous chap says the word. I will show him a thing or two.

His next challenger was a Mrs. W. B. Wright of Philadelphia, who wrote him on the first of February:

Dear Sir:

I saw in the *Item* where you offer a challenge for a race across the Atlantic in small boats. I am a young lady 24 years old and am an American and American descent. I am willing to accept your challenge. I am married, but that has nothing to do with my wishes. I hope to hear from you soon.

He gave her permission to take a man along to manage her boat and asked if she wanted her letter published in the papers. She replied immediately:

Dear Sir:

I received your letter and I was pleased to hear from you. I will mail you my photo as asked. I don't care if my letter and photo is published in the papers. I would like to have the *Philadelphia Sunday Item* get my letter and picture, as some of my friends think I am fooling with them.

I have pluck and nerve. I used to work the knife act. I am a snake, lizard and alligator trainer.

Will you please mail me four of your Boston papers after Sunday, and I will pay for them. I am an American and there is Indian blood in me. I was born in Pointville, N. J., April 4, 1877. As for fame, I have made that for myself in 1897, in Baltimore, Md.

That was the last heard from Mrs. Wright.

A week later Howard received a communication from a Captain D. S. Webster of Chicago expressing an interest in racing in his patented emergency boat, which appeared to be a raft consisting of four inflatable canvas cylinders and a sail. Webster suggested he sail from New Orleans and fall in with Howard around the Bahamas or Bermuda. He hoped Captain Blackburn would call his invention to the attention of his yachting friends.

And that was the last heard from him.

It was now apparent to Howard that he was the butt of a pack of publicity hounds and cranks. Nevertheless, he had no choice but to stick with what he had started. Late in March he deposited a new stake with an official of the Pan American Exposition, which he planned to visit in Buffalo on his return from Portugal. He proposed to race for anything from a hundred to five hundred dollars, winner to take all and donate it to the Addison Gilbert Hospital in Gloucester. His specific target was Nat Martin, whom he offered the privilege of taking another man. And Andrews and Webster could sail with a crew, too, as far as he was concerned.

Still there were no takers. It appeared that if he made it he would be the single-handed sailing champion of the world by default.

All the while that Howard was looking for someone with enough pluck to pick up his challenge, he was engaged in maneuvers on the legal front that can only be described as extraordinary.

He had decided to appeal the jury's adverse decision in the McNary suit, and on the twenty-fifth of March his case was argued before the State Supreme Court by his attorneys, Mayor French and City Solicitor Burke. The opposing lawyer, as before, was Michael McNeirny.

The very next day Howard appeared in the Gloucester court, this time as plaintiff. He was suing another lawyer, Michael Meagher, for five hundred dollars, claiming that four years earlier Meagher had illegally attached goods in his store valued at that amount in lieu of money owed him by the man Howard had left in charge during his gold-hunting expedition.

And now comes the astonishing part of this hassle: his attorney was Mike McNeirny, the same who the day before had been arguing against him in the Supreme Court!

A month later he again displayed his impatience with the subtleties of the law. A newspaper reporter asked him to comment on a rumor that twenty-four liquor dealers in Gloucester had chipped in ten dollars apiece and organized a trust to wage war on after-hours and Sunday bootleggers.

Never heard of such a thing, he snapped. No one had ever come to him for a dollar for such a purpose, and they wouldn't get one if they did. Like others in the business, he had paid his share of fines for illegal activity, and he didn't care how many bootleggers were on the loose.

In early April, Howard abandoned all hope for a race and withdrew his challenge. It had stood for three months without flushing out a single serious contender. He would sail anyway as he had planned all along, he told the papers, and try for a record passage. If he liked *Great Republic* well enough, he might ship her back to America because he was already thinking about taking a third and altogether unique and different voyage, perhaps in 1902.

Great Republic having been taken out of winter storage, overhauled and put in the water, he sailed her to Boston and back on a trial run during the first week in May. She didn't handle to suit him, and he theorized that the trouble was with her ballast. So he had her hauled out again, took off the heavy iron shoe on the keel and substituted a number of lead bars underneath the cabin floor. He also installed two thirty-gallon water tanks.

Sunday, June 9, he decided, would be the day of departure, and it occurred to him that the occasion would be the more festive if he were to push off from Long Beach, a popular swimming resort at the eastern end of Cape Ann. The Gloucester Street Railway ran a branch line out there in the summer, and it would

surely pay him a fine fee for promoting the business it would get
taking thousands of spectators out to see him off; any money he
made, of course, he would turn over to the Addison Gilbert
Hospital.

To his disgust he found that the officials of the streetcar company wouldn't pay him a nickel for the privilege. So he switched
to Pavilion Beach on the Gloucester waterfront, a fine vantage
point for the entire city, if need be. But the East Gloucester
Yacht Club was equally bound that he should start from their
new harbor quarters on Rocky Neck, and in the end he gave in.

Sunday was one of those God-given days of early June. The
lilacs were just coming into purple and white bloom, drifting
their lovers' fragrance out of the dooryards and through the
streets of the city. The trees had that fresh aspect of hopefulness
that comes from the new, unsoiled green of the spring leaf. The
blue sky was clear and carefree, and the breeze suffused the atmosphere with a dry, energizing coolness, not yet laden with the
dull humidity of summer.

Everything was in readiness for the departure, and around
noon Captain Blackburn was able to relax with the reporters.

Forty-two years old, standing six feet two and weighing two
hundred and fifty-six pounds, he was a man still in his prime.
Dressed in his blue serge suit and yachting cap, graying a little at
the temples, his robust face a picture of relaxed self-confidence,
he towered a head above the newspapermen and charmed them
as always.

Was he at all nervous about the dangers that lay ahead?

"I don't fear making this voyage a bit more than you would to
ride a bicycle. I enjoy it, in fact. I am a little too heavy now,
you know, and this trip will take off about twenty-five pounds.
The water and sun with the exercise will harden me. That's what
I want. I expect to make it in about forty-five days. I ought to
strike pretty fair weather this time of year."

In fixing his position at sea, how would he estimate the distance to the horizon, since the deck of his boat was only eighteen inches above water?

"About the same as an ordinary fisherman on a loaded ship, which is about twelve miles. I shall apply all corrections to the altitude, so there will be no trouble to ascertain the position correctly when either the sun or the moon is not obscured. I have a good chronometer, sextant, both general and sheet charts, a patent log and other necessary instruments. I shall only take observations once a week, until near the other side, when both lunar and solar observations will be taken. In ascertaining the longitude, Greenwich time will be used, and this will be done at 8 A.M. and 4 P.M."

Blackburn frowned.

"But there is one thing I did not like."

What was that?

"A business house sent one of their clerks to me and wanted to put their advertisement on my sail, promising to give me adequate compensation. This I took as an insult, for they have not got enough money to induce me to do such a thing. I am not going for money but for my own enjoyment. Had they given the Addison Gilbert Hospital a hundred dollars they could have covered my boat with their ads.

"Then another party out of town offered me two hundred dollars to change the boat's name and call her after a member of their firm, but this was also declined."

The press conference broke up when an open barouche stopped in front of the saloon. Howard, Mayor French, the commodore of the Yacht Club and a leader of the Portuguese community climbed in and were driven across town to the club.

As he stepped from the carriage and strode into the building, the Fingerless Navigator received his usual ovation. During the reception that followed he was presented a bouquet by a little girl, one more expression of the sentiment which surrounded his exploits; indeed, it was considerably more appropriate than some of his gifts, which included a silk necktie, a razor strop, a bottle of lavender water, and from a young lady of his acquaintance a bottle of cologne and a box of linen hankies.

In the absence of any mention of her, it can be assumed that Theresa was not there to see him off.

As the hour of two approached, the party came to an end, and Blackburn, accompanied by the reporters, walked down to the landing and boarded a launch which took them out to *Great Republic*. She was pulling gently at her mooring in the fresh northwest breeze.

At precisely eleven minutes past two the warning gun was fired from the commodore's yacht. The burgees and the American flag were run smartly aloft *Great Republic*, and the immense crowd which had been thronging to the waterfront all morning roared with delight. The pennants were followed immediately by the sails; Howard reefed down the main because the breeze seemed a little stiff for full canvas in the close quarters of the anchorage.

Five minutes later the starting gun was fired. Her mooring was cast off and *Great Republic* was free and away. She had hardly swung into the channel, however, when the wind dropped; he shook out the reef to take full advantage of what breeze was left.

She glided casually down the harbor to the shouts and applause of the thousands who had gathered along the shore, while a swarm of boats wove in and out, surrounding her as she moved along or maintaining a respectful distance — fishing vessels, naphtha launches, yachts, steamers and dories — and there was much tooting and whistling and dipping of flags. This time Captain Blackburn was embarking in the grand manner, and every craft that came alongside received flowers, cigars or a bottle of liquor.

Out the harbor and around by Eastern Point the flotilla worked its way. There was Lighthouse Keeper Bailey at the old stand — just as he had been two years before — ringing the fog bell and shouting good luck and a quick passage through his megaphone.

Off Thatcher Island the Yacht Club launch came alongside, and the reporters jumped aboard. The last choked farewells were

exchanged, and a young lady tearfully pressed on him a last gift
— a loaf of nut cake.

The launch pulled away and joined the fleet for the homeward run to harbor.

He lowered and raised his flag in final salute and was alone.

12
The Second Crossing

THE NORTHERN TWIN of Thatcher's lighthouses bore northwest by north seven miles away in the early evening, and from it he set his course for Portugal — east southeast. In two hours it was dusk, and he went forward with white lanterns and hung them in the shrouds.

It was a deliberate breach of the nautical code requiring red and green riding lights. But his experience on the voyage to England, when necessity and temper forced him to make do with the white, seems to have convinced him that the white lanterns were more visible from all quarters than the colored. He felt safer with them, and anyway, he never bothered much with rules and regulations.

The evening wind was fair and strong, and *Great Republic*'s sheets were straining. But he furled the main, lashed the wheel and told her to sail herself under jib while he went below on unfinished business.

Usually he was as shipshape as any man, but somehow during the rush of the last days before leaving he didn't get around to stowing his gear in Bristol fashion, and he certainly hadn't wanted to delay the departure to do it, thereby disappointing all those people. So he spent most of the night banging around in the cabin, arranging things as they should be.

At two in the morning the lamp in his homemade binnacle went out. The sea was choppy, but overhead the stars twinkled through a clear sky. Roundly cursing the contraption, he stayed in the cockpit and steered by the heavens.

The blasted binnacle was simple enough and suited him fine; he had merely made a box, secured the compass in one side and the lamp in the other, separating them by a pane of glass. He could place it in the cockpit or the cabin, as he liked, for the lamp (if it would only work) threw so much light on the compass card that he could read it from a distance of several feet. He fixed it next morning.

After sunrise the wind moderated, and by noon it was gone. Several coasting schooners passed by on the horizon. The sea was flat, so he turned in, not having closed his eyes for thirty-two hours, and slept until six in the evening. When he awoke it was still calm, and he spent a dull night at the helm, lazing under the stars and going nowhere except when transient puffs of wind whispered along, dying out before they had fairly disturbed the oil-smooth surface of the ocean.

On the third day out he was still barely making headway, ghosting across the northeast rim of Georges Bank off Cape Cod. *Great Republic* loitered past a few schooners fishing but spoke none of them. In the afternoon the tide was setting her off to the west southwest, but early in the evening a breeze stirred from that direction and she pulled herself back on course.

The course he had drawn for Lisbon would take him well to the south of his earlier route to England — a good six hundred miles at its greatest deviation — and he would be longer in the Gulf Stream, a prospect which he disliked intensely. But the weather generally should be more to his taste. And by bearing south of latitude forty most of the distance, he would pick up the welcome sight of the Azores, though he had no plan to put in at the group of volcanic peaks that rise out of the Atlantic a thousand miles from Portugal.

The breeze blew in the first adventure of the voyage, and he wrote in his log:

Saw a swordfish astern, coming straight for the boat. Thinking he might drive his sword through her, I threw a coil of rope on top of him, which made him disappear. In a few minutes there were a dozen swordfish following in the wake of the boat. When they got within ten or fifteen feet of her stern, I would throw the coil of rope on them and they would sink like lead, only to reappear a few minutes later.

There is only wind enough to give the boat steerage way, and every time that the sails slat and jar the boat, I think that a dozen swordfish are ramming her. It is getting so dark that I cannot see whether there are any following her or not, but I will keep throwing the coil of rope all night. How easily one of them could send me to the bottom, as they have only three-quarters of an inch of plank to drive their long swords through.

This made a good yarn except for the fact that a swordfish is generally a pretty easygoing fellow unless disturbed by something — such as a coil of rope landing on his back.

The wind increased, and just after midnight, as *Great Republic* was slipping purposefully through the sea for the first time since dropping Cape Ann astern, she struck something. She shuddered, fell off the wind momentarily, shrugged herself and then resumed her course.

He leaped up and looked hard over the bow at the dark water just in time to see a huge black shape writhe and sink with a splash. It was an enormous sunfish, caught dozing on the surface, indistinguishable from the night murk of the ocean. He had heard stories of such collisions with sunfish; they were grotesque, lazy masses of harmless flesh, sometimes as long as ten feet and weighing a ton, and they packed a jolt when you hit them, no question about that.

An hour later *Great Republic* leaned past a schooner at anchor, her riding lights twinkling through the darkness. It brought back a flood of memories of the old days, and he noted in the log: "I will be glad when I get out of sight of that awful graveyard, where so many of old shipmates and friends are buried in the sands."

It was an eerie night crossing Georges Bank — first the omi-

Sandy Bay Historical Society

Tuning up for Portugal, the portly master of sloop *Great Republic* puts her through her paces in Gloucester Harbor.

The Rudder, *July 1904*

nous swordfish, then the lurking sunfish, and the somehow foreboding lights of the fishing vessel. He welcomed the dawn.

The breeze freshened into a fine sailing wind. With started sheets and canvas billowing off to port, the sloop plunged through the sea, leaving a bubbly wake behind. In mid-morning a brig hove into view, slowly overtook *Great Republic* and crossed her bow at a fine angle on a course just south of his.

She was a stunning sight, that brig. Spread upon spread of ballooning squaresails climbed her masts, and her jibs flew out ahead like winged harbingers of the wind. Her every sheet was taut as a bowstring, and she thundered over the ocean with a singing rush and a pounding roar of foam and canvas.

Still the wind rose, and the little sloop flew. She wanted to leave the sea and take to the air itself, so intent was she on passing the brig. For two and a half hours she kept abreast of the squarerigger, until the ever-widening distance between their rails stretched away to the southern horizon and they lost each other.

It was an exhilarating burst of speed, and he rode her like a chariot for thirty-seven hours, vowing he could stay on deck forever if that was the will of the wind.

But the wind was willful and gathering strength — too much for *Great Republic*. He knew she'd dismast herself before she admitted it, so he hove to and double-reefed the main. Yet the wind whined higher, and late in the afternoon of the fourth day at sea he hove to again, furled the main, took in the jib and broke out the storm trysail, which he laced to mast and boom.

It was a real gale, and the time had come to quit sailing. Sheeted in hard, the stormsail kept her a few points off the wind, which screamed through the rigging and whipped spindrift from the cresting waves across her deck. By eight that night the sea was in a heaving frenzy. Although his boat was bobbing like a cork, he went forward with the riding lights and hung them in the shrouds and then went below and turned in for the night.

The pitching and rolling and banging were more than his exhausted body could take, and at three in the morning he dug out of his bunk, feeling as if he were going over Niagara Falls in a barrel, and poked his nose on deck.

No question that he'd been overtaken by a bagful of wind. Even with the little trysail to steady her, the lee rail was under water, and she was having a hard time keeping her head to the gale against seas that pounced down one after another. He broke out the drag and clambered forward over the bouncing, slippery deck through the driving spray and black night; half underwater himself, he secured the line around the mast and hove the drag over the bow. Then he took in the trysail. Under bare poles now, *Great Republic* fell back the length of the rope until the drag caught her up short; when she felt the steady pull of it, she settled into an easier truce with the storm, and he ducked below again for a few more hours of sleep.

Towards noon the gale seemed to relax, and he tentatively set the stormsail and tried sailing again. But the wind whipped up from the east southeast, dead against his course, and he hove to until late afternoon, when it slacked off for the second time.

At eight in the evening he wrote in the log: "Can see a steamer going west. I am now down to hard pan. All the fine grub that my wife put on board is gone. From this time out I must do the cooking. May the Lord help the crew."

This was followed by a flurry of entries, hastily scrawled when he could snatch a few moments in the cabin away from the gale:

June 15, 5 A.M. A steamer crossed my bow . . . 9 A.M. Saw a steamer going west by south. My steering gear broke down . . . 11 A.M. Saw a large school of porpoises. I am always glad to see those children of the deep . . . 1 P.M. Can see two steamers to the north going west . . . 5 P.M. It has been blowing strong all the afternoon and the sea running very high. Boat doing well. Have completed repairs on steering gear. Will make sail as soon as it moderates . . . 11 P.M. Set mainsail and jib.

June 16, 1 A.M. Took in mainsail and let her go under jib only . . . 3 A.M. Steamer came along, and seeing this little boat running with a white light in each rigging, she came alongside to see what it was and blew her whistle. I went on deck and stood near the light. When they saw me, they changed their course. You do not need any lookout when you have white side lights . . . 10 A.M. Had to heave to. Blowing a gale . . . 2 P.M. Steamer going west. Very rough. I will turn in for an hour or two, as I will have to keep her agoing all night . . . 7 P.M. Nothing in sight. Wind going down, but sea running very high. For the last two days I have been living on smoked salmon, hard tack and water, as it has been too rough to cook anything. I am doing my best to make a quick passage, but so far it has been like stealing a ride on a freight train.

For the rest of that night the wind was light but unpredictable, shifting back and forth between north and west, and it demanded all his attention at the helm and the sheets to keep *Great Republic* on course. By dawn even this erratic breeze was gone, and the boat rose and fell flatly to a slow ground swell.

Since he was now south of the main steamer track, he decided that the time had come to reverse his routine and sail all day, sleeping at night. Hungry enough to eat a dog, he went below and cooked up his first square meal in a week — a big dinner of fried pork, canned salmon, onions, bread and butter, and a mug of steaming tea. Dead reckoning his position, he figured he was south of Sable Island, something less than six hundred miles out of Gloucester.

He was sitting in the cockpit at twilight, musing over his poor progress and idly surveying the innocent face of the ocean that so recently had been contorted by the storm, when he had a large visitor.

It was the steamship *Shenandoah*, heading home for Liverpool. The liner ambled off her course like a friendly elephant come to inspect a kitten. She lay close to him, an iron cliff, her lights burning brightly against the dusky sky, engines throbbing and curious passengers jamming the rail.

An immaculate officer called into his megaphone from the bridge. Who was he, where from and where bound?

He cupped his hands and yelled back — *Great Republic*, Captain Blackburn, out of Gloucester, Massachusetts, bound for Lisbon.

Then from the megaphone: Was he by any chance the chap who sailed across to England a year or two ago?

The same, he shouted back.

Did he want anything?

Nothing but a little wind . . .

A laugh went up from the big ship. The figure on the bridge called a safe voyage to him and yanked three gut-busting blasts out of the whistle. *Shenandoah* lumbered off into the dusk.

It remained calm all night until just before dawn, when it again began to blow, increasing with such crescendo that by noon it was a living gale. What rotten luck! Two days of easterly gales, a day of dead calm, and now another assault from the same quarter, wilder than ever.

The sea was roughing up. *Great Republic* pitched on every wave and buried her nose in the next. She couldn't take all this sail. The jib would have to be reefed. It was a disagreeable prospect. He crawled forward to the plunging bow, where he managed to haul in the sopping headsail, tie the reef points and get it back up. More than once he went down with the bow into green water, which he didn't mind much, as it was warmer than milk. But when he noticed a squad of black fins slicing malevolently through the mad sea around him, his grip tightened.

Back amidships, he furled the main and set the storm trysail. For five hours he tried to make headway, but in the afternoon he gave it up, hove to and went below to ride it out. Even here the sea wouldn't leave him alone and came pouring into the cabin in bucketfuls through the cracks in the closed companionway slide.

Soaking wet and miserable, he sat there, watching the ocean gurgle in and trying to keep from getting bounced around like corn in a popper. At four in the morning, over the screeching wind and the smash of the waves, he heard the blast of a whistle. He pushed open the slide cautiously and between seas jumped up in the cockpit.

It was a freighter. She was riding high and light on the waves, for she had delivered her cargo and was in ballast. She pitched and rolled like an empty box, her lights rising and falling in the darkness. They had spotted his lanterns and swung in as close as they dared.

There was a shouted exchange through the storm. Did he want to be taken off?

No thanks!

But they still stood by, thinking he might change his mind.

Figuring to show them that he knew what he was about and had no need of their assistance, he broke out the trysail again, swayed up the reefed jib and resumed his voyage in the middle of the night and the storm. Rolling drunkenly, the freighter stood off to leeward and followed the bobbing chip with the wild man at the wheel for twenty minutes. Satisfied that he was quite a sailor, crazy or not, they saluted him with three short toots and swung away to the southwest.

He had planned to heave to again as soon as the steamer was out of sight, but *Great Republic* was making some progress in spite of the breaking seas, which she shrugged off stoically, so he drove on. With any kind of luck he could sail out of the Gulf Stream in a few hours, and he was devilish anxious to be clear of it. These easterly gales blowing against the westerly set of the current kicked up vicious cross seas, and he and his boat were taking a hard beating.

"This is the twelfth time that I have crossed the Gulf Stream," he jotted in the log. "I have always got a good ducking in it. I have lost one brother in this same brook."

For the next five days *Great Republic* and her master took their licks. It was a hell of wind and water under shortened sail, sometimes fighting ahead during brief lulls while the storm gathered its strength for a new assault, sometimes hove to while it beat down with the force of a thousand furies. Always they were battered, pummeled, tossed and doused — man and boat as one.

Respite came on the twenty-fifth of June. At three in the afternoon he wrote in the log: "Wind gone down a little. This has been the hardest sixteen days I ever spent on the ocean. This little boat has been jumping from one sea to another like a rabbit most of the time."

The wind backed around to the southwest. At long last it was abaft the beam — a following wind, a wind that was carrying him toward Portugal, no longer a hostile wind bent on driving him back to Gloucester. For nearly a week the black sloop skipped across the middle of the Atlantic while the weather grumbled with squalls but stayed its fist.

Fair skies and quiet seas after so much tempest and tantrum attracted a menagerie to the surface. He never tired of watching the whales, nor did familiarity lessen his wonder at their awesome size. Often their curiosity would lead them to within fifty yards of the boat; when they dove, and the prodigiously long, slowly arching black backs lazily rolled forward and down and sank with a desultory smack of the great flat tails, there were uneasy moments of waiting as he wondered where they would come to the surface — not, he hoped, under his keel by some careless miscalculation. Suddenly, from the least expected quarter, he would hear a deep, wet, sighing huff; if he snapped his head around quickly enough he could see a small cloud of mist and droplets still hovering above the water, a huge glistening back already moving out from under it.

And there were his old friends the porpoises; and sharks, cutting through the water with knives of menace; and Portuguese men-o'-war, protoplasmic sails carrying tentacled armies to their prey; and big sea turtles, dozing amiably in their armor — it was amusing to sail close, reach out and flip them on their backs.

And something else —

July 1, 4 P.M. While sitting on the wheelbox steering, boat making about three miles an hour, suddenly I saw something just abaft the starboard beam lashing the water into foam. I stood up and saw what looked like a coil of very large rope. I hove the wheel down and trimmed the sheets in sharp by the wind. The boat would not fetch it on that tack, but passed within 35 or 40 feet to the leeward of it.

As I draw near I could see that it looked like a large snake, but had a tail more like an eel. It was fully 12 to 15 feet in length. It was holding in its mouth either a small turtle or a good-sized fish, with which it was lashing the water into foam. Its head moved so rapidly from side to side that I could not tell its shape, but am inclined to think it resembled that of a serpent. The tail and parts of the body that I could see plainly appeared to be smooth and of a light lead color.

I put a running bowline into the end of the mainsheet, and when the boat got far enough by to fetch it on the next tack I hove the wheel hard down, and with every hair on my head like so many belaying pins, filled away on the other tack, taking the end of the mainsheet in my hand, and as the boat passed within eight or ten feet of it I tried to lassoo it. But the rope must have struck its head, for without a bit of fuss it sank from sight.

I tacked ship and stood across the spot where it sank, and lay to several minutes with my jib to windward in hopes it might rise again, but I saw no more of it. It was no shark, for a shark of that length would be at least as big around as a five gallon keg, whilst this was no stouter than my mast, which is five inches in diameter. It must have been a baby sea-serpent.

Great Republic dashed on. In the middle of the morning of the Fourth of July the islands of Corvo and Flores — the western Azores — were shimmering on the horizon ahead.

His navigation had been right on the nose, and he was elated. During most of his twenty-five days at sea, he had been cheated out of any chance to make celestial observations and was forced to rely on dead reckoning.

Hoping to run between the two islands, he stood off toward the passage that separates them; but the wind dropped to a breath from the southeast, and *Great Republic* had to bear off to the north of her course. Late that night he beat against rising wind squalls past the dimly seen outline of Corvo, the smaller and more northerly of the crater isles, and squared away for the home stretch.

For a week the weather kept its temper, broken only by alternate fits of squalls and spells of flats, and Portugal lay closer every hour.

And then a languor took possession of the atmosphere. The sea fell completely asleep, its face as bland and characterless as a mirror which the sun stared into stupidly, baking in its own reflected heat like an idiot in the sky. The black sloop was caught in the hot and mindless rivalry of sea and sun. Sails flopping, she drifted with the tide, an orphan of the wind. Her crew, as lackluster as she, lolled and dozed in a half-conscious state of torrid unreality.

July 12, 11 A.M. While on deck with my elbows on the rail, looking into the water, I was startled by the nose of a shark coming within a foot or so of my face. It came out from under the starboard quarter, turned on its side and opened its huge mouth to swallow the shadow of my head and shoulders on the water. But as it got nothing, it swam the entire length of the boat with its belly rubbing against her side, crossed her stem and disappeared.

In less than five minutes it came back the same way, and when it turned on its side again I could see that its belly was covered with red paint from the end of its nose to within a few feet of the tail. It was followed by two pretty fish, each about ten inches in length, with red and white stripes around their body. It was the largest and boldest shark I ever met.

The monster's pals were pilotfish, little jackals of the sea that follow sharks in their hunt for a meal and snap up the leftovers — at a safe distance.

For another twenty-four hours the doldrums hung over the ocean. In mid-afternoon of the twelfth of July the air stirred. A distant mountain range of dark clouds rose out of the sea to the north — higher and higher it curtained the sky, swept overhead, consumed the blazing sun and rolled on and away to close with the southern horizon. The temperature dropped, and with the scudding clouds came the wind, a banshee northeaster.

He clung to the wheel for sixty-two hours as *Great Republic* smashed through the crashing seas, battering onward, under stormsail and reefed jib, dancing a close-hauled jig with the gale. Once and once only did her master heave her to, in the middle of one night for four hours when the tempest was at its frenetic height.

White water poured over the lee rail and up to the cabin trunk. The sails were soaked with spray to their peaks, and the sea squirted into the cabin under the slide. The worst waves came unexpectedly, rising up in a sudden merger of chaotic crests and crashing down on the boat, burying him in water and overflowing the cockpit. Yet she would shake herself free each time and struggle on.

Drenched to the skin and bitterly cold and hungry, he went below only once during those two days and a half, to wind the chronometer and grab a bottle of water and a fistful of hardtack. He steered by compass and navigated by guess and by God, for observations were impossible; the sun was lost all day, and the nights were black as the inside of a boot.

Steamers saw him and rolled in as close as they dared; the men on the bridges tried to take him off, shouted at him over the gale that he was crazy, that his boat would never last through such seas. But he shook his head and stuck with her, although one night, when the bright lights of a passing liner beckoned to him, he nearly gave in; he was on the point of waving his lantern at them, then thought better of it.

The gale tired itself out during the afternoon of the sixteenth of July. The wind slackened a little, and the seas, hesitating, almost imperceptibly responded. At dawn the sun peeked up in the east and came timidly out of hiding.

He cooked a hearty breakfast, set all canvas and commenced

the joyful job of drying out himself and his boat. That afternoon he made his happiest entry in the log:

July 17, 1 P.M. From careful observation taken today, Cape Espichel bears northeast by north, distant 21 miles . . . 3:30 P.M. Have just had my first view of grand old Portugal. Cape Espichel in plain sight. It is a very beautiful cape. Puts me in mind of Cape Virgin, at the northern entrance to the Straits of Magellan. I can well imagine how happy Vasco da Gama, Alvares Cabral and other early navigators must have been when returning from their voyages of discovery to sight this fine old cape. I am as glad to see it as a child is to see a circus. If this wind holds, a few hours more will finish this, the hardest passage I ever made. How so small a boat could make that distance in 38 days with the chance that I have had is a great surprise to me. With such a boat I think I could have beaten any one man in the world.

The wind held as he had hoped, and in four hours he sailed up to a fleet of fishing boats near the shore. By then the breeze was dying and the tide was on the ebb. Thirty miles up the coast was the mouth of the Tagus River, and Lisbon lay another twenty miles inside. There was no use trying to reach his destination that night.

So I spoke a boat which carried a crew of three men and two boys. A man and a boy got into their small boat and came on board. They could not speak a word of English, and I could not speak a word of Portuguese. I gave them some kerosene oil, hard bread, salt pork, tobacco and some canned goods. I then made the old man understand that I wanted him to go up to Lisbon with me.

He offered to do so, but seemed to be very anxious to know how many milreis [equivalent to $1.08] I was willing to pay him. By sign I made him understand that I wanted him to set his price. He did so by holding up one hand and counting the fingers and thumb, which meant that he wanted five milreis. I had no sooner agreed to give him that amount, when up went the other hand. This of course meant ten milreis.

As I was very tired and sleepy, and thinking that if I had him to look after the boat I could get a few hours sleep, I agreed to give him the ten. To my surprise he stuck up the other hand. I shook my head and made signs for him to get into his boat. He then closed three fingers, which meant that he was willing to go for twelve milreis. I consented and shoved his boat away.

I gave him the wheel and went into the cabin, but as he had never steered with a wheel before, he soon had *Great Republic* going all around the compass. So I went on deck and fixed the wheel so that the boat would steer herself, as she had often done before. When he was leaving the wheel he accidentally put his big fist through the glass in the binnacle. It was just as well for a few minutes that he did not understand English.

There was just enough wind to stem the tide, so I went below and went to sleep. The wind soon died out altogether. He came into the cabin and woke me up and wanted me to anchor, but I would not do so as I had no windlass, and two men could never heave that anchor and chain in by hand in that deep water. So I went to sleep again.

But the old man growled so much when he seen that the tide was carrying us to sea that I could not sleep. So I got up, cleaned the cabin, washed, shaved and dressed myself ready for shore. By that time the tide had changed and was carrying us in at the rate of three miles an hour. After we entered the river Tagus we got a fine breeze, which sent us along like a race horse. I saw the American Flag flying on an old fashioned ship. We sailed around her stern. She proved to be the training ship *St. Mary* of New York.

At 2 P.M. July 18th I made fast in the dock just 39 days after leaving home.

He thought the Tagus, with its picturesque villages and beaches, was the prettiest river in the world. Word of his progress must have preceded him to Lisbon, for when he had made fast to the dock and stepped ashore he recorded that the first person to greet him was the son of the Russian consul general, of all people. This young man found an interpreter for him, called a hack and posted them off to the telegraph office, where the mariner sent a cable to the East Gloucester Yacht Club announcing the safe conclusion of his second crossing under its burgee.

It was the fastest nonstop single-handed passage across the Atlantic ever sailed, a record which was to stand for many years.

In spite of the succession of gales and the days on end when it was impossible to make celestial observations, his navigation had been close to flawless. He had aimed for forty-five days between ports; waterfront opinion in Gloucester said he couldn't do it in less than seventy-five. But he beat his own predicted time by six days and the skeptics by five weeks!

The day after docking he dropped in on the American consul, "a fine old gentleman," who directed him to the Grand Hotel Central, which he found to be one of the best in the city. Then he strolled about Lisbon, admiring the parks and monuments, the clean streets and the figured sidewalks.

Invited to the Royal Yacht Club, he was impressed by its fine building and the boats of the members but disappointed at the absence of His Majesty the Commodore, who, he wrote home, "has a splendid steam yacht of which he is very fond. He is away at present on a cruise along the coast. Both the King and Queen are fairly worshipped by the people of Lisbon."

At the bullfight, where he was seated in a box of honor, he thought he had never seen so many people in one building before and wrote: "It was a benefit for Mr. Rafael Peixinho, the champion bullfighter of Portugal. He was the receptor of many valuable presents. John L. Sullivan in the height of his glory was never thought more of in Boston than Mr. Peixinho is in Lisbon. He came to my box and congratulated me upon my safe arrival."

Howard toyed with the idea of sailing *Great Republic* home to Gloucester, but although his health was good, the memory of hardship was still too fresh in mind. He arranged with the owners of the steamer *Peninsula* to carry her to New York for half their usual freight charge (her master turned out to be a former Gloucester fishing skipper). Down at the docks he unstepped the mast, lashed the spars on deck, stowed rigging, sails and binnacle in the cabin, nailed it shut and left her to be hoisted aboard the steamship.

Booking passage for Le Havre on the steamer *Jerome* of Liverpool, he embarked from Lisbon on the fifth of August with a full heart. His reception had been warm, though he couldn't understand why the Portuguese people, wherever he went, took such an interest in him. Perhaps it was simply the unspoken kinship of those who live by the sea.

Nothing was too good for Captain Blackburn aboard the *Jerome*, and with Captain Forbes and his officers and a young English lord returning home from Brazil ("a fine specimen of the English gentleman") he enjoyed four of the most convivial days he had ever spent at sea.

From Le Havre he crossed the Channel to Southampton and immediately boarded the steamer *Columbia,* arriving in New York seven days later.

On the evening of August 19, 1901, deeply tanned and hearty as ever after an absence of ten weeks, he stepped from the seven-forty train at the Gloucester depot into the arms of a cheering crowd of admirers.

13
Inland Voyage

As HOWARD BLACKBURN was triumphantly returning from his second crossing of the Atlantic, Captain William Andrews was preparing for his sixth and most bizarre attempt of all.

With his usual promotional flair, the widower of several years took to himself a young bride during a gala ceremony in the ballroom on Young's Pier at Atlantic City. The new Mrs. Andrews had responded to his advertisement for a female with a "daring spirit" to accompany him on his next voyage; it was to be a honeymoon cruise to Europe in his thirteen-foot *Dark Secret*.

This turn of events caused the *Fishing Gazette*, which had so enthusiastically proposed that Howard be pensioned by the government for his heroic trip to England, to take a second and dimmer look:

Howard Blackburn has no sooner completed his hazardous and foolhardy voyage across the ocean in his tiny sloop, when one Captain Andrews and his bride decided to spend their honeymoon in making a similar reckless experiment. While we all admire physical courage and endurance in a worthy cause, we believe that such useless imperilling of life as this is to be condemned. Such ventures serve no good object, and if Captain Blackburn, who, according to his own story, suffered many hardships, had failed in accomplishing his stint, it probably would have had the moral effect of deterring others from trying to win glory at the absolutely unnecessary and unquestionably uncalled for risk of their own lives.

Notwithstanding these or any other words of warning, Captain Andrews and his mate set sail.

A hundred miles out to sea they were spoken by the steamer *Durango*, whose master reported that Andrews shouted to him that they were showing the world how a Yankee skipper and an American woman could cross the Atlantic to Spain in a thirteen-foot boat:

The poor woman looked as though she had been bleached, so white was she from seasickness or fright. She looked as though she would rather be on the deck of the *Durango*, bound for Baltimore, than to experience any more of what she had passed through. She kept looking longingly at us as far as she could be seen. I could do nothing beyond bidding them a safe voyage and argue to myself that they were both young and old fools.

They were never seen again.

A fortnight after his arrival home, the East Gloucester Yacht Club held a smoker in honor of its most famous member.

It was one of those bittersweet end-of-summer affairs so peculiar to ocean resorts, when everyone is a little wistful about the close of the vacation season and bound to have one last fling before turning back to the routines of inland life. The coincidence of Captain Blackburn's return in time to be present, of course, made this an extraordinary occasion.

The rambling clubhouse on Rocky Neck was brilliantly decorated, and more than two hundred members and guests pressed forward in the hope of catching a few words and shaking the blunt hand that had held the wheel.

The program formally began at eight with a startling blast from Clark's Military Band on the lower veranda, glorious in their uniforms. The music blared and echoed across the harbor, or drifted sweetly through the twilight, according to its mood, and at the concert's end — amid rousing applause — it was announced that chowder was being served.

When the tables had been cleared and the chairs shoved back, the serious business of the evening commenced. Speaker after speaker rose to spread his wings in flights of panegyric, and heavy were the laurels heaped upon the object of the evening's entertainment. But all were agreed that none could match the tribute that came from the lips of the venerable Bert Andrews, liquor and cigar dealer, auctioneer, notary public, justice of the peace and livery stable proprietor, who declared that although he had lived through thirty-four battles of the Civil War and had four bullet holes in his body to show for it, he had not the courage to undertake such a journey as Howard Blackburn had just completed.

At last the moment all were awaiting arrived. The tall, ruddy mariner, distinguished-looking as a senator, got to his feet. The hall rang with applause and cheers, and then a hush fell as he gazed on the throng. He had sat seemingly unmoved during the succession of eulogies. Now he was trying to control a wetness in his eyes. After a few moments he spoke, his deep voice choking:

"Mr. Toastmaster, I never made a speech in my life, and I hope you will excuse me from any further remarks."

Again the walls trembled with ovation as he took his seat, and his friends stood and gave him three cheers and a tiger under the leadership of Bert Andrews.

After that the drink flowed, and there was storytelling and amateur vaudeville and singing, culminated by Mayor French's solo interpretation of "The Art of Making Love."

At midnight one and all joined together for a raucous but sentimental chorus of "Good Night, Ladies!" and the party was declared over. As the celebrants made their various ways home, they agreed it had been a grand evening; that fellow Blackburn was certainly a prince among men.

Since *Great Republic* was expected to arrive in New York aboard the *Peninsula* on September 21, Howard thought he would go down to get her ready for the trip home and take Theresa along to see the first race of the America's Cup Series off Sandy

Hook, scheduled for the following week. He wrote his younger sister Bessy, who had married George Reed, a ship's carpenter in Boothbay Harbor, Maine, to ask if they would let their little Addie come along too.

Her father brought Addie down to Gloucester, but she was so homesick that instead of remaining with Uncle Howard and Aunt Theresa she returned to Maine with him the next day. After she was home, and the papers were full of the great contest between the American defender *Columbia* and Sir Thomas Lipton's challenger *Shamrock II*, Addie was so heartsick that for many days she avoided the playmates to whom she had boasted of the exciting expedition she was going to take with her famous uncle.

At New York, Howard fitted out *Great Republic* and arranged to have her towed to Larchmont, on Long Island, where he planned to embark for Gloucester. Then he and Theresa boarded the steamer *Grand Duchess* to watch the first race.

This was Sir Thomas's second attempt to recapture the cup held by the United States ever since the schooner *America* sailed across to take it from the British in 1851. The New York Yacht Club's *Columbia* had whipped the affable Tea King's first *Shamrock* three straight in 1899, and now he was back with a new boat.

It was a dull day for the first race. There was so little wind that the sleek, slim sloops with their towering triangles of sail were unable to beat around the course within the time limit, and it was declared no contest by the officials. But *Columbia* sailed ahead of her rival, and when she went on to win the series three in a row by the closest margin in the history of the Cup, Howard gave his opinion — in contradiction to the yachting experts — that they were won by the man and not the boat, and that *Shamrock II* was the better boat.

Sending Theresa home by train, he hired a sailor in New York and went down to Larchmont. They cruised *Great Republic* up Long Island Sound and around Cape Cod, reaching Gloucester a week later.

The rest of the year was uneventful. At Christmas, Howard got the names of twenty-five families from the Welfare Department and sent dinners and groceries around to them, as well as to various others of his personal choice. When a reporter stopped by to ask him about this latest beneficence, he declined, with Dickensian modesty, to say anything except that he wished every human being a Merry Christmas. He also presented the Women's Auxiliary of the Addison Gilbert Hospital with a large jar full of pennies that had been accumulating on the bar all year. It was the beginning of another of his rituals. The ladies, wearing white gloves lest they be contaminated by saloon germs, counted the Blackburn coppers one by one; there were seven thousand, one hundred and eighty-one of them.

Long before he sailed for Portugal, Howard's imagination had leapfrogged ahead to a third voyage, and during the winter and spring of 1902 he laid his plans for it.

Having twice demonstrated his ability to subdue the Atlantic, he visualized this next excursion as a different sort of conquest, a far greater test of his ingenuity and, quite frankly, a lot more fun. It would be in the nature of a leisurely Odyssey, with plenty of time to pause, to see strange and interesting places and people, to admire and be admired — in short, a lark.

The plan was to take *Great Republic* down to New York, up the Hudson River and the Erie Canal, through the Great Lakes to Chicago, down the Illinois River to the Mississippi and all the way to New Orleans. Thence he would sail across the Gulf of Mexico to Key West, Florida, and by stages on to Cuba, Puerto Rico and Martinique and across the Caribbean to either Panama or Nicaragua, depending on where the canal was to be built. He would cross from there to South America, cruise down the Brazilian coast, cut back to Florida and return up the eastern seaboard to Gloucester.

His original idea had been to sail north instead of south from Gloucester and penetrate the continent through the St. Lawrence River, entering the Great Lakes via Lake Ontario instead of Lake Erie. His health probably decided him to abandon this route for the more southerly approach; it would be warmer in the spring and summer, and if he were not well on his way down the Mississippi by the following winter, he could easily return to the comforts of home and resume the voyage the next spring.

By May, *Great Republic* had been overhauled, painted and put in the water, and he was ready to go just as soon as he disposed of a small legal matter.

The Supreme Court the previous fall had turned down his appeal from the McNary verdict, and the same Mike McNeirny who had so successfully argued against him then was now arguing for him in his suit against Mike Meagher, the lawyer he accused of attaching his store goods illegally. This time he won. Meagher also appealed to the Supreme Court and was rejected.

Strangely enough, just as Howard had engaged McNeirny to represent him against Meagher at the very same time that McNeirny was suing him on behalf of the McNarys, so had he hired Meagher, even as his suit against *him* was pending, to handle still another minor aspect of his legal affairs.

Having had the satisfaction of watching his lawyer friends perform thus on both sides of a fence of his own construction, he prepared to depart from Gloucester for upwards of two years, the time he allowed himself for his next exploit.

On the afternoon of Saturday, May 17, the *Gloucester Times* man came aboard *Great Republic* for a friendly visit and no doubt a good stiff shot of whiskey. He found that instead of filling every corner of the cabin with necessities, the Captain was leaving plenty of room for comforts and conveniences not ordinarily permissible on an ocean voyage — "As Mr. Blackburn will stop at many ports on his trip and will entertain quite a number of people, the gifts will come in handy." The gifts referred to, which were in addition to his own stock, were the usual farewell presents from his friends, notably this time whiskey and cigars.

At four o'clock on Sunday morning, *Great Republic* dropped her mooring and slipped quietly out of Gloucester Harbor. The predawn waterfront was deserted, except for the usual early morning activity of a Sabbath. Howard had an old friend with him, Captain Matt Greer, who was going to keep him company and give a hand as far as New York.

It was a long beat across Massachusetts Bay and around Cape Cod in the face of head winds most of the way, and not until Tuesday did they drop anchor in Menemsha Bight under the western cliffs of the island of Martha's Vineyard. Wednesday they had a good run off the Rhode Island coast to Block Island, where they lay for the rest of the week, waiting for the westerly to back around.

After a few days of this inactivity, Howard determined to strike out for New York alone, head winds be damned. Leaving Matt Greer to take the ferry for the mainland, he beat *Great Republic* up past Long Island against foul winds and tides, unable to make a harbor until he docked at Brooklyn on the evening of June 2, sixteen days out of Gloucester.

He killed some time in New York, took a short side cruise down the New Jersey coast to Cape May, and sailed back to New York and up the Hudson River, destination Albany.

14
Down the Mississippi

SOME MEMBERS of the Albany Yacht Club helped me to get the boat ready for the trip through the Canal.

First you pass through eighteen locks which lifts you one hundred and fifty feet above the Hudson River. Then you go nine miles before you come to another lock which lifts you fifteen feet. The Erie Canal is three hundred and sixty-five miles long, has seventy-two locks. It has been neglected for the last few years. They expect to have a deep water canal take its place some day.

I had to tow the boat forty miles myself before I could get anyone to take her in tow. Then Captain Howard came along with two light boats. He agreed to tow me to Buffalo for thirty dollars. He carried a crew of three men besides himself and four mules.

One man and two mules would tow the boats for six hours. Then they would run the boats alongside of the canal, when the driver and two mules would come on board, and the other driver with the two fresh mules would take their places and tow us for another six hours.

Each canal boat has a rudder, but they are never used while passing through the canal. They rig up a wheel on the after end of the head boat and run a line from each quarter of the head boat to the bow of the boat towing behind, which then acts as a rudder, and if you want the bow of the head boat to turn to the right, you must turn the wheel to the left, which seemed strange to me at first.

On some of the many bridges under which we passed we found a lot of girls leaning over the rail. They always try to jolly the man at the wheel. Our Captain seemed to enjoy it very much, and could often give them as good as they sent. He was a jolly good fellow and had been through the canal so often that everyone seemed to know him.

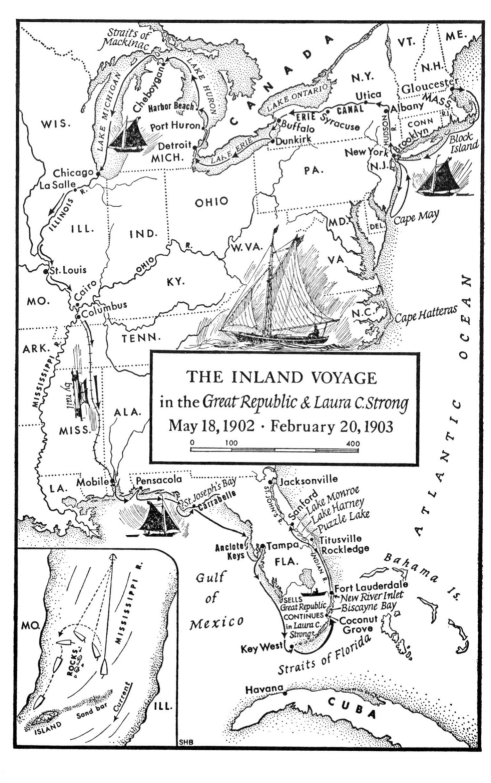

Straits of Mackinac

Lake Michigan

Lake Huron

Cheboygan

Harbor Beach

Port Huron

Detroit

MICH.

WIS.

Chicago

La Salle R.

ILLINOIS R.

ILL.

IND.

OHIO

St.Louis

MO.

Cairo

Columbus

OHIO R.

KY.

TENN.

ARK.

MISSISSIPPI R.

MISS.

ALA.

LA.

Mobile

Pensacola

St.Joseph's Bay

Carrabelle

Anclote Keys

Tampa

FLA.

CANADA

Lake Ontario

N.Y.

Utica

ERIE CANAL

Syracuse

Buffalo

Dunkirk

Lake Erie

PA.

New York

N.J.

MD.

DEL.

Cape May

W.VA.

VA.

N.C.

Cape Hatteras

VT.

ME.

N.H.

Gloucester

MASS.

Albany

HUDSON R.

CONN

Brooklyn

R.I.

Block Island

by rail

THE INLAND VOYAGE
in the *Great Republic & Laura C. Strong*
May 18, 1902 · February 20, 1903

0   100   400

Jacksonville

ST.JOHN'S R.

Sanford

Lake Monroe

Lake Harney

Puzzle Lake

Titusville

Rockledge

INDIAN R.

Gulf
of
Mexico

Bahama Is.

Fort Lauderdale

New River Inlet

Biscayne Bay

SELLS
Great Republic
CONTINUES
in *Laura C.
Strong*

Coconut
Grove

Key West

Straits of Florida

Havana

CUBA

MO.

Mississippi R.

ROCKS

ISLAND

Sand bar

Current

ILL.

ATLANTIC OCEAN

SHB

The girls would hail him just as soon as he hove in sight and say — Oh Captain, what did you bring me from New York? Stop at Buffalo! Don't run nights!

One day our Captain got rattled, turned the wheel the wrong way and run the boat against the bank of the canal. The tow line parted. The mules laid down and tried to roll over and over. My boat nearly drove the end of her bowsprit through the stern of the canal boat.

We got under way after a while, but the head boat leaked so bad that it kept one man at the pump nearly all the time. I helped to pump and steer until we reached Buffalo.

While passing through the canal we saw hundreds of boats tied up waiting for a freight. They would ask Captain Howard where he was bound, and when he answered Buffalo, they would say — you had better tie up here and rest your mules, for there is nothing doing in Buffalo. Our Captain would say — I have agreed to tow this man and his boat to Buffalo. He would often say to me — now Blackburn, if I could only get a load of lumber for New York I would not call the President my uncle.

When we reached Buffalo the newspapers published a history of my boat, and hundreds of men, women and children came down to see her. Some of the gentlemen asked me if they could do anything for me. I thanked them and asked them if there was any way to get a load of lumber for Captain Howard. They said — we will see what we can do for him.

They must have seen Captain Howard, for when I met him on the street he was all smiles and said — now Blackburn, don't be in a hurry to leave Buffalo, for I think in a day or two I will get a load of lumber, and if I do I will draw a part of the freight money and give you back half of what you paid me.

I did not wait but sailed that day for Dunkirk, a pretty little fishing port on Lake Erie about forty miles west of Buffalo. The next stop was at a summer resort on the Canadian side of the lake.

While I was getting ready to go on shore two men from a little steamer came on board and offered to set me ashore. I passed them the flag and asked them to set it, which they did. They then set me ashore, where I remained about two hours.

When I returned to the wharf I found a lot of men who appeared to be excited. I heard some of them say — something is wrong, we had better go on board and see what is the matter. As they were all looking at my boat, I knew that something was wrong with her. So when I looked to see what it could be, I saw the flag union down [upside down, signal of distress]. A man set me on board. I hauled down the flag and left the place at once.

The passage across Lake Erie was one of the hardest he ever made, even harder, he claimed, than the voyage to Portugal. There was all the sea room in the world on the Atlantic, and when it roughed up too much to carry sail he would put out the drag and drift. But when the Canadian gales came whipping across Lake Erie, he had to keep sail on to avoid getting blown into shore, no matter how rough it was.

My next stop was at Detroit, one of the finest cities in the west and the only place I know of where you will find a floating Post Office. A fine steamer collects and delivers mail to the hundred or more steamers that pass Detroit every twenty-four hours.

There is a fine bridge connecting the city with Belle Island on which the city is making a park which will be in time one of the best in the United States. Belle Island before the Revolution was called Snake Island, and to get rid of the snakes every family on each side of the river put a hog on the island, and in a short time all the snakes left the island, which was then called Hog Island.

I had a fine run across Lake St. Clair, but had to butt all the way up the St. Clair River [forty miles], and more than once I had to run the boat ashore to save her from being run down by the steamers, many of them four and five hundred feet long. The captains of all large steamers have orders to sink anything that gets in their way rather than change their course.

My next stop was at Port Huron, where I remained three days waiting for a leading wind to cross Lake Huron. I tried three times to get up over the rapids, but did not have enough wind to do so. Four men from the steamship *Monarch*, laying at a wharf on the Canadian side of the river, took a line from my boat and walked along the shore and towed her over the rapids.

Once out in the lake a little wind will do, for it seems that only a hat full of wind is enough to kick up a bad sea. The strangest part of my voyage across the Lakes was putting the dipper overboard and helping myself to a drink of water. More than once the first day on Lake Erie I would forget and jump into the cabin and take a drink from the water tank.

Before I got across Lake Huron bad weather came on, and I had to run into Harbor Beach [sixty miles north of Port Huron] and remained there two days. The captain of the life-saving station, the harbormaster and everyone I met treated me fine.

My next stop was at Cheboygan on the Straits of Mackinac. From there I run up to Mackinaw and waited two days for the fog to lift so I could get out into Lake Michigan. Once out in the lake, I made for Chicago as fast as a head wind would let me.

I arrived in Chicago before daylight one morning and hove to outside to get a few hours sleep before running into the Basin. In my voyage across the Lakes I heard more thunder, saw more lightning and rain than I did in all my other voyages put together. When I entered the Basin a Mr. Connery took my boat and made her fast to one of his floats. He kept boats to let. The Chicago papers published a history of the boat, and hundreds of people came to see her every day while she laid in Chicago.

He was in Chicago for two weeks, and among his visitors was the Governor of Wyoming, who wanted in the worst way to buy *Great Republic*. Why the governor of a state that didn't have an accessible body of water big enough for a twenty-five-foot seagoing sloop to turn around in had such a hankering for the famous boat, or why Blackburn was willing to part with her at this stage in his trip, is a mystery. In any event, they were unable to agree on terms, and the governor departed for home. But just as Howard was preparing to resume his voyage, he received a letter from the governor offering him within a hundred dollars of his price if he would deliver the boat sixty miles up the lake shore to Racine, Wisconsin. The offer, however, came too late. The mast had been unstepped, and he was all ready for the tow down the Chicago Drainage Canal which connects Lake Michigan at the mouth of the Chicago River with the Illinois and Michigan Canal and the Illinois River.

The Canal is very little used in late years. Its average depth is about three feet of water and two feet of mud. It is ninety-six miles long and enters the Illinois River at Lasalle.

I met a man in Chicago who wanted to work his way down South. I was glad to get him. It cost me eight dollars and eighty-eight cents canal dues.

In towing through the Canal we took turns about. One of us would walk along the tow path with a line over his shoulder; the other end of the line was made fast to the boat. The man on board would steer the boat. [For much of the way they had to drag her through the soft mud on the bottom.] While walking along the tow path, hundreds of snakes would run across the path and sometimes crawl over our feet, many of them six and seven feet long. They would crawl into the Canal and swim over to the other side.

We stepped the mast at Lasalle and started down the river. The Illinois is a fine river; the water is deep, and the current is not strong. We had a fine time going down the Illinois River, but when we hit the Mississippi our troubles began.

We had a book that told us how to follow the channel, from a day mark on one side of the river to a light on a post on the other side. The book was two years old, and the channel had changed so often in that time that the man who wrote the book would not know any more about the river than we did. After we reached St. Louis we got a book that was only one year old, but it was not much better.

In drifting down the river it was a common thing to see a strip of corn field ten or fifteen feet wide and fifty or seventy-five feet long drop into the river. One day we saw a strip of ground with two mules and a hog on it fall into the river. They all drowned.

We often saw a tree fully one hundred feet long and five or six feet in diameter fall into the river and go rolling over and over down the stream; in a short time not a bough was left on it. We would sometimes see a bunch of trees leaning over the river bank as if waiting for their turn to fall in, and many of them did not have long to wait.

One day our book showed us that we had to cross from the Illinois side of the river to the Missouri side. When we got over, there was no day mark to be seen; it had been shifted down the river about a mile.

We could not get back, as the current was running five or six miles an hour.

There was a long bar of rocks and gravel just below us, running out from a point of land that shot out and up the Missouri shore. We could see plenty of water between the point of land and the shore, but thought it was only a cove. It was too late for us to reach it, as there was three rocks between us and the cove. So we let go the anchor.

There was a steamboat on the Illinois side of the river, slowly, very slowly, making her way up the river. It would be no use to set the flag union down, for the steamer could not help us if she wanted to.

We could save ourselves in the punt, but to leave my boat in such a place — the thoughts of it nearly drove me mad. My companion was ready to take to the punt at a moment's notice, for all he had outside of what he stood in was a habit of saying we can't do this and we can't do that.

I knew we could not lay long where we was, as a big tree might come down across the cable any minute and drive boat, anchor and all up against the bar where the heavy driftwood would soon have put an end to her.

I got on the sheer pole [an iron rod secured horizontally to the lower shrouds] and noticed a lot of driftwood going down between the point and the Missouri shore.

I sat down and tried to think of some way to save that boat from such a miserable end. If anyone had pitied me then, I would have cried like a woman.

The upper rock was just about abreast of the end of the bowsprit; the middle rock was abeam; the lower rock was abreast of the port quarter. We had about seventy-five fathoms of cable out. We could have hauled the boat far enough by the cable to be a little above the upper rock without breaking the anchor out [loosening its hold], but how could we, with only an oar, get a boat drawing four feet of water across the current far enough so that she would pass the upper rock, which was about sixty or seventy feet off on the port side?

While setting on the wheel box trying to think of some way to save the boat, we saw a large tree coming down the river. We could see that it would take the cable. We thought it was all off with the boat.

My companion hauled the punt alongside. I hove the wheel to port. The boat answered the helm as if she was under sail and slowly swung over towards the rocks and upstream far enough to bring the upper rock abeam. After the tree had passed us, I hove the wheel amidships. The boat was soon back into her former position. The tree struck the bar, hung there for a few minutes, broke in two and went on downstream.

I said — Vermont, I am agoing to save this boat.

He said — you can't do it. He was born in Vermont; that is why I always called him by that name.

I got a line, made one end of it fast to the cable outside of the hawse pipe, brought it abaft the after chain plate, took it around the mast and hauled it taut. He then slacked away on the cable until all the strain came on the spring line.

I hove the wheel over to port, gave him a knife and told him to lie down on the deck and to cut the spring line the minute I sang out — cut!

In a short time the upper rock was on our quarter. She was still ranging ahead. The water was coming over the starboard rail. To get out of the water, Vermont crawled over to the port side but kept near enough to the line to cut it when I sang out.

Slowly the boat ranged ahead until the upper rock was just under the port quarter. The water was coming into the cockpit. The cable was as taut as a fiddle string. I could hear my own heart beat. Vermont was as white as snow.

The boat no longer seemed to crawl upstream, but she did seem to lay over towards the Missouri shore a little. Every minute seemed an hour. The rock was still under the port quarter. If only the cable would hold for one minute longer, she would have the rock under the starboard quarter.

I could not see the rock from where I stood in the cockpit but knew it must be just under the stern. We could wait no longer, so I told him to cut.

He just inched the rope with the knife, and it snapped like a fiddle string. The boat righted so suddenly that poor Vermont nearly went overboard. I felt the boat quiver as she struck the rock, but she did not stop.

We grabbed the oar and rowed as hard as we could and soon had her going a little faster than the current. I turned the wheel to starboard; she answered the helm, and I knew the rudder was all right. By rowing hard we soon had the boat out into the middle of the stream, which grew narrower and narrower the farther we went. The land on our port hand still looked as if it was connected with the Missouri shore.

It is wonderful how many thoughts can flash across one's mind at a time of great excitement. I could see no outlet but knew there must be one to let such a large amount of water out. As the channel grew narrower, the current ran faster. We rowed as hard as we could with the current, which was running not less than seven miles an hour, and the boat was going about two miles an hour faster than the current.

At last we saw the outlet. It was very narrow, but I knew it must be deep to let so much water through. We kept the boat in the middle of the outlet, and as soon as she passed through it we hove the wheel hard aport. The boat shot into an eddy formed by the island.

We beached her and then sat down to rest.

When we left the Illinois River we had two anchors, one rope cable and one chain. At the first place we tied up for the night on the Missouri shore an Indian come on board. He had a punt. I tried to buy it, but he would not sell it; but just as soon as he saw our folding anchor laying on deck, he offered to trade the punt for the anchor.

As we had to have some kind of a tender, I gave him the anchor for the punt. And now the Mississippi had taken the other anchor, cable and all.

We ripped up the cabin floor, got out a long bar of pig iron ballast, made the end of the chain fast around the middle of it and started down the river again.

We would pick out some place early in the afternoon to tie up at for the night. When we found a place we let go the anchor and brought her up. Then we turned the wheel toward the shore. The current would force the boat against the bank. Then we would get a line ashore, slack the cable so the driftwood could not catch it, fill a bucket with water and set it on deck to settle so we could drink it the next day. In the morning we would draw the water out of the bucket and find a good inch of mud in the bottom.

One evening while he was in the cabin cooking supper he heard someone sing out, "Hey there, stranger! Where bound?" He stuck his head out of the companionway and saw a tall, lean man standing on the bank, a rifle slung over his shoulder.

He remembered having been told in St. Louis that when he tied up for the night farther down the river he might be visited by a moonshiner. So he invited the fellow aboard and offered him a drink of saloon whiskey.

The man tossed it down, smacked his lips and said, "Now that's right smart good stuff! Where did you git it?" He told him a friend up the river had given it to him. The jug was low, and the tall one remarked in an offhand way, "Now I reckon you'd like to have thet jug filled up before you pull out in the morning. Jest leave it over by thet thar tree."

An hour after his visitor had departed into the brush he went over by the tree and investigated. Sure enough, the jug was full.

The Government spends large sums of money every year riprapping the banks of the river. Often while following the sailing or drifting directions in the book from one side of the river to the other, we would find a sand bar running out from the shore instead of a day mark or a light on a post. So all we could do was to wait until she struck. If the water was eighteen inches deep and the bar not more than fifteen or twenty yards wide, we could jump her over it in about two hours by rocking her from side to side.

One afternoon we fetched up, side to, on a sand bar on which the water could not have been more than one foot deep. As the boat drawed more water aft than she did forward, and the current was strong, she was soon heading downstream. We rocked her for about an hour but made little headway. But we got her in on the bar far enough so that all driftwood had to hit the sand bar before it could hit the boat.

Some very big trees came down the river, but none of them came near us. They would fetch up on the bar, hang for a minute and then go rolling over the bar into deep water, which was about twenty-five or thirty yards below us.

I said — well, Vermont, we will have to let her hang until morning; then we will throw the ballast overboard and jump her over the bar.

He said — we can't do it. He asked me to put him ashore so that he could walk to the nearest railroad. He said — I would rather be jumping freight trains than be jumping sand bars.

I said — well, all right, if you want to commit suicide, get into the punt and I will set you ashore.

He asked me what I meant.

I said — don't you know that them woods is full of wild cats and rattlesnakes? I know he was nearly as much afraid of snakes as I was.

He made up his mind to spend the night on the boat.

I promised to land him at the first railroad we seen. He went below and turned in.

I sat on deck watching the big trees as they rolled over the bar. At last I seen one coming down and could see that it would pass near the boat. I got a rope and put a bowline on the end of it, and when the tree was passing the boat I slipped the bowline over the end of the tree, which kept on rolling over and over until the line brought it up.

Then the tug of war begin.

The tree was about three feet in diameter and sixty-five or seventy feet long, but it could not start the boat, which was trembling like a leaf. I could not get the boat down on her side, so I had to hang that big bar of pig iron that we had been using for an anchor on to the end of the main boom, then slack the sheet off until the boom was out against the rigging. That hove her down on her side, and she started and was soon in deep water.

I hauled the boat up to the tree, cast off the line and got the anchor from the boom and let it go. As soon as I could I gave her all the chain and brought her up. As it was nearly dark then, we had to lay there all night and keep a sharp lookout for driftwood, but as luck would have it, none struck us.

When I called Vermont at daylight to help me get the anchor, he could not understand how the boat ever crossed that sand bar without waking him up.

The first place we come to where there was a railroad near it was Columbus, Kentucky. Vermont jumped the first freight train that came along bound south.

The water in the river at Columbus was low and still falling, and the people there told him he would be a fool to attempt to sail any farther downstream in a boat of *Great Republic*'s draft. So he made a deal with the railroad to haul her to Mobile, Alabama, for a hundred dollars. There were plenty of friendly volunteers to help him take out the ballast and load her on the flatcar.

It was October, and he wrote Theresa that he hoped to sell his faithful sloop in Mobile and return home. But he changed his mind when he got there.

15
Ghosts in the Gulf

WHEN I ARRIVED in Mobile I found a stevedore who agreed to take the boat from the car and put her in the dock for twenty dollars. I waited two days for him to do so, but he kept putting it off, and the railroad men wanted the car.

One evening a Cape Cod man whose name I have forgotten came down to see me. He had sailed captain of vessels out of Mobile and was then putting a sewer in the city. When I told him what I was waiting for, he said — you come with me, and I will introduce you to a stevedore, an old friend of mine; we will see what he can do for you.

We went up street and met a Mr. Welch. My friend told him what I wanted, and Mr. Welch said — now Blackburn, all the men that I have working for me capable of doing that job are busy just now, but if you will superintend the job yourself, I will let you have all the men and gear you want.

I thanked him and told him that would suit me all right.

The next morning I took three colored men, two blocks and tackles, two crowbars and four long planks and went to work. In less than two hours we had the boat into the dock and all the gear returned to the store.

A Portuguese sailor who had been fishing out of Provincetown, Massachusetts, some years before came on board and helped me step the mast, bend the sails and ballast the boat. Before the sun went down that day we had the boat ready for sea. And the best of all was she was once more afloat in salt water.

That evening my Cape Cod friend came down to see me. I asked him where I could find Mr. Welch. He said — come with me. We found him in a saloon. When I asked him how much I owed him, he said — give me five dollars and have a drink on me.

The next morning, while I was looking at the monument to Captain Raphael Sims, a big, well dressed man came up to me and said — I have been reading about you in the papers; I am from Pennsylvania and have a friend with me. We have been looking for a man with a small vessel who would take us to a place where there is lots of money buried.

I asked him if he knew where the place was.

He said — I do, but cannot tell anyone until we get out to sea. He said — now if you will take us, I will pay all the expense and give you one-third of what we get. All we want you to do is to land us at the place, and I have something in my pocket that will locate the money.

He then showed me what he called a mineral rod. It was about three inches long and about one half of an inch in diameter. It had a hole in one end about one inch deep.

I told him that I would take the job.

He fitted the boat out with everything that he thought we might need. His friend came on board, and we started down Mobile Bay.

By the time we reached Fort Morgan [on a bar separating the Bay from the Gulf of Mexico], it was nearly dark, so we anchored for the night. I was and had been sick for two weeks from drinking the Mississippi River water.

The next day it blew a gale, and the sea was breaking on the bar so hard that all vessels in the Bay had to stay in, and all vessels outside had to stay out.

After the gale was over, we put to sea. Pennsylvania then told me that he wanted me to land them in St. Joseph's Bay [a hundred and fifteen miles east of Pensacola, Florida, near the mouth of the Apalachicola River]. I got out my chart to see where it was and found that we had to pass Pensacola, and when we got there they wanted to see the city.

So we run up and made fast to a wharf. They went ashore, but told me not to tell anyone where we was bound for. The little man met a girl from Mobile and told her everything, but told her to say nothing about it to anyone.

The next day everyone that came on board told me to have nothing to do with St. Joseph's Bay. When I asked why, some of them told me that the place was haunted.

When Pennsylvania came on board he was as mad as a wet hen. He gave his friend a call down, and the little man left us.

While at Pensacola I met the advance agent of a carnival who wanted me to take my boat and travel with them all over the South. He promised to stand all the expense of hauling her from place to place. They would take her from the car, put her into a tent and give me one half of what money the people paid to see the boat.

I told him that the boat was too heavy for such a purpose, but as I would have nothing to do the next summer I would go home and have a boat built that four men could put on and off a car by hand — that I would sail her across the Atlantic and back to some southern port and then try the show business.

He said — your fortune is made if you do so. Just see how the people here want to see the boat that has crossed the Atlantic.

Among the hundreds of people that came to have a look at the boat was the United States Senators of Florida, state representatives and city fathers.

We sailed for St. Joseph's Bay. We arrived there two or three days later. It was after dark when we arrived. So we anchored just inside of a point on our starboard hand and waited for daylight, and then we crossed the Bay to try and find the place where the old town once stood.

We found it late in the afternoon and begin prospecting at once. He cut down a small bush that had two slender prongs on it. Each prong was about fifteen inches long. He put the mineral rod on the big end of the stick and held the tip ends of the prong, one in each hand.

Up and down the street we went, tearing up what little was left of the brick sidewalks. Whenever the mineral rod bent the two slender sticks in his hands, he would tell me to mark the place. We marked a number of places, so we could find them the next morning.

We then went down to the beach. He walked along the beach one way and I the other, trying to find the point on which those unfortunate people was put to die when the yellow fever attacked them and wiped them off the face of the earth.

While walking along the beach, I picked up a few shells and put them in my pocket, and when I got aboard I put them in a bucket and left them on deck.

When we got ready to turn in we burned some paper to drive the mosquitoes out of the cabin and put some mosquito netting over the companion way to keep them out.

We had not been asleep long when we both jumped up and asked each other what was the matter. Before either of us could answer we heard the strangest noise we ever heard.

Pennsylvania said — in the name of Uncle Sam, what is that?

I said — it must be turtles trying to board us.

We went on deck and look all around the boat but could see nothing but the reflection of Cape San Blas light on the dark, still water of the Bay. We went below again and could hear the noise coming from all parts of the boat.

I asked him if he brought any shells on board with him.

He said — yes, I brought a pocket full and put them in that box — meaning the locker.

I knew at once what was making such a racket. Every shell has a crab in it, but you would not think so when you pick it up, as the crab crawls into the back part of the shell just as soon as anything inches it, and if you looked into the shell you would not see him.

But lay it down on the beach or deck and stand still for a few seconds, and he will first run out two slender feelers, each one about six inches long, and if he finds there is nothing in his way, he will put out four short legs or claws and crawl away.

When we looked in the locker, not a shell was to be seen. They had all crawled through a knot hole in the floor in search of water. What little water there was in the boat was thick with iron rust. So they crawled to all parts of the boat under the cabin floor. They would crawl up between the frames until they struck the deck and then roll down until they fetched up on the iron ballast. The shells striking on the iron made a strong sound.

We ripped up the cabin floor and spent the rest of the night catching the shells as they crawled over the ballast.

Early the next morning we took the pick and shovel and went ashore. We went to one of the places we had marked the night before and begin to dig a hole about two feet square. When we got down about two feet the water came in so fast that we had to give it up and try another place, but it was always the same.

We then went looking for the cemetery, and when we found it Pennsylvania got out his mineral rod and begin prospecting among the brick vaults which had been broken into by men in search of money and jewelry.

The cemetery was on higher ground than what the old town had been built on. The mineral rod would only work at one of the many vaults. He wanted to dig in under the vault. I told him he could have all he found.

While he was digging, I walked around the cemetery looking at the monuments. How strange they looked, standing there among them great pine trees. One of the monuments was erected in memory of the captain of the Boston schooner *Herald*, who had died at sea and was brought to St. Joseph and buried in the cemetery there in 1846.

As night and a reinforcement of mosquitoes was coming on, he soon gave up digging, and we returned to the boat. We had enough of St. Joseph's Bay.

The next morning we sailed for Tampa.

They swung around the capes and put in to Carrabelle, at the eastern entrance to St. George Sound, where he and Pennsylvania parted company. Then he headed into the Gulf of Mexico again for Tampa.

Thirty miles out, *Great Republic* was overtaken by a gale. Too proud to put back, he hove to and dared not open the slide for eighteen hours lest the cabin be flooded by the boarding seas.

He was about fifty miles to the northwest of Tampa Bay when the wind began to lose its strength, and the seas dropped their high crests. He swayed up sail and stood in for Anclote Keys.

Night was coming on, so I went below and laid on the locker to get a few hours sleep, intending to wake up by the time she got within sight of the light, which is visible sixteen miles.

But being worn out by the long watch on deck I overslept myself, and while still sound asleep I heard the cry — *fire!*

I jumped up and knew at once by the motion of the boat that she was in shallow water.

I rushed on deck just in time to get drenched from head to foot by a sea that broke on the boat. Looking ahead I saw the light of Anclote Keys, not more than half a mile away.

I grabbed the wheel and hove it hard up. The boat came around like a top and was soon head-reaching off shore.

I remained on deck the rest of the night, but try as I would I could not help feeling that I was not alone on board of that boat.

It did not then, and it does not now, eleven years later, seem that the cry of fire was a dream. I wonder if those whom we consider dead took everything that once formed a part of their being to the grave with them. I know that most landsmen consider sailors more superstitious than they are. I will admit that we are a bit queer in some things. For instance, no sailor would think of going about the deck of a vessel at sea whistling. I don't know why, but say what you may, it would seem just as much out of place if he did so as it would to hear a man whistling at a funeral.

The following evening, shortly after dark, he anchored in Tampa Bay. After resting at Tampa for a week, he got a tow behind the USS *Hillsboro* out to Egmont Key at the entrance to the bay, where the line was dropped and he stood off for Key West.

While he was taking the sun at Key West he heard from some of the local people what was said to be the true story of St. Joseph's Bay and the mysterious disaster that had turned it into a ghost town.

It had once been one of the most prosperous ports on the west coast of Florida. Vessels putting in there to take on timber were accustomed to pay cash for it, and since there was no bank in the town, the people kept their money in their homes. An epidemic of yellow fever struck the community and wiped out every man, woman and child. But before they died, the householders hid their treasure, every last penny of it.

I remained in Key West about a week and then sailed for Biscayne Bay and Miami. While entering the Bay in broad daylight I run the boat onto a sand bar within thirty feet of the channel and about six miles off shore.

She was making about eight knots when she struck. The tide was falling, so I threw the ballast overboard, and while waiting for the tide to rise, a gale came on, and I had to lay there two nights and two days.

Then Captain Thomas Coleman, the beacon light tender, came along and took me off. I went with him to his home in Coconut Grove.

After the gale was over we returned to my boat, and after two days hard work we got her off and sailed her over to Coconut Grove, where I sold her.

So it was good-by to *Great Republic*. She had taken everything the North Atlantic could throw at her but was no match for the mud banks and sand bars of the Mississippi and the Florida coast. The Biscayne Bay fiasco was the last straw for a man with a notably short temper.

She had been a "hoodoo" ever since they left Gloucester, as far as he was concerned. With his characteristic obstinance he had dragged her, rocked her, jumped her, beaten her, cajoled her and all but carried her on his back to get her this far, and now — finally admitting that she was out of her element — he dumped her.

He wished that he had started out in the first place in a shoal draft boat with an auxiliary engine. Time and again as he traversed the Gulf in company with a fleet of small boats, a storm would come along and he would have to put to sea and heave to; the local boats, with their shallow draft, would duck in close to shore and keep sailing. Consequently, he seemed never able to make his daily objective before dark, no matter how short the distance; something always happened to frustrate his plans.

Furthermore, his health was unreliable; he had suffered three attacks of malaria and was bothered by his rheumatism off and on. So he decided to head for home.

Great Republic's new owner was a gentleman by the name of John R. Strong of Cambridge, Massachusetts, who was vacationing in Coconut Grove but who summered in Gloucester. Howard and Mr. and Mrs. Strong became good friends, and they presented him with a twelve-foot rowboat which he solemnly christened the *Laura C. Strong* in honor of Mrs. Strong.

Trimming down the handles of the oars to fit the palms of his hands and rigging leather straps around them that attached to his wrists, he set out to row to Jacksonville, a distance of some four hundred miles.

Mr. Strong gave me two boxes of cigars and a lot of fruit. I bid him and all the good-hearted people in Coconut Grove goodbye, took a last look at *Great Republic* and started for New River Inlet [outside Fort Lauderdale], rowed across Biscayne Bay and through Flagness Canal which connects New River with the Bay.

There is a chain across the north end of the canal where all boats must stop and pay toll. I rowed under the chain and stopped at the wharf, then went to the house and asked who collected the canal dues.

A lady was in charge. She asked me where the boat was. When I told her the boat was at the wharf, she said — who let that chain down for you?

When I told her that I rowed under the chain, she said — what kind of an outfit have you got, anyway? Come with me til I see that boat.

We went down to the wharf, and when she seen the boat she said — where did you come from?

I told her I came from Miami and was bound for Jacksonville.

She said — what! In that dugout? Why, the alligators will eat you before you get half way to Jacksonville! You had better stay here and help me with that chain. You can have half of all the sweet potatoes we raise and half of all the alligators and snakes we can catch.

She was fully six feet tall, not fat and had a good heart. I told her that I would remove to New River Inlet, which was four or five miles north, and think it over.

She would not take the canal dues and told me that I was making the mistake of my life.

When I reached the inlet I saw a bunch of fishermen mending nets. I heard one of them call me by name, and when I landed they came down and hauled my boat up on the beach. One of the men had sailed out of Gloucester for many years. I remained there until the next afternoon and then rowed for Hillsboro Inlet sixteen miles farther north.

Just as I left the canal and entered the Hillsboro River, two men who was standing on the beach hailed me and wanted to know where I was bound. When I told them they said — you had better come and stay with us tonight, for it will sure rain before morning.

I thanked them and started for the inlet. Then they told me that I would find an old shack on the north side of the inlet and that I could make myself at home in it.

One of the men belonged in London; the other was a Cracker. I asked them if anyone lived at the inlet.

The Englishman said — no, there was only one man that ever tried to live there, and he did not live long; you will find his grave on the south side of the inlet.

Night was coming on, and I wanted to reach the inlet before dark. When I bid them goodbye, they told me to wrap myself up in the woolen blanket and not sleep too soundly, and that if a coon or two ran over me, not to mind it as they are harmless, but if I found a snake was crawling over me I should lie very still until he had passed over.

Every hair on my head was as stiff as a ram's horn, but I would not let them heathens know it, so I said — now, if I should forget when that snake is crawling over me and jump up, what then?

The great long Florida Cracker said — well, I reckon you will get bit.

And when I asked them what I should do when I got bit, the Englishman said — the only thing you will have time to do is say your prayers.

I said — may the devil catch you and all the snakes in Florida before morning — and rowed on to the inlet.

It was dark when I landed on a beach near the old shack, which had a roof covered with leaves and grass. The two sides was made of the same material. Both ends was open.

I stood on the outside, listening. The only sound that could be heard was the Atlantic waves breaking on the beach outside of the inlet and the schools of small fish rushing into shallow water to escape the sharks.

I said to myself — this shack was built to sleep in, and if other men have slept in it, I can do so.

I jumped into it and then stood still and listened. I heard something moving among the dry leaves which covered the ground floor to a depth of two or three inches.

I did not wait to see whether it was coons or snakes but made for the boat as fast as I could and rowed over to the south side, landed everything but the blanket, then rowed into a cove so to be out of the current, drove an oar into the mud, made the painter fast to it and went to sleep.

I landed on a beach next morning near the inlet, and sure enough, there was the grave of the only man that ever tried to live at Hillsboro Inlet.

I spent the day walking along the beach picking up shells. One must always keep a sharp lookout for snakes, which leave their holes on hot days and hide among the driftwood and seaweed which covers the beach. They lay there until a turtle comes ashore, digs a hole in the sand and leaves its eggs and then goes away. Then the snake goes down and eats the eggs.

One evening while I was washing some shells in the river near the inlet, I saw a fight between an alligator and a shark. It was the greatest battle I ever saw.

They rolled all over each other. Sometimes ten feet of the shark's tail would stick out of the water. Then he would roll over, and the alligator, which seemed to have a hold of the shark by the side of his head, would turn a summerset, and when his tail would strike the water it would send the spray ten feet into the air.

The shark semed to be trying to drag the alligator out into deeper water, and the alligator seemed to try to drag the shark into shallow water. But the current, which was running out, seemed to help the shark, for they slowly drifted toward the inlet, and when they got near the point, the strong outrunning current carried them out to sea, still fighting and rolling over each other.

All the time they were fighting in the river I could see the fins of fifteen or twenty sharks which was swimming around in the river, but they did not seem to notice the fight.

I remained at the inlet four nights and three days and then sailed for Titusville on the Indian River.

I had not rowed more than twenty miles when the yacht *Oxidean,* Captain M. Lewis, came along and asked me to come on board. After I got on board he asked me where I was bound, and when I told him he said — why, we have got to pass Titusville on our way home, so you can stay on board and we will tow you up.

The Indian River is wide and shallow, and the current is not strong. We often run aground on an oyster bed. Then they would get a rake and haul up a lot of oysters.

We anchored that night at Rockledge, where I was taken sick. The next morning I got them to set me ashore on the beach so I could lay in the sun all day.

Captain Lewis wanted to take me home with him, but I told him that I would be all right in a few hours. He was a veteran of the Civil War and had settled in New Smyrna, an inlet on the northern end of the Indian River. He did not want to leave me and offered to stay until the next day, but I would not let him do so. He had a young man from Pennsylvania with him who was after the Captain's daughter, and I knew he was very anxious to get home.

I laid in the sun all day, and when night came on I got into the punt and went out into the river to spend the night.

The next day I walked over to a village called Cocoa, and when I returned I found a black snake trying to get the cover off the pot in which I had left some oyster cakes that Captain Lewis gave me. He was not more than five or six feet long, and as I wanted the cakes as much as he did, I went to the boat and got an oar. But he must have seen me coming, for before I could reach him he made off into the bushes. I did not follow him.

I started for Titusville and arrived there two days later. I found a man who agreed to haul my boat over to Salt Lake at the head of St. John's River for five dollars.

The next day, which was Sunday, when we got ready to start a saloonkeeper called us in and gave me a quart of whiskey and said — now, stranger, just as soon as you get bit, drink what is in this bottle, and you will never know whether it was the snake bite or the contents of the bottle that killed you.

On our way over we stopped to have a look at an Indian mound.

While looking it over, I said to the mound — I wonder who built you.

One of the men said — God knows, I reckon it was made before Washington's time.

When the men left me at Salt Lake, there was not whiskey enough in the bottle to kill a mosquito, let alone me.

Late in the afternoon I started for the St. John's River. The water was very high. All of the swamps was full. In rowing across the lake I would pass between two walls of reeds about eight or ten feet high. The only way I could find the river was by following the current.

I rowed down one of them lanes for about two miles. It was not more than thirty feet wide. Looking over my shoulder, I could see that I had reached the end of the lane, for the wall of reeds met another wall running the other way. So I had to turn back.

It was nearly dark when I reached the other end of the lane, so I made the painter fast to a dozen or more of them reeds and sat in the boat all night, for there was not room enough to lay down without landing some of my outfit, and there was no place to land anything, for the reeds was standing in about two feet of water.

I had plenty of company, for there was thousands of wild ducks swimming around, and whenever they got sleepy I would throw a large sweet potato over the wall of reeds. It never failed to drop on a duck's back. When he would make a rush, all the other ducks would do the same. They were too fat to fly, so they had to use their feet as well as their wings to get away. But such a racket I never heard before.

The two men told me before they left me that afternoon that I could not find my way to the river, but by marking places as I went along I could find my way back. They told me not to sleep in the boat, as the water snakes would crawl into a boat, and when they did I would have to get out. They told me to land on some dry ground, if I could find any, and make a fire, burn a place not less than fifty feet wide and as much longer as I could — that I could then lie down in the middle of the burnt place and go to sleep — that no snake would crawl over new burned ground.

As soon as it was light enough for me to see, I started to find another lane that might lead to the river. When I did find one, the current was so feeble that I could not tell whether I was rowing with or against it. I got a long, thin blade of swamp grass and laid it against a reed that was standing alone near the middle of the lane. It slowly bent with the current, and I rowed down the lane to the river. Them swamps may well be called the Dismal Swamps of Florida.

Once in the river I had plain sailing until I rowed into Puzzle Lake. I found the right outlet after a lot of rowing around.

While rowing down the river between Puzzle Lake and Lake Harney, an alligator slid out from among the reeds and passed under the boat, which he nearly upset owing to the shallowness of the water.

On Lake Harney I met some fishermen with whom I spent the night. I rowed all the next day, and just before dark I tied up at Shell Bank, about three miles south of Lake Monroe.

The largest Indian mound in the United States is at Shell Bank. A great number of people must have lived there for hundreds of years to have left such a lot of shells. The mound was opened some years ago by Professor More of Philadelphia. He found so many skeletons in it that he said a great battle had been fought there, and the dead had been piled up and the ground thrown over them.

As all of the outlets from the St. John's River leading into Lake Monroe was blocked with driftwood and heavy weeds, I could not get through. So the gentlemen that owned the farm at Shell Bank hauled my boat over to Sanford free of charge.

At Sanford he took a river boat to Jacksonville, where he sold the *Laura C. Strong*, which he had actually rowed about two hundred miles, for four dollars. He boarded a steamer and arrived home in Gloucester on February 20, 1903.

16
The Third Attempt

TANNED AND TOUGHENED by his travels under the southern sun, Howard shivered with the cold as he stepped from the overheated train at Gloucester into the dead of the New England winter.

He had been home only a few hours before he was visited by the reporter from the *Gloucester Times*. When he had finished telling a few yarns about his adventures, he was asked about his plans.

Well now, first of all he was going to take a good long rest; the attacks of malaria and rheumatism had plain worn him out, and besides, he wasn't getting any younger, having just passed his forty-fourth birthday on the way up from Florida. After he got his health back he planned to write a book about his life, which would be published later in the year. And after that — well, he might just consider another cruise, but it was a long way off.

Gloucester in February of 1903 was as bleak and cheerless as the winter sea. The wind pierced harshly through the city and rattled dry leaves and sand over the snow in little whirlwinds of futility. Wave-broken chunks of harbor ice piled up in a weird Arctic barricade along the high water line of Niles Beach. Down on the desolate waterfront the fishermen, as if berserk, attacked their ghostly shrouded schooners with axes and clubs, smashing savagely at the grotesque coats of frozen spray which the gales of the Atlantic had encrusted on rigging, spars, decks and hulls as if to drag them to the bottom with the burden.

Back in town the people hurried through the streets from one oasis of warmth to another, muffled against the cold, noses pinched, eyes watering. The winter was even worse than usual because of the strike in the anthracite mines the previous year; the city ran out of fuel and had to close the public schools for the entire month of December, and chimneys spewed out a pall of thick black smoke from the soft coal that householders, begrimed with its dust, were forced to shovel into their balking furnaces.

It was a time for a man to haul off his boots, throw another chunk of wood in the kitchen stove and draw up close in his stocking feet and galluses, with thanks in his heart if he was lucky enough not to make his living from the sea in wintertime.

But not Blackburn.

While his relieved family and friends relaxed in the belief that he had at last regained his senses, he took the train down the coast a few miles to Swampscott and secretly presented boatbuilder Gerry Emmons with his plans for a sailing dory capable of being taken across the Atlantic Ocean and back and light enough to be carried on dry land by four carnival roustabouts.

He had been thinking over his boast in Pensacola that the next summer he would become the first man in history to cross and re-cross the North Atlantic single-handed.

Now it was time to make good on it. Probably he would never lay eyes on the carnival agent again, but the commitment had been made, if only to himself, and he was bound he would carry it through. The obsession that kept driving him back to the sea also ordained that this should be the boat . . . a dory. For the anniversary of the ordeal was at hand; it was in a dory, exactly twenty winters ago, that he had bargained his fingers for his life.

The old Cape Ann or bank dory which he knew so well was not the one he chose for this next voyage, however. Not that it wasn't nicely adapted to its purpose; long and heavy, with high, straight-sloped sides and flat bottom, it was meant to be rowed out from a schooner or from shore and back under the roughest conditions with a ton and more of fish. But its stability was due as much to size as to design, and seaworthiness had been compromised for the sake of simplicity and cheapness of construction and the advantage of nesting by removing the thwarts.

What Howard wanted was a faster and abler sailer, and down in Swampscott they had just the thing.

The Swampscott sailing dory had acquired such fame as a longshore work boat that many yachtsmen had taken it over for racing. Given enough freeboard, it was even more sea-kindly than its Cape Ann sister, prettier and swifter under sail. It had round sides and a bit of deadrise on the bottom, which angled up slightly from the centerline to the chine. A centerboard could be dropped down to keep it from slipping to leeward. Like the bank dory, its stability increased with its load. Although both were tender in a wind, tipping rather easily, the round sides and narrow bottom of the Swampscott model provided more resistance when it was heeled over, and hence more reserve stability under sail.

Emmons, the leading Swampscott builder, early in the spring laid the keel for a dory adapted to Howard's specifications. The plans called for a boat sixteen feet, nine inches from stem to stern, five feet wide at its greatest beam, twenty-two inches deep and with a draft of a foot. For extra strength, he gave it twice the usual number of frames. The greatest modification, however, was on the bottom. Instead of a centerboard it would have a long oak keel four inches deep to keep it on a straight course in the hope that it would sail itself when called upon to. Besides the keel, the frames, gunwale, rudder, tiller and bowsprit (which was later discarded) were to be of oak, with cedar planking.

By the end of April the dory was taking shape. It was entirely decked over except for a sliding hatch the width of its owner's hips and a cockpit the size of a laundry tub. He had removed the rudder from its customary position outside the transom and hung it behind the keel, running the tiller post up through a pipe in the counter aft of the cockpit. The dimensions of the cabin were those of a large casket. Wing lockers and a few shelves ran the length of both sides, and there were less than thirty inches between the floor and the overhead.

The builder's men were putting on the finishing touches by the middle of May. The mast was a springy sapling about fifteen feet high, braced with a forestay to the bow and a single shroud to each gunwale. The boat was rigged leg o' mutton fashion; the mainsail ended in a very short gaff at the peak and had two rows of reef points for heavy weather; the jib snapped to the stem and at its clew had a stubby, free-swinging boom known as a club, to which was attached a bridle and sheet blocked to a traveler on the forward deck. Halyards and sheets were rove through extra large blocks to keep them running free and were led back to the cockpit.

It was impossible to keep such a prodigy as this under wraps indefinitely, and word leaked out along the Gloucester waterfront that Blackburn was up to something again. It became even harder to keep the secret when a young German named Ludwig Eisenbraun sailed into nearby Magnolia Harbor from Boston in a nineteen-foot dory to wait for a break in the weather so that he could start alone across the Atlantic.

The cat finally jumped from the bag. The Gloucester papers flushed him out on the twenty-seventh of May.

Yes, he admitted, it was true. He was having a small boat constructed in Swampscott, and she would be launched tomorrow, in fact. He would sail for Le Havre, France, in less than two weeks if all went well — at two in the afternoon on Sunday, June 7, to be exact. When he reached Le Havre, he would sail through the inland waterways of France to Marseilles, sight-seeing along the way. Thence he would proceed westward through the Mediterranean to Gibraltar, where he would pause to inspect "that mighty fortress," and then pass through the Strait and direct his little boat homeward, following a more southerly course to take advantage of the southeast trade winds and to keep clear of the autumn gales to the north. After calling at the Madeiras, he would push on across the Atlantic to Puerto Rico, then on to Cuba and through the Gulf of Mexico to New Orleans and up the Mississippi to St. Louis, where he would place himself and his boat at the disposal of the Louisiana Purchase Exposition the following spring.

When his friends picked up their newspapers the next day and read this, they were aghast. But it was too late to stop him, for at that very moment *America* — as he had grandiosely christened his smallest boat — was being slipped into the waters of Swampscott Harbor.

Full of foreboding, they could only remonstrate, as did young Fred Daggett, that what he planned was suicide. And to Daggett he gave an inscrutable look and rumbled slowly:

"Fred, I don't much care if I come back or not. I'll put my trust in God, for I'd as soon be buried with old Father Neptune as ashore."

The day after the launching he sailed *America* up to Gloucester. She was fast and able, and he was well pleased with her.

For the next week he put her through her paces in the harbor. To his delight he discovered that if the water was not too choppy she would beat to within four points of the wind. Experimenting with the placement of the ballast, he succeeded in tuning her up to such fine balance that she sailed herself as straight as an arrow while he was below in the cabin. Yet she was so tender, even when fully ballasted and loaded, that if he stepped on the gunwale when boarding her she would lay over until the water came nearly to her rail.

Blackburn had no sooner sailed into Cape Ann than Eisenbraun sailed out, destination the Mediterranean. But Howard hoped to cross in fifty days and beat the German in spite of his head start.

Eisenbraun was less than a day at sea when a Captain E. T. Wawn cleared the harbor of Sydney on Cape Breton Island in

the Canadian Maritimes, sailing a dory less than twelve feet long
— destination Europe; but before he had left the bay he gave up
in the face of pounding seas and returned to land.

Every madcap sailor on the eastern seaboard, it seemed, wanted
to jump into a dory and steer it across the Atlantic.

Down in Boston a salt named Joe Chaves was trying to get into
the act. He had rushed off to Swampscott when he read of Howard's plans and ordered a dory as close to the lines of *America*
as he could find. Chaves had the use of only one arm, he told the
reporters, the other having been maimed by a crazed knife-
wielding crew member aboard a schooner a few years back. He
hoped to sail for his native Portugal ten days after Blackburn
and swore he'd get to Europe first.

The epidemic had struck New York, too. There yet a fifth
dory was being fitted out by a William Snyder, also for Portugal.
Eventually he worked up enough courage to leave the land astern;
he ducked timidly from harbor to harbor and abandoned his
voyage altogether in Gloucester, of all places, at the ignominious
end of a coasting schooner's tow rope.

Unperturbed by these potential rivals, Howard stuffed provisions into *America* for a seven-week passage. There were
salmon, beans, tomato soup, chicken, condensed milk, tongue,
ginger, oatmeal, potatoes, salt pork, pickles, tea, sea biscuit and
twenty gallons of water; an oil stove, lantern, kerosene, bedding
and clothing, navigational instruments and charts, tobacco and
whiskey and a miscellany of other necessities. And when he was
done, there was just enough space left for his own massive frame.

And then came the farewell party and the symbolic gifts, by
now an established tradition with his friends. But this time two
stuck out like whistling at a funeral. One consisted of a half a
dozen lace handkerchiefs and a bottle of cologne from a lady; the
other, from ex-Mayor Bill French, was a thousand-dollar life
insurance policy.

Howard and dory *America*, poised to sail.

Phil Kuuse

Off for France, June 7, 1903.

For three days the coast had been shut in under a gray, dripping smother of fog, but on Sunday morning, June 7, the struggling sun at last burned through, and the lingering wisps of mist fled across the harbor before a gentle southwest breeze. By noon every possible vantage point along the Gloucester shore was speckled with spectators.

The launch *Faun* towed *America* from her mooring in Vincent Cove behind the saloon, across the already crowded inner harbor and over to the anchorage of the East Gloucester Yacht Club, where she was left in charge of Joe Oliver, who swore and waved his arms at a swarm of motorboats that appeared to be bent on swamping the dory before she ever got under way.

At one-thirty Howard and Frank Staples, the trusted bartender in whose care he was leaving his business, pulled up at the clubhouse in a carriage and were greeted with enthusiasm by Commodore Ben Colby and Alex McCurdy, who escorted them through the building, past the cheering members and down to the landing. Looking the picture of ruddy health in a dark checkered jacket, blue trousers, blue and white striped shirt, polka-dot tie and yachting cap, Howard received a roaring ovation as he shouldered through the crowd, joking and shaking hands. Theresa was nowhere in evidence.

Just before two there was a shout of "All aboard!" Blackburn, Staples and a party of friends boarded the launch, but it had hardly pulled away from the float when its propeller tangled with a buoy line and the show came to a dead stop. The mess of rope was cut away, the engine was again started, and *Faun* headed for the dory, threading through the flotilla of circling boats. Friends swung aboard *America*, swayed up her sails and hoisted the Yacht Club pennant and then jumped back into the launch, which in the meantime had put out a tow line.

At two o'clock the explosion of the starting gun punched through the sputter of the motor boats and triggered a rising clamor from the crowds, punctuated by a bedlam of whistles, horns and sirens. The launch churned the water. The tow rope tightened and the dory obediently fell in behind, her skipper and Joe Oliver waving their caps.

The swell of acclamation rolled across the water as *Faun* chugged down the harbor with her charge. Launches decorated with rainbows of pennants and crepe cut back and forth across their course, setting up a chaotic chop that tossed the fleet of sail straining to keep abreast against the freshening breeze.

Outside the nearly finished breakwater of gaunt granite blocks off Eastern Point, the sea was choppy from the whipping of the coastal sweep of wind. *Faun* and her tow lay to for a while near the whistling buoy to give the fleet a chance to catch up.

A few minutes before three Joe Oliver climbed aboard the launch. Howard shook hands all around and cast off the line. As he hove the tiller hard over, the following wind caught the sails, and he was off.

The dory leaped through the sea, dashing white little waves of boiling froth from her bow. Her master sat jaunty and grinning on her stern deck with his feet in the cockpit, the tiller firmly pinched behind one thumb, a cigar behind the other.

So unexpectedly fast did she pull away from the fleet that many turned back after a last salute. Off Thatcher Island those that had been able to keep up hove to, gave three quick cheers and watched the tiny triangle of sail scud for the horizon until they could no longer make it out.

17
Close Call

WHILE OLD SAILORS consider the boat remarkably seaworthy, they are outspoken in their belief that Blackburn should not attempt a voyage in so small a craft. The *News* wishes Captain Blackburn a pleasant voyage and a happy return.

Thus did the *Cape Ann News* express the general concern.

Five days later not a single incoming vessel had reported sighting him.

On the sixth day Ludwig Eisenbraun sailed into the Gap Head Lifesaving Station at Rockport on the tail of an easterly gale and the verge of complete exhaustion. He had managed to get three hundred and fifty miles out into the Gulf Stream, where he ran into such rough weather that he gave up and counted himself lucky to get back to Cape Ann.

This didn't sound good, but fears for Blackburn's safety were allayed somewhat the next day when ships coming into port advised that the storm was not unduly severe and didn't appear to have extended eastward to any great distance. Winds were said to have been moderate, though adverse to his course.

But northeast storm warnings were posted on the fifteenth, and wind-driven rain came down in buckets. Blackburn had been at sea, unsighted, for more than a week.

This second storm took an unexpected turn for the worse and pounded and drenched the entire New England coast with a violence almost unprecedented for that season of the year. The beaches of Cape Ann were strewn with debris. The ninety-foot section of a sunken ship's keel was wrenched from the bottom by the wild ocean and cast up. Dead animals were everywhere along the shore among the flotsam of the storm — a large dog with a length of rope still around its neck, three cats, a pig in a bag.

By the nineteenth the anxiety was increasing with every hour. Blackburn had still not been reported. Vessels of all descriptions were limping into ports along the seaboard with accounts of having collided with a procession of ferocious gales extending from Newfoundland to Delaware and as far out to sea as the Grand Banks and beyond. The steamer *Cambroman* docked at Boston from Liverpool with stories of a hurricane that lasted eight hours. The schooner *S. F. Maker* hobbled into Gloucester, and her master told of a battle with mountainous seas and terrible winds off Nova Scotia — the worst in his thirty years at sea.

Blackburn's fate was considered no longer in doubt on the twentieth, when a Gloucester man informed the newspapers that he had just received a letter from his brother which had been posted five days earlier from Vinal Haven, Maine. A member of the crew of the schooner *Hazel Oneita* on a seining trip, the brother had written that on the fourteenth they spoke *America* off Seacock Ledge near Provincetown . . . "we saw Blackburn and he was in the last stages, ready to give up the ship."

But the captain of the schooner was contacted and said the letter was a hoax, that they had never laid eyes on him.

That same day a new storm roared in out of the east. Blinding sheets of rain whipped across the coast, the temperature dropped down to a November chill, and the wind screeched over the land in gusts of almost hurricane force. The oldest residents of Gloucester couldn't remember such a stretch of evil June weather.

The storm swept in from the Atlantic without letup, through the night and all the next day. Blackburn had now been gone two weeks without a trace. It was impossible that a dory less than seventeen feet long could live through such a hell as the ocean had been turned into for ten solid days.

On the morning of the twenty-second of June the telegraph in the office of the *Cape Ann News* awoke with a splutter and spilled out a dispatch from Lockeport, Nova Scotia, a few miles to the east of Cape Sable.

The bulletin concerned the schooner *Springwood*, which had arrived in port from Trinidad. Fifteen miles to the southwest of Sable, three days ago, it had spoken Captain Blackburn in the dory *America*. Afraid that a worrying world presumed him dead, he was anxious to be reported. He had weathered heavy easterly gales. One crashing sea had cracked his hatch, but he had repaired it. He appeared to be well and cheerful and was grateful to the master of the schooner for the gift of five gallons of water, a can of kerosene and some coconuts.

~~~~~

Dropping Cape Ann and the fleet of friends behind, he nosed *America* into the Atlantic on a course that was a hair south of east. He planned to bear well offshore of Nova Scotia until he made the southern edge of the Grand Banks, when he would stand off to the southward into the steamer track and gradually work back to the north of east and France.

Although his progress was slow, all went well until the twelfth of June, when he was struck by the first of a series of easterlies about a hundred and twenty miles out of Gloucester. He took in sail and put out the drag — the same one he had taken to Portugal on *Great Republic*. The dory rode the storm like a duck but drifted back about forty miles. When the wind and seas abated the next day he made sail and beat back over his course to the eastward again.

The second gale struck on the fifteenth. It came in hard from the southeast. Although he was shipping water constantly, he sailed against the gathering storm all day. That night he reached

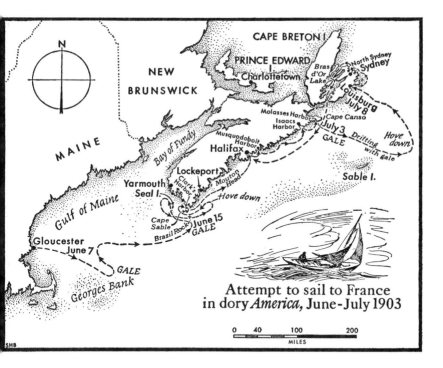

Attempt to sail to France
in dory *America*, June-July 1903

a position south of Cape Sable, but was so wet and tired out that he decided again to haul in canvas and heave to behind the drag.

At two in the morning a boiling sea crashed down on the dory with such sudden force that the drag line snapped. Instantly she was at the storm's mercy. In a matter of seconds her head would be swung, and once caught broadside in the trough he would be rolled over.

He jumped forward in the blackness to the pitching bow. Drenched with spray, he grabbed the anchor and threw it overboard, paying out about thirty fathoms of cable. It sank like lead, but it kept the boat head to; at the same time, it combined with his weight to drag the bow — with him clinging to the forestay — under every wave that rolled down on her.

He crawled aft to the cabin and rummaged out a bucket and an empty beer box. Struggling back to the bow, half drowned in the walls of water that poured over him, he tied the bucket and the box to the anchor cable and paid out another ten fathoms. Cupped against the water and buoyed by the strain of the drifting dory on the cable, they held it nearly horizontal from the bow. The boat settled back into an uneasy compromise with the storm.

Hour after hour and mile after mile, for the rest of the night and all the next day, the dory was beaten back into the Bay of Fundy by the howling wind and the prodigious Fundy tides.

When the gale had subsided enough to risk raising sail without its being torn to shreds, he hauled in the makeshift drag and ran up the main and jib. Then he commenced to beat out of the bay under the gray cover of scudding clouds. The wind was still hard and blowing in from dead ahead. Not a sail was in sight; every schooner for hundreds of miles around had fled for the nearest harbor.

At five in the afternoon of June 19 he had fought nearly clear of Fundy and was passing Seal Island, twenty miles west of Cape Sable. Three hours later he spoke the *Springwood*, the first vessel he had encountered since leaving Gloucester twelve days before.

America was jogging along easily under full sail a mile outside of Brazil Rock the next morning, nine miles to the southeast of Sable. A moderate fog had settled in over the ocean, and the wind was light. He was in the cockpit having breakfast, when through the drifting shroud of mist he made out the shadowy outline of a dory and the figure of its occupant, bent to his fishing. He hove the tiller over to bring her into the wind and bellowed a hail across the water.

The startled fisherman looked up and stared in disbelief. Then he pulled in his gear, took up the oars and rowed alongside. The two men chatted for a few minutes. It was a welcome break in the silent solitude of the sea for both. After they had parted, the fisherman rested on his oars, watching the sailboat move away and disappear in the fog like a phantom.

Bearing northeast off the south shore of Nova Scotia, he was off Lockeport on the twenty-first of June, when early in the afternoon — just as he was running past Ram Island — the wind backed into the east and began to blow. He pointed hard off the land and sought sea room; if another gale was in the making, he had no desire to end up with the driftwood on the rocks of his native coast.

By nine in the evening he was twenty-three miles south by east of Little Hope Island, a dreary pinnacle off Mouton Head, and the third easterly gale in a row was on him like a banshee. He took in the sails and threw over the box-and-bucket drag, closed the hatch, crooked his legs under the cockpit coaming and fought the tiller all night. At dawn, satisfied that he still had plenty of sea room, though he was drifting rapidly back over his course, he ducked below. Heaving himself down on the cabin floor, he fell asleep.

At 10 A.M. an unlucky sea struck the boat and threw her down on her side. The slide was closed at the time, but the top crossboard was laying on the cabin floor, which left an opening two feet long and four inches wide through which the water run into the cabin at a great rate. I tried to push the slide back, but the pressure was so great that I could not open it.

I thought that my time had come at last. All I could do was to lay there watching the water run into the cabin. When that sea struck the boat, she was heading east. It carried her all around the compass until she headed east again, and when she fell into the hollow of the sea, she was half full of water.

My heft on the cabin floor helped to right her. If this had of happened in the night, I would have been willing to take an oath that the boat had rolled over, but I know she didn't, for I could see daylight through the water all the time as it poured into the cabin.

As soon as she was on her bottom again, I got the slide open and crawled out into the cockpit. I looked all around. There was nothing in sight but white foam. The cockpit was full of water. I looked into the cabin and saw a bucket floating around. I grabbed the bucket and began to bail. When I saw a sea coming, I would put my arm into the opening after hauling the slide over. As soon as the sea passed over, I would open the cabin and bail until I had all the water out.

Then I went into the cabin, and what a sight! Everything was upset. The tea, sugar, fine cut tobacco, oatmeal and oil was all mixed together on the cabin floor. I got everything out of the cabin and fixed her up as well as I could. The compass which I carried in the cockpit, the lantern and everything that I had left on deck was gone.

There was nothing to do but lie to the drag and wait. All day the dory drifted with the storm, and all night. The miles fell away as she was pushed back past the coast, past Sable, back again into the Bay of Fundy, losing every hard-fought inch of a week's embattled progress.

At daylight on the twenty-third the wind abated, though it was still hard in from the east, and the sea was less ferocious. Chart and compass gone, provisions spoiled, clothing soaked, he took the drag aboard, tied a reef in the mainsail and headed for land.

As if as glad as he was at the prospect of a refuge, *America* dashed for the coast. At two in the afternoon he sighted Cape Sable when he rose on the backs of the heaving seas. Two more hours, and the town of Clark's Harbor lay dead ahead, scattered thinly along the flat spit of shoreline.

Up went the Yacht Club pennant. The harbor was crowded with schooners and small boats, driven to shelter by the storm. The dory wove through them toward the docks. Still drenching under his oilskins, he perched at the tiller and puffed nonchalantly on a salvaged cigar as if he were only coming in from an hour's cruise. She sprinted smartly up to Scotia Wharf; he spun her into the wind, coasted alongside a schooner and dropped the sail.

He was so stiff and arthritic and tired that his knees buckled and he almost collapsed as he tried to get out of the boat. He caught himself, climbed painfully aboard the schooner and limped across its deck to the wharf.

A boy and two men ran up. And then people were hurrying down from their homes, dashing out of buildings, running across the fields, jumping ashore from boats, dropping whatever they were doing, as the word was shouted through the town. "It's Captain Blackburn!" "He's here!" "Just sailed in out of the gale!" "He's safe!"

Many of the men knew him; they had stopped in for a drink whenever they put in at Gloucester. Everyone had heard of him. Why, he was born and raised only a few miles up the coast at Port Medway! The whole town converged on Scotia Wharf, and in a twinkling he was the center of a crowd. Everyone was pushing and shoving, trying to get in to him, pressing him to come home for a square meal and a warm bed.

He chose to go to the only hotel in the village with W. E. Nickerson, the proprietor. Up the street from the waterfront he limped, accompanied by an excited entourage of townspeople. At the Traveller's Home he shaved and bathed, changed into dry clothes and sat down to his first decent meal in two weeks. After dinner he fought off his surging fatigue and held a reception.

Everybody in Clark's Harbor wanted to squeeze into the hotel, and it was jam-packed as he began to talk. When he told of his battles with the gales that kept knocking him back into the Bay of Fundy and of the time the drag broke and of how he was hove down, they were incredulous. And when he announced that he would refit and continue the voyage almost immediately, they were dismayed.

But the attempts of his new friends to persuade him to abandon what they as seafaring men knew was sheer madness were to no avail. Ironically, the most touching and cogent plea of all tumbled from the lips of the town's young lady schoolteacher, who rushed down to him as soon as she heard of his arrival.

Her name was Gertrude Forbes, and she was his niece, the daughter of his eldest sister Martha. Gertrude begged her Uncle Howard to give up the whole thing. Hadn't he had enough? Didn't he remember how his father had drowned in a small boat — not even at sea, but in Medway River down home? Wouldn't he quit for Aunt Theresa's sake, at least?

He told her, with gruff affection, that she was wasting her breath.

When the last of the people had departed, his host took him to his room and he flopped into bed.

The next morning he went down to the wharf and supervised the removal of everything from *America* for a general drying-out.

When the men was cleaning out the cabin, they found cards of matches sticking to the deck. They said — why this boat must have rolled over! See the cards of matches we found sticking to the deck! A chisel that I had left standing point down on the starboard side behind a board six inches wide that stood on its edge was found sticking into the port side of the boat between the deck beams. It had to turn a somersault to get there.

Whatever had actually happened, he inspected her thoroughly; she was undamaged. Someone found him an oar to replace the one that was lost when he was hove down. Others supplied him with fresh provisions. Frank Simonds knew where he could come by a new compass; they drove three miles in a buggy to get it, but it was so big there wouldn't be room in the cockpit for him, too, so he picked up a dory compass. Mrs. Simonds baked him a cake and gave him a Bible. Captain F. A. Brannan of the schooner *Nellie Harmon*, a coaster on the coal run from Halifax, presented him with a new chart of the North Atlantic and offered to tow him up the coast while he nursed his leg, which was badly swollen and painful.

In the early forenoon of Saturday, June 27, having spent three days and four nights ashore, he bade the warmhearted people of Clark's Harbor farewell and hitched himself aboard Captain Brannan's schooner. Every house flew a flag in salute, and everyone who could walk was down on the wharf to see him off.

As her sails filled, and *Nellie Harmon* moved out the harbor with *America* in tow, a fleet of dories rowed alongside, the oarsmen shouting good-by and good luck until the wind carried the schooner out of range and sight.

Early in the afternoon — they were reaching past Shelburne, a scant twenty-five miles from Clark's Harbor — he unexpectedly decided he wanted to be cast off and left on his own. But Captain Brannan, on whose vessel he was now a passenger, refused.

The schooner dropped her anchor in Halifax Harbor the following day, and he enjoyed a sound sleep that night. The next day was the twenty-ninth; he had been gone from Gloucester for more than three weeks and was still hanging onto land. He arose at the crack of dawn, vowed he was feeling fine and swore to Captain Brannan that he would be delayed no longer. It was time for them to part company. He would follow the coast for a while to see how he felt, just in case he needed to duck into port somewhere for doctoring, and then he would drop Nova Scotia astern and head out to sea.

Brannan shook his head and tried to remonstrate, but it was useless — he might as well be talking to a stone wall. And so he ordered *America* brought alongside, saw her master aboard and let go the line.

Howard Blackburn hoisted the sails, made himself comfortable in the cockpit, cleared the schooner, waved his cap and stood out of the harbor.

Captain Brannan and his crew leaned on the rail for a long while, until the patch of sail was no longer to be seen. They had a sinking feeling in their stomachs.

18
Defeat

He was sick when he sailed out of Halifax Harbor and turned *America*'s bow eastward along the coast. His swollen leg was killing him, and he knew he was in no shape for an ocean crossing. What had started out so finely had turned in three weeks into a nightmare. He dreaded the day — so soon to come now — when he would run out of coastline to follow; then he would have to head out to sea once and for all — or quit. And he dreaded the thought of giving up.

He hugged the coast and that night ducked into Musquodoboit Harbor, a day's run of less than thirty miles. Next morning a new gale whipped in from the east.

It was all he needed to decide him about one thing, at any rate; if this kind of weather was to be his lot, then at least he would shorten his rig and reduce his sail area so as to give himself and his boat half a chance. He sailed into the dock and found a man and his son who helped him unstep and saw seventeen inches off the mast.

The storm proved to be a brief one, and at six the next morning — it was the first of July — he beat out of the harbor. A thick fog had been sucked in behind the gale, and he stood well offshore. Eleven miles off Pope Harbor a schooner loomed out of the soup and luffed up to him. She was the *Iceland*. The lookout thought he was a fisherman gone astray, and they had swung off course to pick him up. But he reported all well, and the big two-master filled away and disappeared in the fog.

Since the wind was fair, he followed the coast for the rest of the day and all night, setting the new compass on the cabin floor where he could see to steer by it under the flicker of the lantern.

Early in the morning he was surprised to hear the plaintive groan of a whistling buoy, rising and falling with the swell off his starboard bow. He ran up to it and read the name. Isaacs Harbor! Good Lord — he was way off course and heading blindly for the rocks! The compass was off at least two points, knocked all out of kilter by the iron ballast beneath the cabin floor.

He altered course to southeast by east and at ten in the morning dashed into Molasses Harbor, a black thunder squall panting down his neck.

Lying at anchor through the day and that night, he gave the whole business some hard thought. Only a few more miles up the line was Cape Canso, the easternmost tip of Nova Scotia. Already he was far to the north of his intended course and getting farther away all the time. Certainly there was nothing to be gained by running up to Cape Breton Island and starting across from there.

It was now or never, fish or cut bait.

At daybreak on the third of July he hauled anchor. The whistling buoy off White Head bore northwest. He steered southeast from it — southeast for Europe.

The wind was fair and the sea calm all day and through the night. At nine in the morning of the fourth he sighted a schooner fishing on a bank called Old Maid's Slipper, sixty-five miles southeast of Cape Canso. He ran up to her and tied alongside. She was the *Colonial* of Lunenberg. Captain Davis welcomed him aboard and urged him to stay for lunch. But the wind held fair and he wanted to push on. After he had walked around the deck and stretched his legs, he swung over the side and cast off.

By late afternoon a curtain of dark clouds was rolling up astern, out of the northwest. He cooked up a quick dinner to brace himself against the overtaking weather.

The storm came screaming down on him out of the nightfall. It exploded, as if a great invisible wall behind him had been burst apart by an uncontainable pressure of air. The wind bore in so fast that at first it took the ocean by surprise and flattened it into a rippled sheet. It dug vicious claws into the unwilling water and rent the smoothness of its surface, and as the wavelets rose up in protest it lifted them from behind. Each fed itself from the hollow and rose higher, and the trough fell deeper, and the wind pushed harder against the mounting wall of water until the sea grew more terrible than the storm itself.

Instead of throwing over the drag and riding it out, he took in the mainsail, closed up the cabin and ran before it with his jib flying. All was blackness. He hunched on the deck with his feet in the cockpit, clutching the tiller with his stumps of hands. The dory was picked up by the sheer, onrushing slope of each rolling mountain of water as it came up astern and hurled forward until the wind struck the jib with a snap and the crest of the wave pushed on under its bottom, and then it seemed to slide backward down the reverse slope, bow pointed high into the wind and flying spray — dropping, dropping into the abyss, the sopping sail all limp, waiting for the disaster of the next one to come down on it.

Just as the first signs of daylight begin to show in the northeast, a fearful sea rose up under the starboard quarter, and as quick as a flash of lightning it threw the boat over on her beam ends and me overboard.

As soon as I could turn around in the water, I grabbed the mainboom, which was lying flat on the water, and hauled myself along until I reached the stern of the boat. Then I let go of the boom and caught hold of the boat, which was still laying on her beam ends. I hauled myself along til I got amidships. Then I threw all my weight onto the side of the boat, which righted at once.

As soon as I got on board, I found that she had a bad port list. All around her as far as I could see, the ocean was covered with foam. I hauled down the jib and put out the drag, then opened the cabin.

There was no water to be seen, but everything was thrown from the starboard into the port side, which gave her a bad list.

I had to take everything out of the cabin and put them into the cockpit while I was straightening up the cabin. While working below, I had to leave the slide open so that I could see. By the time I got through, a lot of water had come into the cabin.

The lantern was still hanging from a beam when he went below, still lit. But the oil stove had upset, and kerosene and sea water sloshed around in the bilge, soaking into all of his provisions except the canned goods. So as to have more room while he was trying to make sense out of this chaos, he had dumped all his clothing in the cockpit; a sloppy sea broke over and carried it away.

As nearly as he could figure, he was a hundred and sixty-five miles at sea, somewhere to the southeast of Cape Canso.

He lay to the drag all day. By seven in the evening the gale had moderated, and he made sail. He ran to the eastward all night, hoping to meet up with a vessel from which he could get provisions to continue. His right knee and both feet were puffed and swollen and afire with pain. He was soaked to the skin. His teeth chattered, and his whole body shook with wave after wave of uncontrollable chills.

Barely after dawn he spied a ship, a long way off. She looked to be at anchor, alternately coming into view and sinking in the sea as he rose and fell on the giant swells. If he could only beat out to her, last long enough to get to her, she would have what he needed to keep going, to hold his strength and spirits up.

She was so far off, and there was so much sea between them, and he was so sick . . . It would take more to reach her, and to go on from her, than he had left.

It was the end.

The wind had hauled around to an easterly, fair for Cape Breton Island. He trimmed the sails to it, lashed the tiller on a course for Sydney and stumbled below. He got the stove going and lay on the cabin floor with it burning at his back. The air was cold enough for November, and the boat was leaking.

The breeze held, and for three days and two nights *America* sailed herself toward land. He lay in the cabin. Now and then he ate a little, and bailed, and crawled on deck to check the trim of her sails.

At the end of the third day, the eighth of July, he made Louisburg on the south shore of Cape Breton. *America* had run to the westward of her course, but she was bringing him back to land.

A dense fog hid the harbor, and he hove to for the night. It burned off in the morning; a passing skipper took him in tow and brought him aboard for a couple of hours before the cabin stove.

He made fast to the lobster factory wharf. The owner carried his clothes to the boiler room to dry them out and placed him in the hands of a friend, who took him home, bathed his feet and legs in hot mustard water, fed him a hearty meal and put him to bed.

The next day he rested, received a few visitors and wearily wrote home: "I did my best, but luck has been against me from the start. A polar bear could not stand such hardships much longer."

A steamer captain towed *America* up the coast to Sydney. They arrived on the thirteenth. The newspaper reporters were waiting for him. He told them he had abandoned the voyage. Age and sickness had finally caught up with him. He sounded beaten . . . "I am going home to Gloucester with my little boat and will never tackle the sea again."

After resting a week in Sydney, he sailed from McDonald's Wharf on the afternoon of the twentieth of July, bound for home by easy stages. A crowd had gathered to cheer him, and a delegation of his friends presented him with a purse. It was a short run across the harbor, and he docked at North Sydney in the evening. The following morning he sailed again.

Taking his time and stopping frequently, he slipped through the narrow entrance of Little Bras d'Or, down St. Andrews Channel, through Barra Strait and across Bras d'Or Lake, to St. Peters, where the tidewater comes in.

I made fast to the schooner *Frank Norton*. As she was bound for Canso, I remained on board. We made the run over in about two hours but met a head tide and wind in the narrows and had to anchor.

Some men passing through the narrows seen my boat. They went into the harbor, where about thirty sail of Lunenberg fishermen was anchored, and told them that I was on board of the coaster, waiting for the tide to turn so that we could get through the narrows. In a short time fifty or sixty dories came out. We gave them a long line, got the anchor, and they towed us into the harbor.

So many people came on board that they nearly sank the coaster. Some of the men asked me to let them take the boat and sail her around the harbor so the people could see her. I did so. They all wanted to see the dory that had lived through so much bad weather.

I went on board of the schooner *Wynot*, where I remained four days. Among the many people that came on board was several operators from the Commercial Cable Company. They asked Captain Wynot, his friends and me out to the Station.

Superintendent F. B. Gerrard took us all through the wonderful place and showed us how they sent and received messages. While he was explaining everything to us, one of the many machines begin to work. He told us to wait to see what news was coming from Ireland. As soon as it stopped, he tore off the strip of paper and read — What cheer, Blackburn; better luck next time! Some of the operators had sent a message to the office in Ireland telling them that Superintendent Gerrard was showing us through the place.

I sailed for Halifax, but as the wind was dead ahead all the way, I called into a good many harbors on the way. While sailing up the coast inside of the islands, a good many boats came out to meet me. They all wanted me to stop a few days with them. But I was too much broken up to do so.

In due course he arrived in Halifax, and he was not there long before Ludwig Eisenbraun also made port. After the failure of his first attempt, the German had sailed again from Boston with a companion. Off Yarmouth he was washed overboard but swam to his boat and was pulled back in by his crewman. They reached Halifax on the twenty-fourth of August, and Eisenbraun and Blackburn met for the first time. He dropped off his mate, took on water and provisions, and four days later headed out into the Atlantic. He put into the Madeiras in two months and reached Gibraltar on the twentieth of November, more than three months out of Boston.

Howard's other rival, Joe Chaves, had been unluckier — or wiser. Accompanied by the fleet of the Harbor View Yacht Club, he had sailed his dory four miles out Boston Harbor, only to turn back with centerboard trouble. Nine days later he started off again, got two hundred and forty miles out to sea, thought better of the whole business, turned around and sailed into Gloucester. Blaming his failure on his boat, he told the reporters vehemently, "I think I'll go down to the wharf and chop it up with an ax."

Howard was in no hurry to get back to Gloucester.

I met an old Gloucester fisherman, Captain John Simmons, who kept a hotel called the French House. A better-hearted man never lived. He asked me if I was agoing to sail the boat home. I told him that I would sell her and go home by rail.

Just then Mr. Miller S. Harvey, an old friend of Captain Simmons, came in. He said — now I will tell you how we can make a hundred dollars apiece. Captain Simmons asked him how it could be done. He said — if Blackburn will stay with us, we will put the boat in the Nova Scotia Exhibition, which opens early in September. Just the thing — said Captain Simmons. Now Blackburn — he said — you stay here with me; you will have a good time.

I did, and after the Fair was over, I sold the boat and came home by rail.

19
Bootlegger

THE CIRCLE WAS COMPLETE. It had started twenty years ago in a dory, and in a dory it ended.

Back home in Gloucester, he talked about the first time he was hove down.

I never gave up hope when on the Banks that terrible night with my dead shipmate in the boat with me, but that I should reach land if I could only get my hands in a position so that they would freeze around the oars.

But when I was cooped up in my little cabin on *America,* unable to open the slide owing to the pressure of the water, I gave up hope and expected that the next wave would carry the boat to the bottom.

So he had lost all hope, just that once . . . and he went back out.

What were those lines from Walter Scott, the ones Captain Collins had used in his little book to catch the horror of Burgeo Bank?

> *No mortal man — save he, who, bred*
> *Between the living and the dead,*
> *Is gifted beyond nature's law —*
> *Had e'er survived to say he saw.*

Strange . . . they seemed to have something to do with so much that had happened since . . . said more about himself than he could. He decided he would publish a picture pamphlet about his experiences and print the lines below his portrait.

He had survived to say he'd seen; had he seen more than any mortal should?

"Do you think you'll go to Heaven when you die?" Fred Daggett asked him idly one day.

"Why not?" he mused. "I've already been through hell."

Six years had been spent, and five voyages, to prove something — perhaps that his survival on Burgeo Bank was no mere trick of fate. Through the irony of his final defeat, did he finally grasp the meaning of his first and greatest victory? Or was there no meaning to any of it, first and last — like a circle that once completed has neither beginning nor end?

The way a rough rock is smoothed over by the ageless action of the sea, he had been sculptured into a monument to himself. To the edge of the sea he returned, and the rest of his days were measured by its coming and going.

Almost imperceptibly he relaxed the disregard which had chiefly marked his attitude toward his wife of nearly twenty years; and Theresa, her husband home again apparently for good, was able to rekindle slowly the natural warmth of her devotion, so long chilled by his neglect.

No small credit for this thaw was due to little Addie Reed, his niece from Boothbay Harbor who had been too homesick on her first trip to Gloucester to see the America's Cup Races. But she grew out of it, and almost every summer after that came down on the ferry from Bar Harbor to visit them in the apartment above the saloon. These annual sojourns of four or five weeks lasted until 1911. All too briefly, they flooded a barren marriage with the joy of childhood. Howard and Theresa looked forward to Addie's arrival for weeks ahead. While she was with them, they concentrated all their frustrated affections on her; she was theirs, on borrowed time.

Her Uncle Howard spoiled Addie extravagantly.

Every morning before going downstairs to open up the saloon he emptied his pockets of the loose change left over from the evening's business. It was a solemn ritual, repeated day after day, summer after summer. As the coins jingled out on the calling card table in the hall, he would instruct the child that this was her spending money for the day and enjoin her not to come home from play with a penny of it left.

Her opulence alone was enough to make Addie the most popular youngster in the neighborhood, but there didn't seem to be enough candy or playmates in the city of Gloucester to spend it on. And so every year, all her efforts and her Uncle Howard's admonitions notwithstanding, she returned to Boothbay Harbor with forty or fifty dollars in bar money.

They had good times, uncle and niece. Sometimes they strolled along the waterfront, and she met the fishermen — the grizzled old Nova Scotians from down home and the jolly, dark-complexioned Portuguese whose talk was so hard to understand — and she noticed how they came up to him wherever he went and how respectfully they treated him.

Sometimes they went sailing in the harbor, and she never forgot one time, out by Norman's Woe Rock, how they sat in the boat — both lost in the fascination of it — watching the shiny black backs of the porpoises as they frolicked around them.

And occasionally on a Sunday, if it was sunny and there was not too much breeze, Aunt Theresa packed a picnic dinner and joined them with a friend or two for an outing on the water.

One day she glimpsed another side of Uncle Howard, and it scared her.

It was late in the afternoon, and she was skipping down Main Street on the way home, when she came to a Chinese laundry. It was a corner of mystery in her life, as indeed such establishments were for most people in those days . . . and a little frightening. But this time curiosity got the better of her and, screwing up her courage, she paused in the open doorway for a quick look inside. The proprietor looked up from his ironing and flashed a smile: Whose little girl was she? Upon learning who her uncle was, he beamed from ear to ear and told her he was honored by her presence because Captain Blackburn was a very brave and kind and great man.

Addie ran home and raced up the stairs to the apartment. Uncle Howard was in the sitting room and asked her what she'd been up to that day. Breathlessly she poured out the story of her visit with the laundryman and what he had said.

Howard jumped out of his chair in a rage and shouted: "Who does that goddam Chinaman think he is, talking to my niece!"

Aunt Theresa rarely got her temper up about anything; her greatest anxiety was that Addie should always behave as she thought Uncle Howard would want her to, and she gave her the strictest orders never to upset him under any circumstances. For some reason of her own she wanted the child to become well founded in the history of Boston, and many were the day-long excursions to the city, Theresa dragging her tired niece along on interminably dull tours of public buildings and historic sites.

If Addie's visits helped to round off the square corners of her aunt's and uncle's domestic life, it remained a strange one all the same. Theresa was as good a housewife as he was a provider, but of companionship each offered the other — or was able to give — precious little.

Theresa doted on her husband. She always drew his bath for him, and while he was splashing in the tub laid his clean and pressed clothes out on their bed. She was an energetic house-keeper and an excellent cook, taking great pains to prepare his food exactly to his taste. Yet a man usually climbed up from the saloon and carried his tray down to him, for they almost never ate together.

Theresa was lonely, perhaps because she was a woman easily offended and not given much to talk. She had few friends, and Howard had many, but they entertained them separately and had practically no common social life. They saw so little of each other during the day, in fact, that they often communicated entirely by written messages. It was a standoffish marriage, yet it worked after its fashion.

The sea was his mistress, after all — his real love more than his wife could ever be. In his opinion, women, salt water and boats didn't mix except very rarely and in very small quantities, a view which he felt was amply borne out, to his regret and amusement, in the summer of 1907.

President Theodore Roosevelt — a corker in Howard's book — was coming down to Provincetown, forty-five miles across Massachusetts Bay on Cape Cod, to lay the cornerstone of the Pilgrim's Monument.

Everyone in Gloucester that could get away left home the day before, so to be at Provincetown when the President arrived. I chartered a boat to take my wife and a few of our lady friends over to see the President. The boat was a good sailer and had a fine cabin.

All went well until we got about half way across the Bay, when the wind breezed up, and the boat, which had a great overhanging bow and stern, begin to throw the spray.

All the ladies went below, and if only they would have remained there we could have anchored in Provincetown early that evening. But in a short time they made a rush for the deck and said — we can't stay down cellar any longer. Then each one selected a place where she would get as much of the spray as she could.

As we did not want to see them get wet, we had to keep off for Hull, where we remained all night. Early the next morning we sailed for Provincetown and arrived there just as the President was leaving. We remained in port until the next morning, then sailed for home.

As soon as we got out from under the lee of Race Point, the spray begin to fly, and as the ladies would not go down cellar, we had to keep off for Plymouth.

As soon as we anchored, they all went ashore to see Plymouth Rock. The gentleman in charge of the Rock told them that if they stood on the Rock and wished for anything, they would be sure to get it. So each one mounted that famous old boulder and wished for everything but a fair wind.

We remained in Plymouth two days, then sailed for home with a strong fair wind. By the time we got abreast of Norman's Woe Rock it was blowing half a gale, and the sea was running wild.

Just as we reached the end of the Breakwater, a nice little sea caught the boat under that overhanging stern and lifted it high in the air. A two hundred and fifty pound lady setting on the weather side lost her balance and nearly turned a somersault in the cockpit. By the time we got her into a place of safety, we saw another large wave doing its best to overtake us. But before it could do so, the boat shot around the end of the Breakwater into smooth water, and the wave dashed itself into foam against that wall of Cape Ann granite.

The wet years paraded by, and the saloon prospered. And although Howard kept up his tireless charities — dispatching jars of pennies to the ladies at the hospital and Christmas dinners and coal by the ton and clothes by the storeful to the poor — he was always able to afford a sailboat and almost always had one.

It was mighty pleasant and sort of a comfort to have a little yacht of one style or another moored out there behind Five Pound Island in the inner harbor, a stone's throw from the saloon, and he owned a succession of them, starting with an eighteen-foot sloop he had someone build for him during the spring following his last voyage.

In December of 1909 (it happened to have been a dry year for the saloons, happily rare of late) a report circulated around Gloucester that Captain Blackburn was planning to build a new boat. This inspired the usual speculation, and although his fifty-first birthday was just around the corner, inevitably it was said that he was going to sail her across. The reporter from the *Gloucester Times* dropped around and inquired if there was anything to the story.

Not a thing. I am going to have a boat, a new one, a nice little twenty-six foot cruising craft, but I have not decided upon her other dimensions as yet.

You see, it is this way. I like the sea. I like a boat. And I have planned to cruise along the coast the coming summer in my new boat and stop at Bar Harbor and other summer resorts and sell sea shells.

You would be surprised to see the way the summer people and especially the western people crowded in here last summer buying shells. Of course this place was fitted and used for a bar room, and still retains that look, and for that reason a good many people pass it by. But for all that, I have seen the place in back of the bar crowded with nice ladies seeking shells, day after day last summer.

No, there is nothing doing in the ocean-crossing business this time. But when I get everything ready about the boat I will let you know, and when she is in the water you must come out with me for a sail.

In the spring Howard went over to Bishop's yard (probably Hugh, who had built *Great Western*), and soon the new boat was taking shape. She had grown in his mind's eye and was thirty feet in length overall, twenty-four on the waterline, with a nine-foot beam and a draft of five — about as long as *Great Western* but a trifle wider and deeper. Otherwise, she had the unmistakable mark of her heritage . . . just in case he should decide to take her across.

Christopher Columbus, as he christened this handsome female, had a short bowsprit and departed from tradition by carrying only one jib. Her flush deck was bordered all around by a six-inch rail. He installed a storage hold amidships, another departure from the earlier boats, which was reached through a hatch and which foreshortened the cabin quite considerably. Her sawed frame skeleton was heavily clad with yellow pine planking an inch and a quarter thick in unbroken lengths of lumber from stem to stern, without a single butt.

For a decade he moored *Chris* at his back door where he could keep an eye on her — content, apparently, to head her out the harbor for a day of sailing when he had a mind to.

The saloon was closed down for three of the next five years, up through the outbreak of the first World War, a dismal portent

When Gordon Prince bought *Christopher Columbus* in 1921, he covered Blackburn's midships hatch (left) with a cabin trunk but for a while kept the original rig (below).

Chris shows wholesome lines (right) on Dion's ways at Salem in June, 1921. (All photos, Gordon C. Prince.)

of the '20's. In 1911 Gloucester was dry again; in 1913 Howard turned the business over to a friend whose application for a license, for reasons now unknown, was rejected; the following year he himself applied and was turned down for the first time in his career, again for reasons undisclosed. But in 1915 whatever difficulty had arisen had been taken care of, and he was back at the old stand.

Scarcely a year had passed, however, when he dropped into one of those occupational pitfalls which were the dread of saloon-keepers. In the spring of 1916 an irate woman sued him for five thousand dollars.

It seems that this lady's husband and a companion had been splicing the main brace with carefree regularity in a Gloucester bar one balmy April evening, and upon emerging they encountered a policeman who remonstrated with them. A sidewalk debate ensued, during the course of which the officer attempted to convince the companion that he should accompany him to the station to have a talk with the sergeant. Whereupon the husband of the lady in question offered to referee the discussion with a knife, which he directed at the law. The policeman prevailed, however. The man was taken to jail, and then to court, where he was sentenced to an extended term in prison. His wife, convinced that he had taken leave of his wits in Blackburn's saloon, sued Howard on the contention that he was ultimately responsible for her husband's misbehavior, as a consequence of which he languished behind bars and she at home, deprived of his support.

The suit dragged along for three years without coming to trial because of one technicality or another. Finally, a month after Congress passed the Volstead Act over President Wilson's veto, it was dropped altogether; possibly the weary plaintiff concluded that Captain Blackburn was about to receive his just deserts according to the will of the people.

If so, she was right, but there was some confusion as to just what the people wanted.

The arid winds of temperance had been blowing up from the Bible Belt for a generation, and as early as 1914 the Southern Democrats had shoved a prohibition amendment through the House of Representatives. In July of 1919 the Wartime Prohibition Act, passed in the patriotism of conflict and out of the necessity for conserving alcohol and grain for gunpowder and food, had taken effect. For the Anti-Saloon League and the drys everywhere, it was the golden opportunity to put the barrooms, those corrupters of the workingman, enemies of industry and spoilers of the home, out of business forever.

By January of 1920 the rolling snowball had reached huge dimensions and was squashing everything in its path. John Barleycorn was on the run, and when, on the sixteenth, the last of the required number of states ratified the Eighteenth Amendment, a surprised nation woke up to the fact that in its fervor to close down the saloons it had thrown the baby out with the bathwater. It was now a constitutional offense to manufacture, sell, transport, import or export any beverage containing more than one in two hundred parts of alcohol. The thought was sobering, but too late.

At about this time his doctor advised Howard in forceful terms that for the sake of his heart he should forswear liquor for the rest of his life. Being a man of unswerving purpose once he made up his mind to something, and with the law of the land giving force to his resolve, he did.

Although the inevitable was almost upon them, the citizens of Gloucester, in a last futile gesture of legal defiance, marched to the polls a month before Prohibition and voted overwhelmingly wet.

Having thus expressed themselves on a matter of deep principle, a small but increasing contingent of the voters commenced to search for other means by which they might be enabled to carry on their opposition to what they considered Federal intrusion in home rule. It was not long before Gloucester achieved a reputation as one of the most energetic and efficient ports of nocturnal entry for bottled liquids containing something more than one in two hundred parts of alcohol on the east coast of the United States.

At first it was a mere freshet, pumped from an obscure spring by occasional independent dissidents who had discovered that their efforts were in the nature of easing a piece of candy from the relaxed fingers of a sleeping child. The Treasury Department was totally unprepared for the assignment of enforcing the popular will against itself; the police of Gloucester were vastly outnumbered and generally unenthusiastic about this phase of their work; and Cape Ann was ideally situated for such clandestine endeavors, with its numerous remote coves, inlets and salt marshes, cluttered harbors and infinitely anonymous fleets of boats engaged in the ebb and flow of a daily variety of presumably legitimate occupations.

More springs appeared, and more freshets, and their confluence was a mighty river which flowed from the sea into the land. Its source became known as Rum Row, a bold fleet anchored on the international edge of the three-mile limit with a liquid cargo that magically found its way into the holds of swarms of small craft which scuttled back and forth from the coast like excited ants around an open jam pot.

These were trying times for Marshal Daniel H. Casey.

On the twenty-third of July in the year 1921, stung by intimations that he had been less than energetic in his efforts to restrain the activity which had become a way of life around Glouceser, he ordered raids against five suspected speakeasies.

In the back room at Blackburn's his men found a pitcher containing one cup of whiskey, which they seized. Scarcely pleased with this discovery, they apologetically arrested the proprietor, who nailed them scornfully to the wall with his piercing stare. The next day Judge Sumner D. York regretfully found him guilty of liquor keeping and fined him fifty dollars, which he paid on the spot.

There was strong feeling in the city, especially among the fishermen, that Marshal Casey had gone too far this time. Captain Blackburn was no rumrunner or bootlegger, just a man whose only means of making a living for the past thirty years had been taken away by a law that everyone was ignoring. While big-time operators were doing as they pleased under the noses of the cops, Blackburn was merely selling a little drink now and then to a few cronies, quiet as you please and not bothering anybody.

But Gloucester was booming, and the case was soon forgotten. The fishing industry had been rejuvenated overnight, and largely at night. Tucked beneath many a hold full of fish was a tidy fortune in booze, and many a vessel was fitted with a false bottom for the conveyance of a cargo more precious than mackerel or cod. For every speeding lobster boat that was stopped by a shot from the Coast Guard across its bow, and for every schooner that was nabbed off Thatcher's with the goods, two more took its place; and for every gallon of booze that was confiscated, a thousand slipped through to a thirsty America.

There is no evidence that Howard had anything to do with the rumrunners except as a minor customer. But whenever a fast little smuggler slipped away in a hail of police bullets and disappeared down the Annisquam River, he must have chuckled.

In May of 1923 he received from the City Council a license to sell soft drinks. This permitted him to dispense "near beer," a nonintoxicating beverage containing less than one half of one per cent of alcohol and hence legal. Since the laws of nature rule against the fermentation of beer with such a low alcoholic content, brewers made real beer under government supervision and then extracted enough alcohol to render it legal.

Anyone with a handy supply of alcohol and a healthy contempt for Prohibition could "needle" near beer and restore what Uncle Sam had taken away.

Ten months passed.

It was a quiet Saturday afternoon, the first of March, 1924. A large touring car droned down the road from Boston, bumped across the drawbridge over 'Squam River and wound along the waterfront to Main Street. It pulled up in front of number two-eighty-nine, Howard Blackburn's soft drink parlor.

Two Federal Prohibition agents got out, crossed the sidewalk and entered the front door, pausing to glance through the big window at the paintings of the proprietor in the dory on gale-swept Burgeo Bank and the photographs of the boats he had sailed alone across the Atlantic Ocean.

Behind the long mahogany bar stood a giant of a man who looked about sixty-five years old. His great frame, somewhat angular because of his years, was as erect as a mast. Although he was in shirtsleeves and galluses, he was carefully dressed in rather old-fashioned clothes. His neck, still thick and muscular, had a dewlap where he had lost flesh and was banded by a starched wing collar around which was knotted a neat silk four-in-hand.

His head . . . it was a sculpture chiseled by an Olympian hand, bony, with craggy jaw and massive brow. The face of the man was an unfathomable mask. It seemed unaccountably ruddy and weathered for one who lived ashore. His thick mustache drooped just a trifle over the corners of his mouth and then took an upturn and dwindled away past his cheeks, like the bow wave of a ship. His snow-white hair was closely cut at the sides and neatly parted on the left.

Inside the thumb stub of one maimed hand was stuck a half-smoked cigar. His sea-blue eyes fixed them with a steady, quizzical stare.

One of the agents asked him if he was Captain Howard Blackburn. He said he was. The agent pulled a paper from his pocket and told him it was a warrant for his arrest and that they wished to search the premises.

Howard stood calmly by as they entered the rear room and started tapping and examining the walls. In a few minutes they found what they were looking for. It was a cleverly concealed opening. They removed the section and found a hidden tank, from which they drained off approximately twelve gallons of liquor.

The agents informed him that he would shortly receive a summons to appear in the Federal District Court on charges of violating the National Prohibition Act. Then they departed.

The case of the United States of America *versus* Howard Blackburn opened before Federal Judge James M. Morton, Jr., in Boston a month later, on April 3. The defendant was gaunt with strain. He was charged on two counts: that on the first of March he possessed twelve gallons of liquor, more or less; and that on the twenty-fifth of February he had sold one pint of liquor, more or less.

There is no record of the testimony at the trial. But it was reported that the evidence for the defendant's arrest was obtained by a third Federal agent who had frequented his place for several weeks under the guise of a retired sea captain.

He pleaded guilty and was fined fifty dollars. Under the circumstances, his sentence was extremely light; it was said later that Judge Morton persuaded him to swear on oath that he would never again engage in bootlegging. So far as the record shows, he never did; he was a man of his word.

The case was closed, but his trial had just begun.

Almost immediately Howard applied to the City Council for renewal of his soft drink license. There were three others, two of them old saloonkeepers like himself.

On April 30 the Council convened for its regular weekly meeting in the   mid-victorian brick   City Hall overlooking the harbor. Presiding as usual was Mayor William J. MacInnis, a handsome and popular lawyer of about forty and a strong temperance man.

When the time came to consider the soft drink license applications, the mayor read aloud a communication from Marshal John Parker, his equally handsome but not so popular chief of police, who for sixteen months had been going after the bootleggers hammer and tongs.

He was convinced, Parker wrote, that all four of the applicants, three of whom (including Blackburn) ran near beer saloons, were using their soft drink licenses as blinds for bootlegging. He advised the Council to turn them down.

Here was a hot potato. The Council decided to defer action until the next meeting.

The following week Mayor MacInnis introduced an order that no soft drink licenses would be granted near-beer saloons. It was opposed by Aldermen Henry Parsons and Harry Pew, but they were overridden by a majority of three to two, and the mayor ruled out all four applicants.

It so happened that Henry Parsons was the son of old John Parsons, the bewhiskered, rum-fighting mayor who had given Blackburn such a hard time with his Parsons' Purge nearly forty years earlier. Henry had inherited his father's political knack, if not his crusading spirit. He was a colorful, gangling, horse-faced jokester who looked and talked like a hayseed but was as smart as a fox. Sixteen years before, he too had been Mayor of Gloucester; he had his doleful eye on the job again, and he could spot a good political issue a mile away.

Billy MacInnis knew that Henry was going to make trouble over the license question at the Council meeting in two weeks, and that it was all going to revolve around the figure of Captain Blackburn. So he wrote a little speech and kept it in his pocket.

The Council chamber was filling rapidly with spectators the evening of May 21 as the aldermen concluded their regular business.

Henry Parsons brought up the matter of the soft drink licenses for reconsideration.

There were no such places of resort as near-beer saloons in

Gloucester, he said; he and Alderman George Nelson had visited the shops of all four of the applicants and found only counters, like all stores — no bars.

At this, the mayor arose and read another letter from Marshal Parker reiterating his position, referring to Howard's recent conviction and continuing:

I believe that if any man in our city has a right to sell liquor that man is Mr. Blackburn, but no man has that right and no man can legally give it to him . . . As City Marshal, I shall always do my best to enforce all laws . . . Friend or foe, high or low, will be dealt with alike and will surely be prosecuted if the evidence can be had to do so.

What the department needs most is the cooperation of our citizens. Rum-running in boats, taxis, etc., has added burdens on the department, and with no additional officers to cope with the situation and the lack of help from our citizens who are often in a position to do so, greatly handicaps the department in liquor law enforcement. No chief of police or police force can fully carry out the provisions of laws without the cooperation of the people.

By now the chamber was packed with spectators, and the atmosphere was getting tense.

Mayor MacInnis took his statement out of his pocket and started to read. After noting pointedly that he was not a candidate for re-election in the fall, and that as far as he was concerned there had been about enough lip service to law enforcement, he went on:

When Howard Blackburn first came to Gloucester, it was difficult for newcomers to get a chance on a fishing vessel. "He met my father, Captain Murdock MacInnis, who helped him to ship, and they went on the same vessel. Mr. Blackburn told me this story over a year ago. I have always been fond of Mr. Blackburn, and upon hearing this story from him, I have been more so than ever."

The mayor described his bravery and suffering on Burgeo

Bank, his maimed hands and his first lone voyage to England . . .

"The world gazed on this venture with mingled admiration and respect for a man who carried on despite physical disabilities and who was bound to conquer the very ocean on which he had years before suffered such privations.

". . . During all these years he has been a quiet but effective dispenser of charity. No needy and deserving person called on him in vain. In the giving of charity he always avoided notoriety. It can be said of him that he observed the Bible injunction not to let his right hand know what his left hand was doing. If any person deserves good of the city of Gloucester, the people of Gloucester and the Municipal Council, it is Howard Blackburn.

"On the other hand, here is the record and the recommendations of the City Marshal. The members of the Municipal Council are not free agents. Every member has taken an oath to uphold the law.

". . . I state this whole matter plainly, although I am very loath to do so on an occasion of this kind . . . My personal preference would be that this particular case did not come before me for a decision, but since it is before me, I wish to have all angles of the matter clearly understood from the standpoint of principle and duty. This is a government of laws and not men. The law is no respecter of persons. Public officials should not set up themselves, nor their opinions, nor their political present or future, to take the place of law.

"What other recommendation could Marshal Parker make in these cases? We know he is right. I reiterate my intention to support Marshal Parker and will vote against granting any of the licenses which the City Marshal disapproves."

The mayor sat down, and the crowded chamber was hushed as Henry Parsons rose to his feet.

The alderman looked around him and said that of course he had no written speech. He knew that Captain Blackburn had a court record, and he was also aware that the marshal had admitted that in the past he had approved the granting of soft drink licenses to men he suspected of bootlegging. Then he came out with it, with what everyone had been waiting for:

"You all know Howard Blackburn. Why can't we give Mr. Blackburn a chance and stretch one little point?"

A rustle moved through the spectators, and the chamber buzzed with whispering.

"That's just it," shot back Billy MacInnis. "You've stretched a good many points!"

"So have you," drawled Henry, putting on a comical expression. "But I haven't got quite as much oil as you."

There was a burst of laughter from the spectators.

"All I want is a square deal," he continued. Then, drawing himself up and looking around him again — "I'm as temperate as any man in Gloucester."

"That's the lip service," the mayor broke in.

"You know where I stand," glowered the alderman.

"Yes," snapped the mayor. "You stand on both sides!"

This exchange concluded in another outbreak of laughter, and Alderman Nelson got up. He was the key man who had sided with MacInnis two weeks ago. Had Henry been able to bring him around?

He and Alderman Parsons had visited Captain Blackburn's place a few days ago, he said, and they found that all of the saloon equipment had been cleaned out except the counter, which was necessary in any business. Now, since Captain Blackburn had taken an oath never to sell liquor again, the Council, in his opinion, should give him a try.

Henry had brought him around.

Alderman Pew got to his feet. The citizens of Gloucester would approve, he believed, if the aldermen just shut their eyes and granted the licenses.

At this, the mayor was unable to restrain himself. Harry Pew was probably the most honest alderman he ever knew, and "when

Mr. Pew said let's shut our eyes, that well-known phrase comes into use — he said a mouthful."

Pew went on to read from a magazine article about Blackburn and concluded by asserting that there was nothing wrong with approving the licenses and that the Council would not be breaking much of the law by voting to give him one.

With that, the debate ended, and the licenses were granted by rollcall votes of three to two.

The following Sunday the Reverend Albert A. Madsen, minister of Trinity Congregational Church, delivered a sermon on the subject of the Council's action. He said he could not understand why a man who had simply made a courageous fight for his own life should be given any special privileges when the men of the Grand Army of the Republic, the veterans of the World War and so many who had made sacrifices and given their lives, not only for themselves but for others, were not asking for special treatment.

He then read Howard's criminal record to his parishioners.

This was just what Henry Parsons was waiting for. He announced he had decided to run for mayor in the fall and leaped back into the fray as Blackburn's champion. In a flutter of letters to the newspaper, he let the minister have both barrels: he had only suggested that one little point be stretched in view of the mayor's eulogy to Blackburn and the captain's oath to the judge . . . "Now that's the story, and if I have committed a crime I am willing that St. Peter light the match that will burn me up with hell fire and brimstone, for I make no excuses, no apologies, and will follow the same line though the earth crumbles, the sea roars, and I become a relic of the past, despised and forgotten."

Henry was elected, and one of his first acts as mayor was to fire Marshal Parker. The police chief had laid himself wide open for it: a few days earlier, while testifying in court, he had been forced to admit that for more than a year he had been getting the goods on bootleggers disguised as a girl — and a flapper, at that.

The gales of controversy had swirled around Howard Blackburn that spring of 1924. When the skies cleared again, he was an old man.

20
Indian Summer

CAPTAIN BLACKBURN had taken a liking to Jimmy Clancy next door, and it was a feather in the kid's cap to be allowed to run errands down to the grocery store for the old gent. When the Captain invited him up to his sitting room to listen to the news of Lindy's flight across the Atlantic, he didn't have to be asked twice.

Jimmy was thrilled that May day in 1927 to sit with the man who had crossed the ocean all by himself in a little boat and hear the voice through the radio static tell how the aviator had just accomplished the same feat in an airplane.

Sitting there in his easy chair, his tired old legs propped on a stool, smoke curling up from the cigar stuck behind the butt of his thumb, listening so intently — did he recall his prediction for the new century, a few months before he sailed for Portugal so long ago, that in a hundred years men would be spanning the Atlantic in flying machines — and chuckle to himself? That was the year before Charles A. Lindbergh was born.

Had time passed him by, after all — faster even than his imagination could look ahead?

Or was time the sea, and he the sailor still?

Among those who discerned some enduring quality in the old man was a wealthy yachtsman and summer resident of Gloucester named Henry A. Wise Wood, who knocked on his door one summer day of 1928. He brought with him Miss Margaret

Fitzhugh Browne, a rising young artist, and told Captain Blackburn he had commissioned her to paint his portrait, provided he was willing to sit for her.

Howard was glad to oblige and for a few weeks during the early autumn walked down to his favorite waterfront spot on the wharf of the Independent Fisheries Company every sunny day and posed patiently, seated on the gunwale of a hauled-out dory. His fishermen cronies would pause to watch the progress of the painting by the hour, exchanging jokes with the subject and helping to steady the artist's easel — already ballasted with a bar of pig iron — when a puff of wind tried to blow it over.

At last the portrait was done, and all pronounced themselves satisfied; Miss Browne had caught the massive tenacity, the weathered ruddiness of the rocklike features, the hint of humor and the blue squint of the fathomless eyes.

The paint was hardly dry before Howard began to suspect that something more than the desire of an admirer to have his picture was afoot. He was informed that on November 8 the Governing Board of the Cruising Club of America had unanimously elected him an honorary life member. Furthermore, the club would cruise to Gloucester next summer to pay him its respects.

He was quite overwhelmed by this news. The Cruising Club was the aristocracy of American blue water yachtsmen. He was one of only eight men to have been thus honored in its history, including but two others this year — the great Rhode Island yacht designer and builder, Nathanael Herreshoff, the Wizard of Bristol, and Ralph Munroe, a pioneer cruising man of the Florida coast.

Only then did he learn that Wise Wood had commissioned the portrait for the club; when the members sailed to Gloucester to pay him tribute, it would be presented in solemn ceremony to the Master Mariners' Association, the select society of veteran fishing skippers which had admitted him to honorary membership a quarter of a century before.

This was the beginning of the Indian summer of his life. An officer of the CCA has recalled:

"One would almost think the man was superhuman. I remember him at Cruising Club dinners in Boston. A big man, taciturn, with granite features, he obviously had a warm affection and respect for the older members. It was an honor to the club that he belonged . . ."

Although Howard was seventy the next February, his election to the club and the opportunity it gave him to swap yarns with men who were even older than he and still active at the helms of their boats rolled back the years and filled him with excitement. If his peers could still steer out to sea at three score and ten, then so could he — and show them a trick or two in the bargain.

He traveled down to Boothbay Harbor and paid a visit to his brother-in-law George Reed, the ship carpenter. Could George come up to the Essex shipyards and build him a boat? Reed was all for it, but when he arrived in Essex and found he would have to join the union to work there, his Down East dander rose up and he turned on his heel and went home.

But Howard would have a boat, and he clumped down to see Marian Cooney of the United Sail Loft on the harbor not far from home. Cooney was a boatbuilder as well as a sailmaker and was glad to have the job. In late April of 1929 the keel was laid.

Howard delighted in walking down to the yard to watch the progress, and he always had a pocketful of fine cigars for the workmen. Finally the great day of the launching arrived. It was around the Fourth of July, and a friendly gang of fishermen crowded the wharves and the decks of schooners at their berths.

She was a pretty little black sloop, about thirty feet long, with a nearly straight stem and stubby bowsprit, beamy and full in the stern. A good, deep sea boat she was, as usual, and similar in most respects to her illustrious predecessors — with one exception: her mast was hollow. A stick built like a pipe was something new in those days. Gordon Prince, a Cruising Club member who had bought *Christopher Columbus* from him in 1921, asked Captain Blackburn later how he liked it. Howard replied:

"Well now, I don't know. I've never been shipmates with a hollow mast before."

Wearing his cap against the sun and puffing proudly on his cigar, he went down to the wharf with Addie Forbes, another schoolteacher daughter of his sister Martha. The boat was strung with a colorful panoply of flags and pennants.

The order was given, and the workmen knocked out the wedges. The fishermen cheered, and as the stout sloop slid past her, Addie whacked it on the bow with a bottle of champagne and cried: "I christen thee *Cruising Club!*"

Two weeks later, when the yachts of the Cruising Club of America sailed in by Eastern Point and dropped their hooks in the quiet water of the inner harbor, imagine the surprise of those on board to discover in their midst, swinging at her mooring in gallant welcome from the man they came to honor, the little sloop *Cruising Club!*

The fine fleet of lovely ladies — schooners, sloops, ketches, cutters and yawls — had stood up the New England coast from Block Island, across Buzzards Bay, through the Cape Cod Canal and over to Gloucester for their two-day rendezvous on July 19 and 20. The yachting writers were there, and the photographers, and at a fine gathering the portrait of Captain Blackburn was unveiled and presented to the Master Mariners' Association by Commodore Alexander Moffat of the Boston Chapter of the Cruising Club.

Commodore Edward Crabbe of the New York Yacht Club presided and said that no living man more than Howard Blackburn represented the high traits of heroism and courage that characterize those who follow the sea.

And then Howard was introduced. After the applause and cheers and whistles and table-thumping had ceased, he allowed as how he'd rather cross the ocean again than try to make a

Gloucester Master Mariners' Association

Portrait, sitter and artist.

Cape Ann Historical Association

speech; he thanked the Cruising Club from the bottom of his heart for the honor, complimented the artist on the portrait and sat down.

Later the Master Mariners were invited aboard the yachts for refreshments, and Commodore Crabbe was host to Captain Blackburn on his schooner *Windjammer;* and when the guests had returned ashore, the fleet hauled anchor, spread its canvas and sailed away.

Howard was a familiar figure around the harbor during the rest of the summer at the wheel of *Cruising Club,* and in September he joined the yachts that sailed out beyond the breakwater to watch the last of the great Gloucester schooners race.

The famous Fishermen's Races, dating back to 1892, had been revived in 1920 with the first of the international matches between the best of the boats in Gloucester and Lunenberg, Nova Scotia. Sail was fighting a losing battle against the inroads of steam and diesel, and the rivalry of these two old fishing ports grew hot and often bitter after the launching in 1921 of the apparently unbeatable *Bluenose* of Lunenberg. There was no international match that fall of 1929. In company with niece Addie Forbes, Howard was persuaded to watch *Progress* beat her local rivals from the cabin of the Goodyear airship *Mayflower;* it was his first and last voyage aloft, and he had a grand time looking down from the belly of the blimp on Cape Ann and the scudding sails offshore.

These were the days when he enjoyed the full measure of his fame. The world came to his door.

A month or so after the races he was visited by Sir Wilfred Grenfell, the English medical missionary whose work along the coasts of Labrador and Newfoundland was known throughout the world. The Grenfell Mission's supply schooner was hauled out for repairs at Rocky Neck at the time, and Captain Kenneth Iverson, who already knew Howard, brought Sir Wilfred over to meet him. They talked for a long while. Howard greatly ad-

Champagne in hand, Addie Forbes poses with her Uncle Howard before christ-
ening *Cruising Club* at the United Sail Loft wharf on June 26, 1929. Below,
the launch. (Photos, Annie Forbes.)

Cruising Club feels the master's touch as Howard Blackburn, at seventy, takes her for a quiet round of Gloucester Harbor with a couple of cronies in the summer of 1929. (Adolph Kupsinel photos, courtesy Gloucester Camera & Photo.)

Back at the wharf. (Kupsinel photos.)

mired the man who had done so much for the Newfies, the special objects of his gratitude, and his famous visitor inscribed for him one of his books — "from a friend whose whole heart goes out to men like him who go down to the sea in ships."

There were others.

Secretary of the Navy Charles Francis Adams, avid yachtsman and winning skipper of the America's Cup Races in 1920, sought his friendship and came under the spell of his personality. So did Commander Donald B. MacMillan and Captain Bob Bartlett, the renowned Arctic explorers. John Hays Hammond, the eminent mining engineer and financier who summered in Gloucester, spent many hours with him and wrote that he was "one of the most undaunted sailors America has ever known." And Sir Thomas Lipton, whose dogged sportsmanship in trying to recapture for England the America's Cup with his succession of *Shamrocks* had endeared him to the land of his rivals, he too came to visit, for he had heard of the great sailor down in Gloucester.

A very special friend, however, was neither a yachtsman nor an adventurer, but a writer of sea stories. James Brendan Connolly more than any other man kept alive the story of Howard Blackburn and told it to the world long after the memories of others had faded.

In his youth Jim Connolly had been an Olympic track champion, but his great love was the sea, particularly the sea that was sailed and fished by the men of Gloucester. During his long career he wrote hundreds of short stories and novels full of action and humor and the salty talk of the Gloucestermen he loved, and through them all was the smell of the fish and the feel of the ocean. A tall, lean man of dynamic energy, he spent many summers in Gloucester, and the one he most admired and always visited was Howard Blackburn.

It was a warm friendship, and Connolly couldn't resist repeating in one of his books a conversation he had with Howard on a September day in 1924.

Alain Gerbault, a Frenchman, had just arrived in New York after single-handing a forty-footer across from Gibraltar, and Jim was reading the newspaper account to Howard. The old sailor broke in: "How long was he comin', did you say?"

"A hundred days."

"A hundred days!"

"A hundred days."

"A hundred days? What d' y' s'pose kept him?"

In March of 1930 the last schooner ever to be built for the Gloucester fishing fleet slid down the ways at Essex. The *Gertrude L. Thebaud* was a lovely, long, sleek vessel with mighty masts and an enormous spread of sail, and Howard had followed her planning and construction with intense interest. He knew her principal owner, yachtsman Louis Thebaud, and Captain Ben Pine, who would be her skipper. It was common knowledge that when she wasn't off to the banks on a fishing trip, the two would be scheming how to take the Fishermen's Cup away from Captain Angus Walters, the stubborn and crafty master of the *Bluenose*.

Summer came and went, and on the sixth of October *Bluenose* sailed haughtily into Gloucester. The first match was scheduled in three days. Although the Cup was not at stake, the harbor was a chaos of boats moving out beyond Eastern Point to see the race.

Among them was *Cruising Club*. Howard had a party of friends aboard and was at the helm. But he was not watching his course; in fact he was bearing down on a Coast Guard patrol boat. Chief Boatswain's Mate Emerson Cudios tried to move his craft out of the sloop's way. He shot forward, backed up, shouted a warning — but it was too late. With a splintering crash, *Cruising Club* rammed the Coast Guard, and when she fell away, her broken bowsprit dangled from the forestay and her jib drooped like a forlorn piece of laundry.

Howard was abashed and apologetic; yes, he should have been looking where he was going. Fortunately the damage was confined to the bowsprit, and he continued on out of the harbor under mainsail to watch *Thebaud* beat *Bluenose*, to his utmost satisfaction.

For the rest of the series he was the guest of the Coast Guard aboard one of its boats. The second match was started and called off several times and was finally won by the Gloucester schooner. Although she raced *Bluenose* twice again, in 1931 and 1938, she was never able to take the Cup away.

As for *Cruising Club*, she was fitted with a fine new bowsprit, compliments of the Coast Guard.

Right about this time Howard let a few friends in on a secret: next summer, by thunder, he was going to make another voyage; he was hard at work on his plans to sail *Cruising Club* across to the Mediterranean — alone, naturally.

There was all hell to pay. What, Theresa demanded to know, was a man of almost seventy-two thinking of, to even talk of such a thing? Finally, after nearly forty-five years of marriage, she put her foot down: if he was determined to be such an old fool, then she would go along too, because he needed someone to take care of him. His nieces and his friends remonstrated with him, but it was no use. He was oblivious to all and kept right on happily preparing for his next voyage.

In desperation the hand-wringers turned to the doctor for help, and that wise man had a talk with his patient. Go if you must, he told him, but remember your heart and your age; you'll have to take someone along to manage the boat just in case you should happen, by some outside chance, to become ill; otherwise, stay at home — doctor's orders.

Faced with this ultimatum, he capitulated. If he couldn't sail single-handed, as he always had, then he wouldn't sail at all. Sadly he abandoned the dream and sold his beloved *Cruising Club*.

That winter Theresa sickened. She was not ill for long, mercifully, and on April 29, 1931, at the age of sixty-eight, she died.

LONE VOYAGER

Deeply affected by her death, Howard buried her in the Catholic cemetery and returned to his lonesome home.

The Indian summer was over.

Suddenly he was overwhelmed by his age and by the ancient injuries to his tough old body. He engaged a housekeeper, and Annie Forbes, a nurse in Boston and the third of his Forbes nieces, came up more frequently and for longer visits to help him get about. He even talked of selling his property and moving into a fishermen's rest home, but his lawyer dissuaded him.

His legs bothered him increasingly, and the doctor told him to rest with his feet raised higher than his head. So he had a special frame built for the purpose. Someone suggested that his arthritis would mend if his teeth were out; there was nothing wrong with them, but he trudged off to a dentist and had them pulled, and of course it did no good.

Yet for more than forty years he had stubbornly refused to be operated on for the old double hernia he had suffered trying to lift Tom Welch's body onto the landing at Little River. When the intestine popped out again, as it did increasingly in his old age in spite of the truss he wore, he always worked it back by himself.

Not long after Theresa's death he went down to Beverly and — though his friends advised him against it — had his left knee operated on in the hope that it would relieve the pain. Instead, the joint stiffened like a board. He came home and was confined to quarters, so crippled that he had to crawl up the stairs to bed from his sitting room, dragging the stiff leg behind him.

The doctor advised him to walk as much as he could; perhaps it would restore some life to the knee. And so he summoned a carpenter and supervised the installation of a wooden railing for support, around three walls of the bedroom and across the foot of the bed. He was very proud of the job.

One day the old legs gave out, and he collapsed on the floor. Nan Forbes tried to help him up, but he was too heavy.

"Go to the window and call a policeman — they all know me,"

he ordered. One was passing on the sidewalk below, and she called to him. The officer rushed up the stairs two at a time and got Captain Blackburn to his feet in a jiffy. They all had a good laugh over it.

The weeks and the months dragged on. The country was sliding into the depths of the Depression. Three thousand unemployed walked the streets of Gloucester. Some of them were old friends and came to see him; some were not and came because they knew he had never turned anyone away. His front door remained unlocked, and he kept a hundred dollars in a table drawer for visitors who looked as if they needed the cash more than he did.

In the bitter winter of 1932 — it was January — he gave a hundred dollars to the Fishermen's Institute and told the chaplain to buy two hundred and fifty meal tickets for the men. And then he proposed that an unemployment relief fund be raised by asking those who had jobs to give a fraction of their wages for the benefit of those who didn't. The idea caught the public imagination and grew into a city-wide project.

How much had the old man given away over the years? Some said fifty thousand dollars. No one knew.

Through the spring and the summer he was incarcerated in his apartment over the old saloon from which the clink of the beer glasses and the hum of the sturdy voices and the laughter had been gone for ten years now. The boredom and inactivity were relieved by an occasional visitor and the attentions of Nan Forbes, who came down from Boston as often as she could.

Indomitably he clung to the hope that his health would improve and that once again he would be able to put on his cap and coat, descend the stairs and walk down to the wharves and the sea.

But late in October he suffered a paralytic stroke. It confined him to bed and affected his speech. Nan came to stay with him.

It was damn annoying. He couldn't seem to make the words come out as he meant them to. He would say no when he intended yes. And once when he wanted Nan to open the curtains so he could see the world outside, he muttered: "Reef the main-sail."

Shortly after three o'clock on the afternoon of Friday, November 4, 1932, Howard Blackburn gasped and died. He was seventy-three years old.

Every flag in Gloucester was flown at half-mast — the flags on the Customs House and the city buildings and the stores, and from the balconies of the houses and all along the wharves and on the vessels.

The funeral procession formed in the street outside the rooms of the Master Mariners' Association at half-past one on Sunday afternoon. The men moved into line — the old schooner captains and the fishermen, two hundred and fifty of them — and the Coast Guardsmen, forty of them. And then the pallbearers, six old friends, all sea captains. And the honorary pallbearers — Charles Francis Adams, Secretary of the Navy of the United States, Congressman A. Piatt Andrew and Jim Connolly, Grenfell and MacMillan, Bartlett and Hammond and Wise Wood and Thebaud, and Leonard Craske, the sculptor, and Tom Carroll and Tom Gorton, the powers of the fishing fleet.

To the slow dirge of muffled drums the procession marched down Main Street, past the silent crowds that filled the sidewalks. It halted before the black-draped brick building with the man's name over the glass front that had once been a saloon.

The pallbearers broke their ranks and walked inside. They emerged with the casket. The two cornetists played "Rock of Ages" as the men lifted the coffin gently into the hearse.

The cortege moved back up Main Street, stepping slowly, only the shuffling sound of the marchers' shoes on the pavement to be heard above the roll of the drums, past the silent crowds, past the glimpses of the harbor, and over to Middle Street, where it stopped before the church.

Every pew was filled, and the air was sweet with flowers. The minister spoke simply of him, and the choir sang.

It was in Fishermen's Rest, back among his own, that he had asked to be buried. As the casket was lowered into the fresh earth, a bugle sounded Taps. And as the summons to sleep drifted away, it was answered by another from afar, and the clear notes were carried across the fields by the eternal wind, and out to the sea.

Chapter Notes

Legend has it that the fore-and-aft-rigged prototype of the schooner was invented in 1713 in Gloucester by Captain Andrew Robinson. As his new boat slid down the ways into the harbor, a spectator exclaimed: "Oh, how she scoons!" Upon which her designer declared: "Then a scooner let her be."

There is evidence, however, that the rig — so peculiarly adapted to coastwise sailing — had already been in existence for many years on both sides of the Atlantic.

The first five of the news items appeared in the *Cape Ann Advertiser* between February 2 and March 3, 1883 — three of them in the same issue. Reports of individual loss of life, and even loss of vessels, were far more commonplace and were given less space by the Gloucester newspapers of the period than highway fatalities receive today.

The loss of two hundred and nine Gloucestermen in 1883 was not unusual. Two hundred and forty-nine were lost in 1879, including a hundred and forty-three who went to the bottom aboard thirteen schooners during a two-day gale on Georges Bank in February. That was a particularly bad year; one out of every twelve Gloucester fishermen was taken by the sea.

CHAPTER I

The *Grace L. Fears* was built at Gloucester by David Alfred Story in 1874. She was typical of the extreme clipper type in vogue at the time, having low, hard bilges, low bulwarks and a shallow hold, and in the summer carrying a large spread of sail. The *Fears* measured 84.5 tons net, 81 feet overall, 22.9 feet beam and 8.4 feet depth of hold.

During her record trip the previous year the *Fears* took aboard a fare of 98,825 pounds of halibut and 3000 pounds of cod, for which she stocked, or collected, $6016.50. According to the traditional mode of settlement whereby the boat (owners and master) and the crew (except the cook, who was the only man aboard on wages) split fifty-fifty, each crew member's share was $206.30 and the cook earned $253.94. She arrived back in Gloucester on March 22, 1882, after a trip of five weeks and a day, including a five-day "freeze-up" in the ice at Canso, Nova Scotia.

Captain Alec Griffin went on to make his mark as one of Gloucester's famous skippers. In *American Fishermen* James B. Connolly told of Griffin's doubts one trip about the soundness of his new masts, imported from outside New England because native tall timber was running out.

"He was off the Nova Scotia shore, on his way to the Grand Banks, when he ran head into a northeast winter gale. 'A good chance right here,' said Captain Alec, 'to find out about those new sticks of mine.' He hauled his vessel up by the wind, and drove her with all sails set, first on one tack and then on the other, for fifty miles in a living gale. Well, his new spars were still up there. 'They must be all right, at that,' said Alec."

Many were the rugged fishermen who sailed with the *Grace L. Fears.*

One nasty day in November 1880 Bill Lee and Jack Devine were hauling their trawl on the Banks when a sudden steamroller sea roared down, threw them overboard and half filled their dory. Devine grabbed the gunwale, pulled himself back aboard, secured the trawl to the bow to keep it head to, and began bailing furiously.

But Lee had been hurled fifteen feet into the ocean. Dragged down by the weight of his boots and oilies, he fought to the surface, only to sink again. Two or three fathoms under water he came in contact with the trawl by some quirk of fate. He started to haul himself hand over hand toward the dory. And then fate grinned again; a dangling hook caught his forefinger and jabbed clean through it by the bone. Trapped in the depths by the very line that was guiding him back to life, he reached his free hand up the trawl to the length of his arm and tore the hook from the flesh.

Just as he broke through the surface and clutched for the bouncing gunwale, his lungs bursting, a second hook snagged a leg of his oilskin trousers. With everything he had left in him, he seized the gunwale with both hands, ripped out the hook as he lunged over the side, and fell senseless into the bottom.

When Lee came to, Devine wanted to row him back to the *Fears*. But his bleeding and exhausted dorymate would have none of it, and they finished hauling.

CHAPTER 2

Howard wrote in his autobiography that when he withdrew his hands and feet from the tub of brine, the Lishmans "showed me the tub and said — just see what a lot of frost came out of your poor hands and feet! The ice on top of the water must have been a good half inch thick."

This is patently impossible and was therefore omitted from the text. The freezing point of such a strong brine would have been several degrees below that of fresh water and probably well below the temperature of his frozen parts.

The Lishmans drew the water from the icy river — and may even have thrown some snow in with it for good measure. Howard may have convinced himself that the resulting slush on the surface was of his own making.

Mountain climber Bradford Washburn, director of the Museum of Science in Boston and an authority on frostbite, says that the traditional treatment used by the Lishmans was the worst possible and remains current today, the best medical evidence to the contrary. The patient's extremities should have been immersed in warm water — about 110 degrees Fahrenheit — instead of in ice-cold brine.

Blackburn said later he thought a skilled physician might have been able to save the fingers of his left hand and probably those of the right, with the exception of the little finger that was mangled from pounding the ice. This seems unlikely. The wonder is that he survived at all.

Reading the newspaper stories of the ordeal, a William Litchman of Marblehead, Massachusetts, was struck by the similarity of his name to that of the Lishmans. All he knew of his own family was that when he was a child in 1834 his father had brought him down from Newfoundland to Marblehead, gone fishing and then disappeared. As a shot in the dark, he wrote Frank Lishman in Little River.

"I think it is all likely you are my brother," Frank replied. "If so, you are minus a part of one of your fingers, as I remember a man named Organ cut it off by accident making kindling."

William was indeed minus a forefinger. He traveled to Newfoundland, and the brothers were reunited after fifty years.

CHAPTER 3

When I visited Nova Scotia in the course of my research, I found the Blackburn homestead intact and occupied. The stair treads were worn nearly down to the risers by generations of pounding feet.

Port Medway, however, was the ghost of its past, having barely three hundred scattered inhabitants. A few retired fishermen remembered Howard; they had quaffed beer in his saloon down in "Gloss-ester."

Clyde R. Blackburn of Ottawa, Canada, a retired newspaperman and distant cousin of Howard's, uncovered for me the information that the *Sophia Catherine* displaced thirty-four tons and was built at Lunenberg, Nova Scotia, in 1843. She was first registered at Halifax, then again at Liverpool in 1854 in the names of John Blackburn and David Day of Port Medway.

Mr. Blackburn recalled that his father had told him he had some kind of proof that the crew of the *Sophia Catherine* did not, in fact, eat their dog. In the absence of the *corpus delicti*, the point remains moot.

Blackburn may still have been sailing with the *Polar Wave*, in which he shipped when he came to Gloucester in 1879, when the following incident occurred.

It was March 24, 1880, and the schooner was fishing on Banquereau Bank, according to an account in the *Fishermen's Own Book*, "when the wind suddenly shifted and it set in extremely cold while six of her dories were out. The vessel got underway and found five of the dories without difficulty, but the other, containing George Nelson and Charles Ray, remained undiscovered until morning. These men had hauled up and rowed away from the vessel instead of towards her. They soon discovered their mistake, as a strong light was set in the rigging of the vessel, and they remained within sight of it all night. They threw overboard their fish and gear, but were unable to make headway against the wind and sea to the vessel. The next day they were seen by the crew, who went to their succor. When found at three o'clock, P.M., Nelson was dead, having died from the exposure at about nine, A.M."

CHAPTER 4

Fast and beautiful the clipper schooners were — and terribly dangerous, being susceptible to a knockdown in a gale or squall due to their shallow draft and heavy rig. Captain Collins had sailed many of them and knew their qualities. Appalled by the fearful losses among this type, he campaigned successfully in the '80's for modifications in hull design and sail plan which led to the development of the classic, and much safer, Gloucester schooner of the early twentieth century.

Captain Collins was the founder in 1884 of the Watercraft Collection of fishing vessel models in the Smithsonian Institution at Washington, D.C.

The Gloucester Fishermen's Institute reported in 1895 receiving from Howard the gift of "an old flint-lock musket, charred, brine-eaten and encrusted with patches of coral formation; supposed to have been on a vessel burned at sea by the British in the War of 1812. It was hauled up on a trawl in 40 fathoms, 60 miles southeast of Matinicus Rock [off the Maine coast] by William Grant, December 22nd, 1894."

CHAPTER 5

No sooner had the Klondike broken into the headlines than the reporter from the *Gloucester Times* sought the views of Captain

Solomon Jacobs, the King of the Mackerel Killers, and the interview appeared on July 27, 1897, in the same issue that carried the first news of Blackburn's plans. Sol Jacobs, who had been everywhere and done everything in his schooner, the famous *Ethel B. Jacobs*, had this to say:

"My first idea of the wealth of that region was during my last sealing voyage. I touched at the mouth of the Yukon, and two miners came on board and asked for passage to Seattle, which I gave them.

"While on the passage I had frequent talks with the miners. They said they had been pan mining up the Yukon for two years and during that time took out about $40,000 in gold. Of this amount it cost them $18,000 to live, and they had the remainder with them, which they showed me."

Captain Sol went on to describe the rigors of the territory and his plans to send a small expedition after gold. But he seems not to have gone through with it. Mackerel was his fortune; he could smell a school ten miles to leeward on a foggy night.

"The people do indeed like pluck," said the *Gloucester Times* of Blackburn and his gold hunters. "There's something about a plucky man or woman which is contagious. They carry with them a certain power which brings about success. In many instances it is as capital in business, for pluck will command capital. Men with money to loan look for good plucky men with whom to make their investments."

The provisions Cook Nelson stowed aboard the *Hattie I. Phillips* are typical of the fare to be had on a round-the-Horn voyage at the turn of the century. They included: 11 barrels flour, 450 pounds sugar, 200 pounds butter, 75 pounds lard, 40 pounds tea, 60 pounds coffee, 10 pounds baking powder, 30 pounds rice, 50 pounds bacon, 50 pounds evaporated apples, 5 cases condensed milk, 25 pounds raisins, 20 pounds currants, 20 gallons molasses, 24 boxes magic yeast cakes, 20 bushels potatoes, 5 bushels turnips, 2 barrels cabbage, 1 bushel beets, 1 bushel onions, 40 pounds rolled oats, 10 pounds oatmeal, 20 pounds squash, 30 dozen eggs, 1 barrel corned beef, ½ barrel herring and 200 pounds pollock, plus unspecified quantities of beef, salt pork, clams, beans, peas, apples, pears, blueberries, tomatoes, pickles, vinegar, biscuits, baking soda, cream of tartar, hops, ginger, pepper, cassia, peppermint, lemon and vanilla flavoring, nutmegs, mustard, ketchup, table sauce, pepper sauce and chocolate.

It must have taken formidable talent and stamina to wheedle three squares a day from the smoky galley cookstove for sixteen men, pitch and roll, for a hundred and twenty-nine days. When they arrived in San Francisco, Blackburn wrote home that Nelson "has given us full and plenty of the best of grub, which greatly helped to make the voyage a pleasant one."

CHAPTER 6

If one grants the authenticity of a yarn in *Gloucester by Land and Sea,* Josh Slocum was not the first man by a long shot to at-tack his enemies by the sole-stirring device which has been associated with his name.

It seems that the same Captain Andrew Robinson who is said to have invented the schooner did considerable Indian fighting off and on for the colonial government. Around 1723 a band of savages surprised him and his crew of two as their sloop was lying at anchor and carried them off. The Indians killed his men, but during the night Captain Robinson managed to slip away, boarded his sloop and raised sail. Unfortunately the wind was light, and his foes overtook him in their canoes.

"On board the sloop he had 'a large quantity of scupper nails, well known for their peculiar shape; being short and having a sharp point, and a large flat head, with a sharp edge.' These he sowed broadcast on the deck, and the Indians, swarming on board with hideous yells, got their feet so full of nails that they could not stand, and floundered about until the resourceful skipper, his own feet protected by stout sole leather, knocked them on the head and threw them overboard. This so appalled their comrades that they paddled away as if the devil were after them."

Waterspouts, which Howard described in a letter home, actually consist more of rain than sea water. The phenomenon is caused by local whirlwinds sweeping up spray from the ocean, which causes condensation of atmospheric vapor. The columns are partly salt water and spray but largely rain and vapor from cumulus clouds above. The notion that a waterspout can be dispelled by gunfire is an old mariners' superstition.

CHAPTER 8

The dory *Centennial* that Alfred Johnson sailed to England in 1876 is still in existence. "Centennial" shipped her back from Liverpool, tried exhibiting her with indifferent success and resumed fishing. When he got to be master of his own vessel, he sold his fares to the Gorton-Pew Fisheries and gave them his famous dory after he retired. A few years ago it turned up in Marblehead — under the porch of a summer hotel — where it remains, forgotten by all but the proprietor and a few guests.

Since Blackburn seems not to have put any flour aboard *Great Western*, and since it is hardly likely that he did any baking, the inclusion of saleratus (sodium bicarbonate) in the list of stores suggests that as a cook he was a great sailor.

Commenting on the departure of *Great Western*, the *Gloucester Times* declared that "as a man Mr. Blackburn is above reproach. His charity is proverbial, and great and good works are ascribed to him by the poor of our city. The love and esteem in which he is held by the public at large manifested itself on Sunday."

CHAPTER 10

The fate of *Great Western* is a mystery. Perhaps she still cleaves British waters of a summer by another name, her owner unaware of where she comes from and how she got there.

CHAPTER 11

For his second transatlantic crossing Howard simplified his diet drastically, relying heavily on canned goods and cutting down on items that required cooking or elaborate preparation. *Great Republic's* stores included: 6 cans of chicken, 18 of salmon, 6 of lobster, 12 of kidney beans, 3 of oxtail soup, 3 of vegetable soup and 12 of condensed milk; 6 pints of pickles, 10 pounds of sugar, 2 bags of salt, 2 pounds of Indian meal (corn meal), 1 bushel of potatoes, ½ bushel of onions, 11 pounds of butter, 30 pounds of lean pork, 2 corned shoulders, ½ pound of pepper, 8 pounds of tea, mustard — and two can openers.

CHAPTER 12

Howard always stuck to his story about the "sea serpent." Gloucester people have been sea-serpent-conscious ever since Colonel Thomas H. Perkins and Mr. Daniel Webster came down from Boston one August day in 1817 and viewed with their own eyes from the shore of the harbor a serpent which had been disporting in Cape Ann waters for several weeks.

The statement that the crossing to Portugal was "the fastest nonstop single-handed passage across the Atlantic ever sailed, a record which was to stand for many years," is, I believe, justified — although claims of this sort are invariably open to dispute.

While it contains some discrepancies, the most complete log of transatlantic crossings in small boats that I know of appears in Humphrey Barton's *Atlantic Adventurers*. To be sure, Barton states that Rudolph Frietsch crossed from New York to Ireland in 35 days in 1894, but the forty-foot *Nina* sailed on August 5 and appears to have docked at Queenstown on September 13, making a passage actually of 40 days. Joshua Slocum sailed *Spray* from Yarmouth, Nova Scotia, to Gibraltar on the first leg of his circumnavigation in 1895 in an elapsed time of 34 days. But he lay over for four days in the Azores. This spoiled his chances of an easy nonstop record, although it reduced his sailing time to 30 days, an amazingly fast trip.

Blackburn's record of 39 days seems to have stood for thirty-eight years. In 1939 Francis Clark took his thirty-foot cutter *Girl Kathleen* from New York to Cornwall in 33 days, the previous year having crossed from Portsmouth to Savannah, Georgia, in 79. This was the first known single-handed round trip. I exclude R. D. Graham's 24-day voyage from Ireland to Newfoundland in *Emanuel* in 1933, since his course was more than a thousand miles shorter than the average.

Claims for records are influenced by many factors — varying distances, weather, seamanship, sizes and models of boats, and in some instances lack of verification. But by any measure, Blackburn's physical handicap alone makes it hard to dispute that he was the most indomitable single-handed sailor of whom history has a record.

CHAPTER 14

The trip down the Chicago Drainage Canal must have been malodorous in the extreme. The canal had been completed only two years earlier. The works involved reversing the flow of the Chicago River into Lake Michigan in order to carry the burgeoning city's sewage down to the Illinois and Mississippi rivers.

In recalling his encounter with the rocks and the island in the Mississippi many years later, Howard appears to have reconsidered his statement that the steamboat laboring upriver "could not have helped us if she wanted to," for in 1929 he wrote in *Yachting*:

"When once above those rocks she could have anchored and attached a line to a piece of board. The current then would have brought it down to me. I could have made it fast to my boat, and the men on the steamer could have hauled me up above the rocks, which lay between my boat and the middle of the river. But they evidently thought such a small boat was not worth saving. The salvage would not pay them for their trouble. So they blew their whistle three times and passed slowly on up the river."

CHAPTER 16

A leading yachting writer of his day, George Story Hudson, went down to Gloucester for a "gam" with him shortly after Captain Blackburn returned from Halifax. Howard discussed his various boats at some length, and Hudson's resulting article was published in the magazine *The Rudder* in 1904. The description of *America*, which Hudson said was designed to "float on the sweat of an ice pitcher," provides additional details which may interest the nautical reader:

The pin holding the tiller to the rudderhead was set up with a nut, and Howard carried duplicate pins and a wrench. The rudder swiveled on the deadwood with heavy straps, and the keel projected under the heel of the post.

Aloft, the main and jib halyard blocks, jibstay and sister hooks of the shrouds were secured to a wrought-iron eyeband. "This sister-hook scheme, he says, was the best wrinkle he had aboard. When properly moused they cannot get adrift and may be removed with little trouble, if need be. The captain has no use for turnbuckles to connect shrouds and chain plates. Lanyards of tarred hemp are his preference, because they ease the mast in hard winds and rolling seas. He is afraid turnbuckles may strip their threads and leave him in the lurch."

As for running rigging, the main and jib were hoisted with a two-part purchase of fifteen-thread line, the topping lift and jib downhaul being twelve-thread and the jib sheets nine-thread. Blocks were several sizes larger than the rope that was rove through them so they would render free in wet weather, and all rough places that came into contact with lines were burnished to prevent chafing. Sails were of yacht drill.

America's drag was a "stout canvas bag with an iron ring to strengthen and hold open the mouth. The cable is bent to a thimble in the bridle eye, strain on the inboard end being relieved by a spiral steel spring. The cable is made fast to a big cleat and to the mast. There is a trip line and plenty of chafing gear at the chocks. The skipper says this sea anchor is as essential to successful ocean voyaging as the boat itself."

All in all, Hudson judged Blackburn the most ingenious man he had ever known when it came to the construction and fitting-out of small vessels for transatlantic crossings.

CHAPTER 18

No record can be found of how Howard shortened his mast seventeen inches at Musquodoboit Harbor. He probably sawed it off at the bottom; when it was restepped he would have had to take up on the jibstay and shrouds and probably reef the mainsail. Of course he could have "topped" it, but he would have had to retaper the masthead to fit the eyeband. One thing is sure: he didn't cut a piece out of the middle.

America can be traced up to 1927, when a letter appeared in the Liverpool, Nova Scotia, *Advance:*

"Following his return to Gloucester, the *America* remained in storage in Nova Scotia for twelve years, when she was turned over to the captain of a schooner in the coconut trade with Utila Island [one of the Bay group off the north coast of Honduras]. Offered down there at whatever price she might bring, she came into the possession of Captain Dwight Hunter, Jr., who at once installed a motor.

"More recently the *America* was bought by the Utila Salt Company. A modern engine is being installed, and before long she will be ready for sea again, probably to be used on the run from Utila to La Ceiba, 20 miles, and to Ruatan Island, 24 miles distant."

CHAPTER 19

The verse Captain Collins selected to describe Howard's first ordeal is from Canto IV of *The Lady of the Lake,* by Sir Walter Scott.

Mrs. Addie Dolloff, Captain Blackburn's niece (Addie Reed), told me this story:

Once when she brought her two young sons to Gloucester for a visit, Uncle Howard perched one of them on his knee, picked up his pipecase and, holding it after the fashion of a pistol, said the ruse had been the means of his saving the lives of some men in San Francisco many years before.

Mrs. Dolloff could recall no more, and I was able to find nothing by way of substantiation.

CHAPTER 20

Howard Blackburn's apartment was closed and locked after his funeral, and a week or so later — before his nieces had an opportunity to return to Gloucester to go through his effects — it was broken into.

China and glassware were smashed, linen and clothes ripped to shreds, furniture broken and general devastation inflicted. The rooms were left a shambles. Priceless letters and documents were pulled out of desks and drawers and torn to pieces.

The vandals were never brought to justice.

Sources

THE CORE OF THIS BOOK was constructed from a page-by-page search of some fifteen thousand issues of Cape Ann newspapers, all of which except the *Gloucester Times* are defunct. The rest was filled in from innumerable other sources — newspapers, periodicals, pamphlets, books, documents, records, photographs, correspondence, travels and interviews.

The greatest stroke of luck was my discovery among the literary papers of the late James B. Connolly at Colby College in Waterville, Maine, of the typewritten copy of an original manuscript by Howard Blackburn. It was the laboriously penned account of some incidents of his youth and voyages, written probably in 1913 and presumably for Connolly. Connolly wrote an article based on the story of Burgeo Bank which appeared in the *Saturday Evening Post* in 1926 and the following year as a chapter in *The Book of the Gloucester Fisherman*, along with a summary of the voyages. Then the hundred-odd pages of memoirs were apparently forgotten for another thirty-five years.

The first-person extracts in the text are almost exclusively taken from this manuscript, including all of Chapter 14 and Chapter 15 except for brief interpolations of narrative. In rare instances there are excerpts from Blackburn's letters and logs. The manuscript extract is unadulterated by editing, save for minimal changes in spelling and punctuation for clarity's sake, and is published here for the first time with the kind permission of Colby College.

BOOKS AND PERIODICALS

ATKIN, WILLIAM   *Of Yachts and Men.* New York: Sheridan House, 1946.

BARTON, HUMPHREY *Atlantic Adventurers*. New York: Van Nostrand, 1952.

BERTON, PIERRE *The Klondike Fever*. New York: Knopf, 1958.

BLACKBURN, HOWARD The Adventures of Captain Howard Blackburn. *Yachting*, May-August, 1929.

CHAPELLE, HOWARD I. *American Sailing Craft*. New York: Kennedy Brothers, 1936.

——— *The National Watercraft Collection*. Washington: United States National Museum Bulletin 219, 1960.

CHURCH, ALBERT COOK *American Fishermen*. New York: Norton, 1940. (Text by James B. Connolly.)

COLLINS, JOSEPH W. *Fearful Experience of a Gloucester Halibut Fisherman, Astray in a Dory in a Gale off the Newfoundland Coast in Midwinter*. Boston: F. A. Varnum, 1884.

CONNOLLY, JAMES B. *The Book of the Gloucester Fishermen*. New York: John Day, 1927.

DAMON, FRANK C. Story and Experience of Howard Blackburn. *Salem News*, August 26, September 9 and 15, 1932.

HALE, WILLIAM *A Fearless Fisherman*. Gloucester: Cape Ann Breeze Print, 1895.

HALIBURTON, THOMAS C. *An Historical and Statistical Account of Nova Scotia*. Halifax: Joseph Howe, 1829. Vol. II.

HAMMOND, JOHN HAYS *The Autobiography of John Hays Hammond*. New York: Farrar and Rinehart, 1935.

HAWES, CHARLES BOARDMAN *Gloucester by Land and Sea*. Boston: Little, Brown, 1923.

HUDSON, GEORGE STORY A Fearless Singlehander. *The Rudder*, July, 1904.

PARKINSON, JOHN, JR. *Nowhere Is Too Far: The Annals of the Cruising Club of America*. New York, 1960.

PRINCE, GORDON C. The Rejuvenation of the "Christopher Columbus." *Motorboat*, May 25, 1922.

PRINGLE, JAMES R. *History of the Town and City of Gloucester, Cape Ann, Massachusetts*. Gloucester, 1892.

PROCTER, GEORGE H. *The Fishermen's Memorial and Record Book*. Gloucester: Procter Brothers, 1873.

——— *The Fishermen's Own Book*. Gloucester: Procter Brothers, 1882.

SLOCUM, JOSHUA *Sailing Alone Around the World*. New York: Dover, 1956.

STANFORD, ALFRED *Men, Fish and Boats*. New York: Morrow, 1934.

NEWSPAPERS

Boston Herald

Boston Journal

Boston Post

Cape Ann Advertiser

Cape Ann Breeze

Cape Ann News

Cape Ann Shore

Gloucester Times

Gloucester News

Illustrated London News

Liverpool [Nova Scotia] *Advance*

New York Herald

New York Times

Salem News

MISCELLANEOUS

Addison Gilbert Hospital, Gloucester: *Annual Report for the Year June 1, 1901 to June 1, 1902.*

The Century Dictionary and Cyclopedia (ten volumes). New York: The Century Company, 1902. (An invaluable source of contemporary information.)

Pamphlet of photographs and drawings illustrating incidents of his life, published privately by Howard Blackburn.

Flyer printed in connection with the presentation of the Margaret Fitzhugh Browne portrait of Howard Blackburn by the Cruising Club of America to the Gloucester Master Mariners' Association in 1929.

Fearful Experience of a Gloucester Halibut Fisherman, in Program of the 250th Anniversary of Incorporation of Town of Gloucester, 1892.

The Fisherman. Monthly magazine of the Gloucester Fishermen's Institute, July 1895.

Autobiographical manuscript by Howard Blackburn (around 1913) in the James Brendan Connolly Collection at Colby College, the gift of James A. Healy.

Acknowledgments

MY SPECIAL GRATITUDE goes out to Howard Blackburn's nieces, Miss Annie J. Forbes of Mill Village, Nova Scotia, and Mrs. Addie Dolloff of Boothbay Harbor, Maine, whose fine perception and long memories gave me insight into the lives and personalities of their uncle and aunt which I would otherwise have missed; to Philip Bolger and Captain Thomas Morse of Gloucester, naval architect and fisherman respectively, who read this manuscript and supplied invaluable technical advice; to Richard Hunt of Gloucester, who provoked my interest in the subject and suggested many sources of information; and to Arthur H. Thornhill, Jr., of Little, Brown, whose encouragement made this book a reality.

In addition, I thank the following agencies, institutions and individuals for their assistance in its preparation. Others, too numerous to be listed, are the objects of my deep appreciation.

Boston Public Library
Cape Ann Scientific, Literary and Historical Association, Gloucester
City Library, Gloucester, England
Essex County Probate Court
Essex County Registry of Deeds
Essex County Superior Court
Gloucester City Clerk and Assessors
Gloucester Fishermen's Institute
Gloucester Master Mariners' Association
Library of Congress
Marine Historical Association, Mystic Seaport, Connecticut
Mariners Museum, Newport News, Virginia

Massachusetts Supreme Court
National Archives and Records Service
Newburyport Public Library
Peabody Museum, Salem
Public Archives of Nova Scotia, Halifax
Sandy Bay Historical Society, Rockport
Sawyer Free Library, Gloucester
United States Department of Naturalization, Boston
United States District Court, Boston

Fred Adams, Secretary of the Cruising Club of America; Miss Elizabeth L. Alling; Clyde R. Blackburn; Robert F. Brown; Miss Margaret Fitzhugh Browne; Howard I. Chapelle; James P. Clancy; Miss Charlotte D. Conover, Librarian, Mrs. Alan G. Hill, Reference Librarian, and the staff of the Sawyer Free Library; Emerson Cudios; Fred Daggett; Captain Eldred Glawson; Fred Head; Pierre M. Hulsart; Captain Kenneth Iverson; Herbert Kenny; Philip Kuuse; Boris Lauer-Leonardi, Editor, *The Rudder;* Mrs. Addison B. Le Boutillier; Miss E. Marguerite Letson; William J. MacInnis; John R. McKenna, Librarian, Colby College; Orlando Merchant; Donald F. Monell; F. T. Nickerson; Walter E. O'Donnell, M.D.; Charles Olson; Mrs. Ben Pine; Gordon C. Prince; William N. Ratcliff; Captain C. William Sibley; Reverend H. Robert Smith; William H. Taylor, Managing Editor, *Yachting;* James Walen; Bradford Washburn; Philip S. Weld, Gordon Abbott, Jr., and the staff of the *Gloucester Times.*

Appendix to the Second Edition

This section of new material is arranged as it relates to the chapters.

1

When he first rowed up Little River, Blackburn turned back after about three quarters of a mile, not only because the current was strong against him and he could see no signs of life, but because he was afraid his frozen fingers would break off on the oars. So he declared in an undated manuscript account, dictated to a Mr. Gaffney, that came to hand too late for the first edition, one of two such given me in 1963 by Mrs. Burton Johnston from the effects of her late husband, "Dixie," a *Boston Globe* newsman and admirer of Blackburn. During the worst of that winter, Howard recalled, "two of our men went over the mountains to a place called Dog Cove where they got some hard bread that had been damaged with kerosene oil. It was all the people could spare."

On March 24, 1934, while single-dory trawling from the haddocker *Imperator* out of Gloucester 35 miles southeast of Sable Island, Manuel Joseph was separated from his vessel in a squall and drifted 48 hours before he was picked up by the *Delawana II* of Lunenburg, Nova Scotia. Back in Gloucester the young fisherman told the *Times* (April 16): "And always before me was the thought that a man named Howard Blackburn had gone through a similar experience and reached shore with his dorymate dead in the bottom of his dory. If he could do it, why couldn't I?"

2

Three months before his death Howard told Frank Damon of the *Salem News* that strange story of burying his fingers with Tom Welch at Burgeo. Netta H. Baxter of Lynn, however, who was born near Little River, has written me that Joseph Small of Burgeo was her uncle and "had Capt. Blackburn's fingers in a bottle, in his office, for many years. I understand that he finally sent them to Capt. Blackburn at Gloucester."

4

"Mr. Howard Blackburn of this city has purchased the fine schooner yacht *Elfin* of Boston parties. She is a handsome craft of 10.62 tons register. Mr. Blackburn has entirely refitted and painted her and she is doubtless one of the beauties of the fleet." (*Cape Ann Advertiser*, August 7, 1891.) A month later *Elfin* served as the judges' boat for an open regatta of the Cape Ann Yacht Club in Gloucester Harbor.

"On Saturday [June 17] a young child named Robeshaw fell from the wharf into the dock in the rear of Howard Blackburn's. Mr. Blackburn saw the accident and ran to the rescue, jumping on a raft to reach for the lad, but it sank under him and he found himself in the water. Nothing daunted, he saved the little one and was soon on shore. It was a brave act and, considering the crippled condition of Mr. Blackburn's hands, meritorious in the extreme." (*Cape Ann Advertiser*, June 23, 1893.)

"This true tale," wrote columnist Henry Bollman in the *Gloucester Times* of December 20, 1957, "was told me by an aged man who saw it happen. It seems that on a cold, snowy day before Christmas, a tiny urchin peered into the doorway of the warm Blackburn tavern. The boy had no overcoat, and his toes showed through the holes in his badly worn little shoes. The giant Blackburn looked down at the small boy, and immediately said to a patron at the bar, 'John, you tend bar for a while, I'm going out.' He picked up the lad and carried him to a clothing store, and bought him the finest warmest woolen clothes that money could buy; a thick brown overcoat, heavy stockings and sturdy shoes. Then he took him into a restaurant and ordered all the hot, nourishing food the boy could possibly stuff into his empty stomach. Finally, he called for a horsedrawn hack and drove the boy home.
"At the door of a shabby tenement he was met by the boy's mother. It so happened that she was one of the 'temperance ladies' bitterly opposed to Blackburn's business. In a rage, she tore the warm clothing off her frail little son, and threw it at the feet of Blackburn.
"'Take it back!' she screamed. 'I refuse to accept anything from a rum seller!'
"Sadly the big man returned through the snow to the tavern and, as he entered the door, tears flowed freely down the rugged features of the grandest, kindest, most generous man in town. He had no children of his own, and he loved them all, especially that freezing waif."

7

All the gold the Blackburn expedition found "could be put in one eye without any serious inconvenience," Lewis Lexington (born on the centennial of the battle) Berry wrote Mr. Houghton from Dawson City, Alaska, in June of 1899. A copy of the letter was sent me by his daughter, Mrs. Mabel Berry Buker of North Billerica. After they struggled back to the frozen-in *Eclipse*, Berry wrote, the members of the Gloucester Mining Company divided their treasury of $100 and their provisions and broke up. When the ice on the Yukon cleared in May, Lew and a few others took *Eclipse* down the river to Nulato, where they evidently sold her and went their ways. Berry returned home and married his childhood sweetheart.

In "Schooner to the Arctic" by Otis Rowell, as told to Arthur W. Nelson in the June 1944 issue of *The Alaska Sportsman*, Rowell related that he lost three toes from frostbite that bitter winter of 1898-99, and all his teeth from scurvy, which he said was widespread owing to the lack of vegetables. He claimed only seven of the expedition lived to return to the States. Home again in Massachusetts, Rowell took up farming. The article was sent me by Mrs. Alice Story Selmer of Bainbridge Island, Washington, daughter of one of Rowell's mates on the venture, Fred H. Story, who raised his family in Alaska, she wrote, and died in Seattle in 1947. Frederick E. Head, on the other hand, came back to Massachusetts, became a locomotive engineer with the Boston and Maine Railroad and died in Essex in 1975 at the age of 98.

8

Two days after the launching of *Great Western* and insouciant as ever though scheduled to sail for England only ten days hence, Howard took the train to New York on June 8, 1899, and watched James J. Jeffries knock out the Englishman Bob Fitzsimmons for the world heavyweight championship at Coney Island the next day, according to an item in the *Gloucester Times* of June 9.

13

John Fairfield Thompson of New York, honorary chairman of the International Nickel Company of Canada, wrote me in 1963 of a memorable meeting one blowy day in 1902 while camping out with his family at Indian Point on Sagadahoc Bay, at the entrance to the Kennebec River, on the coast of Maine. "All day the storm increased so that by late afternoon it was striking the coast and the waves were going up in the air higher than the trees. As we watched, a small sailboat came down the coast with a pocket handkerchief for a sail and about half that large a jib. It pulled around into the lee where we had some boats and waved to us, evidently asking if he could use our anchor, as we had pulled our boat up on the beach. That evening after dinner my father and I went out to pay a visit and found a man opening soft shell clams to cook a stew for dinner. We were struck by his absence of fingers. It was Blackburn, and we spent two or three hours with him that evening and he told us of his transatlantic trips...He was a very pleasant man to talk to, not what one would call 'a show off,' and I still remember a pleasant evening with him."

If the year 1902 is correct, Howard must have been cruising east in *Great Republic* shortly before embarking on his inland voyage on May 18. Soon after his return from Portugal, incidentally, he informed the *Gloucester Times* (August 22, 1901) that he intended to change his sloop over to a schooner rig for the inland voyage - an uncharacteristic notion that fortunately he thought better of.

15

It appears that after John R. Strong bought *Great Republic* from Blackburn at Miami, probably in January 1903, he returned her to Gloucester and entered her in *Lloyd's Register of American Yachts* from 1904 through 1907, when he was living in Cambridge. George Olson, a Gloucester boat builder, was listed as her owner in 1908. From 1909 through 1911 she was not in *Lloyd's*. In August 1910 this classified ad ran for a week in the *Gloucester Times:* "SLOOP - For sale, sloop Great Republic, in which William Blackburn crossed the Atlantic, has auxiliary and is in good condition, no reasonable offer refused. Inquire at 10 Stanley Court." The address was Olson's. *William* Blackburn... such is fame. Then from 1912 through 1924 *GR*, as succeeding generations of owners came to call her, was back in *Lloyd's* under the ownership of Strong, who had moved to New York. Throughout this score of years Strong also had the 39-foot yawl *Alice*, which he kept at Marblehead.

Strong's attachment to *GR* was largely sentimental, judging from the statement of her next owner, the yacht designer and builder William Atkin, that when he bought her from Strong in 1924 she had been in storage on Long Island for at least 14 years, first at Port Jefferson, then at Cold Spring Harbor. Atkin brought the famous sloop to his own yard at Huntington. He was amazed to find her sound, he wrote in *Of Yachts and Men*, in spite of years of neglect. "She is a mystery because the yellow pine used in her construction has kept as well as the oak, and a trifle better than the white cedar. She is framed with double bent oak frames; two pieces 5/8 inches by 1 1/8, finishing 1 1/8 inches by 1 1/4 inches; has a white oak keel and deadwood; yellow pine planking above the water line and white cedar below. She has black iron floor timbers; iron keel fastenings, and copper rivets in the planking; a black iron rudder post and a wooden well; bronze stuffing box, shaft and propellor, and (to add to the complication) an iron fitting at the heel of the rudder. Now why she had not eaten herself up [by electrolysis] during those 24 years is a mystery to me."

A month before sailing for Portugal Howard told the newspaper that he was replacing the 1400-pound iron shoe on *GR*'s keel with 4800 pounds of lead as inside ballast to improve her balance. He must have changed his mind about the lead since he informed G.S. Hudson (*The Rudder* of July 1904) that he had filled the bilge with cement mixed with boiler punchings; Atkin found it under about 200 pounds of loose iron and wrote that "I considered this with apprehension. Many of us have a belief that cement in the bilge spells decay. I was much relieved, after breaking out a considerable amount of this cement which was as hard as stone, to find that the wood and the iron floor timbers beneath were in the same condition as they were the day Archie Fenton launched the sloop...I should not hesitate to use the same kind of ballast in a new boat."

To raise headroom below, a cabin trunk had been added, perhaps by Olson. Atkin refinished the cabin, replaced the auxiliary with a two-cycle, four horsepower Barker that cost him four dollars and gave *GR* new spars and sails, shortening the foot and head of the main and lengthening the hoist. Atkin was attached to *Great Republic* though he faulted her design - "too full aft, and too fine forward. This seems to be a characteristic of the Friendship sloop model of which *GR* is a modification. The result of these unbalanced ends is that in rough water the bow jumps too much." Off the wind she would not stick to a course untended, though she held better on a beat.

During William Atkin's tenure he enrolled *GR* in the fleet of the then-fledgling Cruising Club of America. He sold her to William Smythe of Essex, Connecticut, who that year or the next passed her on to Llewellyn Howland of Padanaram, Massachusetts, the yachting writer who 11 years later would launch the first of the noted Concordia yawls built by the company he founded. His son Waldo, who succeeded him in the firm and was about 18 at the time, has written me that he could never get the one-lunger to start, "except once when I needed it most, going into Menemsha. At the critical moment she popped a few times and got us in past the tide. On one cruise we tried for a whole week to get her from Edgartown to Nantucket against a fresh southwest wind. We never made it but had fun trying." His last sight of *GR* she was heading west out of Buzzards Bay: "the engine was running fine, the lone crew and helmsman was seated aft amid a number of five gallon cans, and he looked very grand and happy in his derby hat."

On July 25, 1928, William A. McLean of New Haven bought *Great Republic* from Llewellyn Howland for $1100 for his 18-year-old son Bassett, who wrote me from Bath, Maine, that he kept her that winter at Essex, Connecticut, where in the spring he replaced the engine with a Gray and then shifted her to a yard at West Haven. "The highlight of the summer of 1930 or 1931," Mr. McLean recalled, "was a visit to Gloucester and taking Capt. Blackburn out for a 'sail.' I put sail in quotes because there was not a breath of air! Perhaps it was just as

Great Republic was ripe for her first restoration when William Atkin found her in "Boss" Abrams's yard at Cold Spring Harbor in 1924 and perched his sons for a snapshot. Below, the results. (Photos from *Of Yachts and Men.*)

Kate and Ri Mann sail *Great Republic* in Long Island Sound, probably 1934, shortly before converting her to the marconi rig photographed years later (below) for another owner by Peter Barlow.

well because Capt. Blackburn was a heavy man. Seymour Bradley and I had to give him a hand getting aboard and ashore. No one was around on the wharf. I recall he said 'Where are the reporters and photographers?'"

Truman L. Bradley, Seymour's brother, writes from Clearwater, Florida, that McLean kept up the sloop beautifully, with dark blue topsides and gold leaf and scroll. "When we would poke into any New England harbor, there were always numerous yachtsmen who would row over to visit and admire her." On one cruise to the eastward the brothers sought out her first owner in his Gloucester saloon. "The delightful old gentleman came down for supper aboard his former cross-Atlantic home and regaled us with his experiences in building and sailing the *GR* to Spain. (He never mentioned Portugal.) According to him, he had a lot to do with the design and building of the *Great Republic*, and her lines and construction reflect his Nova Scotian background. She was a bit difficult to windward - wet and made a little leeway, but she was always sea-kindly."

In 1933 McLean sold *GR* to Kenneth B. Millett of New Rochelle, New York, who moored her at Larchmont. From 1934 through 1938 *Lloyd's* registered her to N. Freydberg of New York City. However, Dr. Lawrence T. Waitz, a later owner, reports that she was actually owned by the late Riborg G. Mann of New York, who kept her at Threemile Harbor and in 1934 hung a marconi mainsail on a taller mast; this is confirmed by Lefferts A. McClelland of Florida, Mann's sometime sailing mate. Thus, after 34 years, was the old gaff rig bastardized. Mann conveyed *GR* in 1938 to three New York advertising men, Allen Flouton, William Maillefert and Harry W. Bennett, Jr. According to Bennett, they replaced the rudder and two frames and rebuilt the cabin, "and what a delight she was. She would sail two points to the wind, dance along in a light breeze and could stay out in weather that would usually send most sailors to harbor." They kept *GR* at New Rochelle and Threemile Harbor, and for a season or two at Marion, on Buzzards Bay, where Bennett's two daughters learned to sail in her (one, Joan, married Senator Edward Kennedy of Massachusetts). Flouton, Bennett writes, was the last of the trio to enter the service in World War II and reluctantly sold *GR* around 1944.

Jeff Brown and Jim Mulcahy of Old Greenwich, Connecticut, were the buyers, according to Waitz. Then in 1947 they sold her to John Leonard of Levittown, New York, who sold her in 1948 to Stanley Groffman and Dr. George Lapin of Jamaica; these two moored her at Port Jefferson and Wading River and in 1949 passed *GR* on to Larry Waitz. Waitz replaced 46 frames and part of the stem, refastened extensively, repowered her with a 16-horse Gray engine and reregistered *Great Republic* with *Lloyd's*. He sailed out of Port Jefferson, Oyster Bay and Hempstead Harbor and informs me that "the little sloop steered herself very well on the wind and we always affectionately remarked that Blackburn was steering."

Her last voyage took *Great Republic* from Lindenhurst, Long Island, in 1970 to Larry Dahlmer's boat shop in East Gloucester, 1976.

Fred Broszeit

Photo by Jerry Klinow

On passage to the Gloucester Armory, the largely restored Blackburn sloop puts in at Wheeler's Point Boat Yard for cradle work on December 16, 1976 - seventy-six years old.

In 1956 Waitz sold *GR* to Frederick W. Webb of Mamaroneck, who had her at Oyster Bay and Riverside, Connecticut, and in 1960, when she was 60 years old, handed her over to her seventeenth (counting Freydberg) consecutive owner, Pierre M. Hulsart of Huntington, Long Island. Pete gave her a new deck, cabin trunk and 30-horse Universal engine in 1962. My wife and I sailed with the Hulsarts one day the next summer. They were the last of the string to have *GR* in the water. In 1968 Hulsart sold her to Thomas J. D'Amico of Haworth, New Jersey; in 1969 he sold her to Frederick D. Broszeit of Lindenhurst, Long Island.

Keel and floor timbers had gone to rot from exposure to rain and snow when I found *GR* in Lindenhurst. Several of us kicked in $500 to buy her at a token price from her generous owner in November of 1970 and gave her to the Gloucester Historical Commission, intending eventually to raise the money to restore the old sloop as a memorial to Blackburn. James and Nancy Thompson of the Wheeler's Point Boat Yard trailered her home in December at cost, as they have around Gloucester since, for free. Commission Chairman Julian Hatch and I raised about $1000, not enough to get under way (nor could we find a home for her), and the project was laid aside until 1975, when the City acquired the old State Armory on Prospect Street and approved the Historical Commission's request to exhibit *GR* there, once restored. I made an appeal for funds that brought in another $8500, including a grant of $1000 from the National Trust for Historic Preservation, its first ever for vessel restoration.

Great Republic was moved into the boat shop of Laurence A. Dahlmer on the same Smith Cove where she was built by Archie Fenton 75 years earlier. Rotten keel, deadwood, frames, garboard planks and rudder box were replaced. The bogus deck and cabin were ripped out, and Larry built a new deck, cockpit, wheelbox, companionway and rails as faithfully as possible from photographs and contemporary descriptions, with the advice of the naval architectural historian William A. Baker, consultant to the National Trust.

On December 16, 1976, *Great Republic* was moved into the Gloucester Armory to await sparring, rigging and the finishing touches, a seemingly indestructible monument to that nearly indestructible first of her twenty owners over three quarters of a century.

19

George Story Hudson concluded his interview in the July 1904 *Rudder* magazine: "Captain Blackburn has just finished another sea-going boat to replace the *America*. She is 18 feet on deck, seven feet beam and draws 30 inches. She is a keel craft with ballast ᵐented under the floor. Her general plan is like others of the fleet I ᵉ described, excepting there is a low house forward and a hold amidship for storage. I would not be a bit surprised to hear of his starting for the coast of Spain in this new ship, though the purpose for which she was built is not disclosed."

He of course did not embark for Spain. The *Gloucester Times* reported on June 6, 1904, that "Captain Howard Blackburn sailed for a cruising trip down east and along the Maine coast in his 20 foot boat yesterday afternoon. It was originally his intention to take a companion along with him, but the party whom he had engaged backed out at the last moment, so Capt. Blackburn decided that he would go alone. The lone mariner will spend the summer in pleasure cruising and in fishing, catching anything that will come along. Capt. Blackburn hoped that the bill providing for a bounty on dogfish would have become a law, as it was his intention to spend his time in exterminating some of these pests."

I have not been able to track down the name and fate of *America*'s successor. Possibly she proved not to her master's liking, in which event he may have sold her after a season or two, leaving himself boatless, because in the summer of 1907 he rented a boat to sail the party of ladies to Provincetown, and in September of 1908, I discover, he chartered the auxiliary sloop *Morning Star* for a two-day cruise to Plymouth with friends (*Gloucester Times*, September 5). Furthermore, he complained in announcing his plans to build *Christopher Columbus* (*Times*, December 11, 1909) that his "last boat was an open one and not comfortable for cruising."

The sloop Blackburn launched in April 1910 - presumably *Christopher Columbus*, though not identified in print that I can find - was 30 feet overall and measured 5.14 tons net. Gordon C. Prince of Wenham bought her from him in April 1921 for $300 and sailed her up to Fred Dion's yard at Salem for refitting, as he describes in his article in *Motorboat* magazine of May 25, 1922. *Chris*, as everyone called her, was ballasted in Blackburn fashion with a mixture of cement and boiler punchings in the bilge, and pig iron, all of which Prince broke out. To lower the floor and raise headroom, he had 1200 pounds of the iron cast for an outside keel, stowed another ton of it inside and left the remaining 900 pounds ashore, which lightened her without affecting her stiffness. He broke through the midships storage hold into the cramped forward cabin, where Howard had a pipe berth and a stove, and built a small trunk 14 inches high abaft the slide. Prince installed a five-horse Lathrop turning a quarter wheel, replaced the Blackburnian deadeyes and lanyards with turnbuckles, and the wheel with a tiller, and extended the bowsprit outward seven feet so as to supplement the jib with a forestaysail set from the stem. The result was an extra turn of speed and a better balanced rig while reefed. His entire investment, including new sails, came to $1080.44.

Prince cruised in *Christopher Columbus* as far as the Maine island of Grand Manan and then sold her after a couple of years to William Bell Watkins. Mr. Watkins wrote me from Mt. Desert, Maine, that she was "strong and able...She would be called a sloop but really was a cutter as her mast was stepped aft of where a sloop's would be. I personally like the cutter rig as it has a much shorter main boom which does not trip up so easily in the sea when rolling. Also it puts the weight of the mast farther aft. However, with the headsails taken in she had a strong weather helm and could not be kept off. Going into harbor I had to keep one headsail on her. I had her for a number of years and liked her."

Dr. F. C. Grant owned *Chris* in the early 1930's and wrote me that she "was a splendid little sea boat and great fun to sail. I cruised in her for three or four years and went to Nova Scotia twice." Dr. Grant did not recall to whom he sold her, except that she was around Southwest Harbor, Maine, for a while, and that is as far as I have been able to trace *Christopher Columbus*...save for the following interesting sidelight:

In his *Letters of E. B. White* (New York: Harper & Row, 1976) the essayist wrote an undated (probably summer of 1932) note from East Blue Hill, Maine, to Bernard Bergman, managing editor of *The New Yorker*, mentioning that "I am going to make a rent payment on the Christopher Columbus - a black sloop built by a man with no fingers. To cross the Atlantic. She tends to broach to in heavy weather, but is tight." In a footnote he stated that she was originally called *Great Republic* and gave some brief background on Blackburn.

After I wrote Mr. White a correcting letter, he replied from North Brooklin, Maine, on January 26, 1977, that "for forty-five years I've been living a harmless dreamlife, thinking that the boat I sailed in that summer was the one Blackburn crossed the Atlantic in, and that her name had been changed. The man from whom I chartered *Christopher Columbus* was named Grant, and he was summering in Northeast Harbor. I don't think it was Grant who told me wrong, I think it was someone else along the line. But your letter and enclosures cleared up two things I've long wondered about. First, when I would come across a picture of *Great Republic* it never grabbed me. She didn't look just like the boat I'd remembered from that summer. Something about the stern seemed different. Second, I've never understood how anybody would want to start across the Atlantic in a sloop that was so hard to manage downwind. *Christopher Columbus* had a very deep forefoot. She went to windward well, but when running broad off, she could be flighty. If the breeze freshened, it was sometimes difficult to keep her off the wind, and I almost ran her, all standing, onto Naskeag Bar one afternoon when passing inside Hog Island. Just squeaked out of it by getting forward and lowering the peak. I have an idea *Great Republic* better-behaved boat off the wind or Blackburn would never have

Off Magnolia in September, 1921, *Christopher Columbus* looks definitely cutterish in the long bowsprit, double headsails and high-peaked main favored by Gordon Prince, her new owner, handlining (below) outside Thacher's Island. (Photos, Gordon C. Prince.)

made Portugal. (All this can be taken with a grain of salt: I'm not a gifted sailor, and perhaps I'm doing *Christopher Columbus* an injustice.)..."

Extraordinary how opinions differ! Commodore Alexander (Sandy) Moffat told me that while cruising east in *Chris* with Gordon Prince, she would sail herself for long stretches off the wind - the only tillered boat he had ever seen do so - a talent he attributed to some extent to her cutter rig.

The mystery member of the Blackburn flotilla is the sloop *New England*. I can find no written evidence of her existence, but Frederick E. Kluge of Gloucester told me in 1968 that he acquired her from the late John Alexander, fish dealer and founder of the Beacon Marine Basin in East Gloucester, around 1912; Kluge said she was built by Blackburn, a claim confirmed to me by the late Charles P. McPhee, who grew up next to the Blackburn saloon, and by David Carter, who told me his Uncle Manuel Burnham crewed on her for Howard. Kluge described *New England* as about 28 feet overall, nine feet beam and three-plus draft, cedar-planked on oak frames, long and straight keel, rather straight and full in the bow, wide stern, flush deck, all ballast inside, bowsprit, double headsails, gaff rig, tiller-steered, with black topsides and three bunks below. He put in a five-horse Knox engine, renamed her *Ruth*, went lobstering and yachting, and sold her around 1916 to a buyer from a nearby town, identity unremembered. "She couldn't turn worth a damn," said Kluge, "but boy could she hold on the wind!" In view of the fact that Howard had *Christopher Columbus* from 1910 until 1921, when did he build *New England*? Could she have been the successor to *America* of 1904, larger than life in the memory of Mr. Kluge 50 years later?

20

Cruising Club (31'8" overall by 9'6" beam by 4'8" draft) was launched from the wharf of the United Sail Loft on June 26, 1929. On July 4, the *Gloucester Times* reported, Captain Blackburn planned to embark on a shakedown cruise to Portland and Boothbay Harbor. Apparently he didn't, because the *Boston Herald* noted on July 22, two days after the Cruising Club of America rendezvous, that he would be sailing in her for Bar Harbor momentarily. There is no evidence that he ever did.

Cruising Club's collision with the Coast Guard boat probably occurred during the American fishermen's races at Gloucester on August 31 and September 1 and 2, 1929, (the last of which Howard watched from the airship *Mayflower*), not during the October, 1930, races, as stated in the text, because an item in the *Gloucester Times* of ʾlay 17, 1930, has come to light to the effect that Blackburn had sold sloop to J. F. Phipps of Cohasset, who was installing an engine and building a cabin trunk, and had renamed her *Longonot*. For her subsequent history I am indebted to William H. Taylor, late managing editor of *Yachting*, Pierre M. Hulsart, John Giannoni, Charles Freyer and Coast Guard records:

Phipps sold *Longonot* after a year or two to James Ford, owner of a boat yard on Manhasset Bay, Long Island, who renamed her *Blackburn* and sold her to Albert Olsen, foreman of a nearby yard at Port Washington. From Olsen she passed to Howard M. and Robert W. Hill of Bayside, at the tip of Little Neck Bay, and was assigned Coast Guard No. 10G47; she had a Universal 20-horse engine driving a shaft through the port quarter. Howard Hill sold *Blackburn* to John A. Shirreffs of Port Washington, a relative, on June 20, 1953. Shirreffs restored her name to *Long 'o 'Not* and sold her to John Giannoni of Brooklyn on November 11, 1954. Giannoni renamed her *Smuggler*, sailed and cruised in her out of Port Washington and on March 16, 1959, sold her to Charles Freyer of East Northport, Long Island.

Now thirty, *Seascape*, as Freyer named her, wanted thoroughgoing repairs. At the Northport Boatyard he stripped off her main deck, broke out the Blackburnian ballast of cement and reframed her by epoxy-gluing together three 1/4-inch oak battens and throughfastening each of these ribs, thus laminated in place against the planking, with Everdur bolts. He did away with the break in the deck (frequently a rot trap and unusual in a Blackburn boat) by carrying the line of the original foredeck, which he preserved, back to the stern four or five inches above the afterdeck, which flattened her after sheer. An earlier owner had added a two-ton lead keel; figuring that if cement was good enough for Blackburn it was for him too, Freyer poured 1000 pounds of it back in the bilge. He cleaned the outside planking with lye and wrapped the entire hull from rail to keel with Dynel synthetic fabric bedded in epoxy, likewise the deck and trunk with a heavy plastic covering.

In November, 1961, Freyer and a companion set sail in *Seascape* from Long Island for the Caribbean, having in mind a circumnavigation. A few days out, they ran into a gale and lost Howard's hollow mast. The Coast Guard towed them to Bermuda where they found a massively solid replacement, reportedly 90 years old, and resumed their voyage. In the Caribbean they undertook diving and underwater photography jobs and eventually parted. Freyer sailed *Seascape* throughout the West Indies for two years, then brought her back to New York in April 1964.

On June 3, 1965, Charlie Freyer cleared Block Island singlehanded for England, arriving at Plymouth on July 7. After a sojourn in Britain he and *Seascape* sailed to Lisbon, thence to the Canaries, making the passage back across to Barbados in 32 days. And then, according to his

The rejuvenation of *Seascape*, ex-*Cruising Club*, proceeds at the hands of Charles Freyer (standing) at Northport, Long Island, in October, 1959. Below, his method of laminating and throughbolting new frames. (Photos, Charles Freyer.)

Cruising Club, ex-*Seascape* back home off Manchester after 46 years in July, 1976, in her Florida rig (above), and inside the Gloucester breakwater, rerigged and repainted (below) in November, 1977.

account, it was Barbados to Trinidad, the Panama Canal, Acapulco, San Diego and San Francisco for another sojourn. Returning, they skirted Central America after passing through the Canal, then sailed through the Gulf of Mexico to Miami and on to City Island, New York, by the Inland Waterway. Next, *Seascape* took Freyer via the Leeward Islands and Trinidad just across the Equator to Belem, Brazil, and back by way of the Leewards, Puerto Rico and Bermuda. After his marriage in 1972, he and Margaret sailed from Norfolk, Virginia, to West Palm Beach, where they made their home, later on shorter cruises to Key West, Nassau and Cozumel, Mexico.

Our telephone jingled on the evening of July 6, 1976, and Charles Freyer introduced himself with the announcement that he had just arrived in Gloucester singlehanded from West Palm Beach in *Cruising Club*, ex-*Seascape*, having decided to give up the sea, bring her home after 46 years and sell her, possibly to the guy who wrote the book about Blackburn. He had her all in tropical white, except for a light green cabin top, rigged with a tiller and Gunning self-steering apparatus. Six days later Becky and I bought her.

Cruising Club carried her ninth owners on a nine-day cruise to Monhegan Island, Maine, and back that September. In the spring of 1977 bits of rot here and there were taken care of and other repairs made with the assistance of Larry Dahlmer; the cockpit was enlarged, wheel and wheelbox were restored, rails were replaced, the jib was adapted to furling gear, and stanchions and lifelines were added. Topsides reverted to black and the deck to a good old Gloucester buff. And the Coast Guard, succumbing finally to an avalanche of evidence, waived its requirement of a builder's certificate and officially documented *Cruising Club*, pedigree and all.

In August of 1977 *Cruising Club*, ex-*Seascape, Smuggler, Long 'o 'Not, Blackburn, Longonot*, and *Cruising Club*, took the two of us on a three-week cruise down east along the Maine coast as far as Bar Harbor and Frenchman's Bay and return. She had left 20,000 miles of water behind her keel under Charlie Freyer, but she was not loath to show her latest owners that she was as kindly an old sea boat as ever. And though deservedly out to pasture, it seemed fitting, back in Gloucester again, that *Cruising Club* should complete the little voyage to Bar Harbor that Captain Blackburn had yearned to make but couldn't, 48 years earlier.

Blackburn gave Dixie Johnston this note from James B. Connolly, postmarked Chestnut Hill, October 17, 1931:

Dear Howard: I have just been listening to a radio man telling about you and your adventures. He makes out that he knows you very well. Colonel Goodbody he calls himself...These radio chaps are a great lot for stealing stuff. He used stuff in his talk that he took from my Book of the Gloucester Fishermen, things that had never been in print except in my book. Nowhere has he paid you anything for making use of your history. If not, he should have, and unless you say no I'll get after him and the radio station for taking things out of my copyrighted book without permission. I hope you are coming on in good shape.

Your Friend, Jim Connolly

Besides the loss of his fingers, the second joints of his thumbs, two left toes and three right, and the heel of his right foot, the rest of Blackburn's toes were left misshapen. Whether the damage to his feet contributed to his knee injury in San Francisco I can't make out, but he contracted chronic inflammation and water on the knee there that kept him on crutches for eight months after his return to Gloucester. Early in his voyage to England he was almost incapacitated by the gross swelling in his right knee and foot - the foot most maimed 16 years earlier. His legs served him for the crossing to Portugal and for most of his inland voyage (during which he caught malaria), but a factor in the failure of his attempt in *America* was the recurrence of swelling and intense pain in both feet and the right knee. Nan Forbes said that when she first knew her uncle in 1912 he walked briskly and enjoyed it, and didn't complain of his feet. But the old injuries caught up with him with age. Shortly before he died he told Frank Damon of the *Salem News* that pieces of bone had been removed from his knee at the Beverly Hospital. His notably inaccurate obituary in the *Gloucester Times* claimed that he had been operated on for a bone infection in his left leg; it may have been the right (the hospital record has been destroyed), suggesting that the fragments might have been broken off in the old San Francisco injury and were the probable cause of his chronic water on the knee.

Along with his old injuries Howard had arthritis and a hernia to contend with. He was addicted to beef, and to sauerkraut which he and a friend made in a crock in the saloon, and he used salt with a vengeance - a habit his physician prevailed on him to give up. He told an English reporter in 1899 that he had been a teetotaler for six years (he had a case of whisky on board *Great Western* that he didn't crack); perhaps he backslid, because Miss Forbes said he drank heavily until he quit permanently in his fifties (he was 50 in 1909) on doctor's orders, for the sake of his heart. Yet he smoked to the last. The cause of his death is certified in city records as myocarditis, pulmonary edema and probably chronic interstitial nephritis.

A few months before Howard Blackburn died, he said he wanted to live out his days in Snug Harbor, the retired sailors' home at Staten Island, New York, where a number of old Gloucester fishermen were berthed. The president of the U. S. Fisheries Association, W. F. Morgan, Jr., arranged for him to bypass a long waiting list, but by then his health would not permit the move, and his friends persuaded him to abandon the idea.

GLOUCESTER BOOKS BY JOSEPH E. GARLAND

LONE VOYAGER
The Life of Howard Blackburn

THAT GREAT PATTILLO
The Life of James William Pattillo

EASTERN POINT
*A Nautical, Rustical and Social Chronicle of
Gloucester's Outer Shield and Inner Sanctum, 1606-1950*

THE GLOUCESTER GUIDE
A Stroll Through Place and Time

GUNS OFF GLOUCESTER
Cape Ann in the American Revolution

BOSTON'S NORTH SHORE
*Being an Account of Life among the Noteworthy,
Fashionable, Wealthy, Eccentric and Ordinary, 1823-1890*

BOSTON'S GOLD COAST
The North Shore, 1890-1929

DOWN TO THE SEA
The Fishing Schooners of Gloucester

ADVENTURE
Queen of the Windjammers

EASTERN POINT REVISITED
Then and Now: 1889-1989

BEATING TO WINDWARD
*A voyage in the Gloucester Daily Times
through the stormy years from 1967 to 1973*

GLOUCESTER ON THE WIND
*America's Greatest Fishing Port
in the Days of Sail*